SHE'S AT THE CONTROLS

Music Industry Studies

Series Editor: Sarah Raine, Edinburgh Napier University
Founding Series Editor: Dave Laing†, Honorary Research Fellow at the University of Liverpool and Senior Research Associate at the University of East Anglia

In recent years, there has been a rapid growth of interest in the music industry, from policy-makers, educationalists, the media and others. This new series aims to satisfy the demand for in-depth knowledge and analysis of all facets of the industry, from recording to live music and the publishing sector. It will include both historical and contemporary approaches and draw on contributions from economics, geography, sociology, legal studies, cultural studies and other disciplines.

Published:

Beyond 2.0: The Future of Music
Steve Collins and Sherman Young

Forthcoming:

Elements of Music Management
Sally Gross

Local Acts, Global Success: How Ireland Produces Popular Music
Michael Murphy and Jim Rogers

The Handbook on Music Business and Creative Industries in Education
Edited by Daniel Walzer

Venue Stories:
From Backroom to Rave Room, from the Toilet Circuit to the Town Hall
Edited by Fraser Mann, Robert Edgar and Helen Pleasance

SHE'S AT THE CONTROLS

SOUND ENGINEERING, PRODUCTION AND GENDER VENTRILOQUISM IN THE 21ST CENTURY

HELEN REDDINGTON

SHEFFIELD UK   BRISTOL CT

Published by Equinox Publishing Ltd.

UK: Office 415, The Workstation, 15 Paternoster Row, Sheffield, South Yorkshire, S1 2BX
USA: ISD, 70 Enterprise Drive, Bristol, CT 06010

www.equinoxpub.com

First published 2021

© Helen Reddington 2021

All rights reserved. No part of this publication may be reproduced or transmitted in any form or by any means, electronic or mechanical, including photocopying, recording or any information storage or retrieval system, without prior permission in writing from the publishers.

British Library Cataloguing-in-Publication Data
A catalogue record for this book is available from the British Library.

ISBN-13 978 1 78179 651 1   (paperback)
         978 1 78179 652 8   (ePDF)
         978 1 80050 049 5   (ePub)

Library of Congress Cataloging-in-Publication Data
Names: Reddington, Helen, author.
Title: She's at the controls : sound engineering, production and gender ventriloquism in the 21st century / Helen Reddington.
Description: Bristol : Equinox Publishing Ltd, 2021. | Series: Music industry studies | Includes bibliographical references and index. | Summary: "She's at the Controls gives a socio-historical examination of the roles of women studio professionals in the UK music industry based on interviews conducted over six years with 30 female studio practitioners at different stages of their careers and working in different genres of popular music including reggae, hip hop and pop"-- Provided by publisher.
Identifiers: LCCN 2020046467 (print) | LCCN 2020046468 (ebook) | ISBN 9781781796511 (paperback) | ISBN 9781781796528 (pdf) | ISBN 9781800500495 (epub)
Subjects: LCSH: Women in the music trade--Great Britain. | Sound recordings--Production and direction--Social aspects--Great Britain. | Popular music--Production and direction--Social aspects--Great Britain. | Women sound recording executives and producers--Great Britain--Interviews. | Women sound engineers--Great Britain--Interviews.
Classification: LCC ML82 .R415 2021 (print) | LCC ML82 (ebook) | DDC 621.389/3082--dc23
LC record available at https://lccn.loc.gov/2020046467
LC ebook record available at https://lccn.loc.gov/2020046468

Typeset by S.J.I. Services, New Delhi, India

Dedicated to my daughters, Isobel and Florence

Contents

Acknowledgements	ix
Introduction: "Why are there so few women producers?"	1
1 Starting Out: Early Engagements with Sound, Music and Technology	19
2 Becoming Professional: Entering the Music Industry	39
3 Specialization and Entrepreneurship	56
4 The Workplace Experience and Relationships with Clients and Colleagues	74
5 Male Culture and Studio Territory	95
6 Gender Ventriloquism: Songwriting, Production and the Mediation of Women's Voices	119
7 Fighting Back Against Stereotyping: The Case of EDM	140
8 Education, Inspiration and Potential for Change	162
9 Conclusion	180
Bibliography	194
Producer Biographies	207
Index	213

Acknowledgements

Thanks to Dave Laing, for being such a great friend and mentor, sadly missed; to Peter Nelson and Mary Fogarty, for a chance and very encouraging meeting in Edinburgh; Sarah Killick, whose transcription work gave me the impetus to start the book; Sarah Raine, for patient and thorough editing; all the producers and engineers, not just for their time and their fascinating interviews, but also for sharing their contacts with me in such a positive and generous way; to David Scott, David Sheppard, Kienda Hoji, Fola Philip, Ruth Barnes, Pierre Champagnie, Sally-Anne Gross, Jane Abernethy, Shelia Preston, Sacha Taylor-Cox, Jenny Adlington, Simon Zagorski-Thomas, Simon Frith, Victoria Armstrong, Denise Stanley, Tami Gadir, Marion Leonard and Sheila Whiteley, for both direct and indirect help and support.

Introduction: "Why are there so few women producers?"

At the time of writing, a "studio" can be anything from a mobile phone or a small portable recording device or laptop, to a fully-fledged multi-track studio that can accommodate an orchestra. This variety of different working environments means that the skills developed to operate one may not be transferable to the other, although principles and terminology associated with the recording process may provide a common language of practice to communicate and work with (see Bayton 1998 and Porcello 2004, for discussions about technical language in the studio). In London, in particular, there are large studios that can accommodate orchestras (RAK for instance, or Abbey Road, both in the St John's Wood area). Many different factors define the roles of those who record and shape the sound: budget, available time, the confidence and experience of the artist, the end result (the intended audience), fashion and "cool" (the reputation of the studio and the auteur nature of the person responsible for the final sonic impression), and the use-value of the music (is it for primarily reflective listening or intended for dancing to, for instance?). The latter is a particularly intriguing point for discussion. I attended the Art of Record Production conference in Oslo in 2014 at which there was a panel discussion on mixing. Two of the panellists worked in digital recording environments and were mixing for mobile phones, which at the time they regarded as the major listening device for pop music. A third, however, was setting up a large analogue studio because, he said, his clients were predominantly adolescent bands who had been listening to their dads' progressive rock albums and wanted that big retro sound that was only achievable through the use of vintage techniques. Thus, it can be seen that every part of the chain of production, from initial means of recording to the ways in which the music will be heard, is variable and draws on historic as well as cutting-edge technologies.

Reflecting this, the women that I have interviewed for this book possess many different skills. Some define themselves as engineers, with technical expertise in the recording, mixing or mastering of music being at the forefront of their practice. Others are more concerned with the aesthetics of the end product, making decisions about sonic identity based on what audiences for a particular genre of music might want to hear. Often, a combination of these skills and flexibility in the ways in which they are used has been an essential working practice. Generally, a recording engineer will have the skills to set up instruments with appropriate microphones, route audio signals into and out of a mixing desk or computer (plus associated hardware), and place the recorded sound into an organized whole with the use of equalization, compression and other external hardware or plug-in features of the studio. A mix engineer is responsible for optimizing the recorded sounds often with specific instructions about a target audience who expect certain sonic features related to a defined genre of music. A mastering engineer is responsible for finishing-off the end result of the session so that it is of a standard to cut a vinyl record, manufacture a CD or make a radio show or podcast, all of which have specific audio requirements. A producer is responsible for running the whole process, from choosing the studio (whether laptop or old school), finding additional musicians, often writing arrangements, making final aesthetic decisions, orchestrating personalities in order to get recordings of the most positive and skilful performances of the artist(s) involved in the project, and sometimes hands-on work at the mixing desk or computer. Having established an understanding of the contemporary producer and music production, it will also be useful to set out a brief overview of recording technology's history later in this introduction.

It had never occurred to me when I was a teenage music fan to wonder why record producers were always men, or even what they did and why they matter, although I had heard of Sam Phillips, Phil Spector and Berry Gordy. Equally, I had heard that there was something special about what they did and who they were. In the early 1980s, Elton John married his sound engineer, Renata Blauel from Sydney, whom he had met in England while recording his *Breaking Hearts* album. Commentators were taken aback by the marriage, which took place on Valentine's Day of 1984, because it was already widely known that John was gay. What surprised *me*, however, was that such a thing as a female sound engineer existed, and that she was respected enough to work at such a high level in the music industry. Much later, in 2009, I met a woman engineer from Hastings, Terrie Harris, who told me that she was the only female engineer in Britain. I knew this to be untrue, because I had met another in London, Felix Mackintosh. However, that conversation provided the stimulus for this research, combined with years of frustration at the drop-out rate of female students from studio training at the various universities where I had been teaching. The sense of isolation that she expressed in this statement was a common thread to the interviews that I undertook in subsequent years, especially in the early stages of the careers of some of the older interviewees who found themselves in the position of being "token achievers" (Potter 1997: 30).

After the conversation with Terrie, I sought out other women that I had interacted with during my musical and academic career and began to interview them. I was driven not only by curiosity but also a feeling that their experiences were unique, valuable, pioneering and, because of their often "backroom" nature, had not been sufficiently documented in detail. Following the leads of Finnegan (2007), Cohen (1991), Bayton (1998), Leonard (2016), Gadir (2016), and building on my own previous research into women punk instrumentalists (2012), I decided to forefront the ethnographic aspects of my work before contextualizing this by examining the reasons why we should feel disturbed by the control of male gatekeepers over what we hear in popular music. This approach also builds on research by, for instance, Green (1997), Whiteley (1997, 2000), Bayton (1998), Wolfe (2012, 2016, 2019), among others. Because I am a female musician and producer myself, this undoubtedly has had an effect on the conversations we had, and I am aware that my authorial voice is strongly affected by my own engagements with the music industry throughout my life, both as a performer and as a producer. However, I feel that my reflexive insider position benefited the research by establishing a level of informality during the interviews. This in turn encouraged candid and open responses to my questions and the consequent closeness to authenticity that they provide. However, I was equally aware that insider research could be fraught with pitfalls: there can be a mistaken sense of objectivity (McRobbie 2000) that is sometimes counteracted by statements of cultural, gender and educational factors (see, for instance, Nehring 1997), or unconscious bias because of insider knowledge (see, for instance, Costley, Elliott and Gibbs 2010; Saidin and Yaacob 2016). Throughout this research, I reflexively and actively negotiated my insider and outsider roles.

My own research into the concealed roles of women in music making was first published in 2007 and was focused on British punk rock in the 1970s and 1980s. The research presented here differs from this publication in that it is a snapshot of a current situation; I have been interviewing women producers since 2010 and presenting my ongoing research results in different contexts since then, feeding in the responses to the development of my thesis. When I discussed this project during my role in higher education, there was often aggression from male (and sometimes female) students, who would insist that everything is now equal in the music industry. However, the gender imbalance of music industry student cohorts would often be extraordinarily biased in favour of males, and I would feel sorry for the lone female in the class. Conversely, in some HE situations, women students recommended underground female producers that I might not otherwise have heard about. I also have also presented papers based on this research formally at conferences such as the *Art of Record Production* conference at Leeds Metropolitan University in 2010, the *Performing Prejudice* symposium at Newcastle University in 2013, and the *Music, Gender, Difference* conference in Vienna in 2013, the IASPM *Studying Music* conference at Edinburgh University in 2014, the Musician's Union *Working in Music* conference in Glasgow in 2016, and the *Art of Record Production* conference in Aalborg in 2016, amongst others. Aspects of my research have also been published in a chapter in *Music Entrepreneurship* (eds. Allan Dumbreck and Gayle MacPherson, 2016), and in an article for the *IASPM Journal* special issue on "Gender Politics in the Music Industry" (2018).[1] I will now present an overview of recording technology's history, and its current environments and roles.

Recording Technology and the Move to Accessibility

A short summary of changes within recording practices will provide a backdrop to the issues discussed later in the book. There are many detailed histories of recording that cover perspectives that it is not possible to delve into deeply here, for instance Chanan (1995), Kahn (1999), Massey (2000, 2009), Milner (2009), Frith and Zagorski-Thomas (2012) and Schmidt Horning (2013).

Recording and storing sound have fascinated us for centuries: Douglas Kahn describes an episode in Rabelais' *Gargantua and Pantagruel* (written in 1532), in which the sounds of battle become frozen in a block of ice, only being released later when the ice melts. At a time when printing was just being developed and when words were preserved only in visual form, this recording of actual *sounds* was also a concern of Plutarch, a contemporary of Rabelais (Kahn 1999: 205–206). Any form of recording, whether through writing, drawing, film or sound, raises issues of power that are centred on who is doing the recording and the implications of the archive, whatever form that takes. Conceptually, the idea of saving sounds (and specifically, the emotional meaning of sound) has been a challenge that was difficult to resolve until Thomas Edison developed technology that enabled both recording and playback. The commodification of this process was gradual as the uses of recording not just for record-keeping but also as an art form became apparent. The ability to multi-track and layer sound, originally developed in the 1940s by Sidney Bechet (copying disc to disc), and Les Paul (tape to tape, using army surplus equipment after World War II and encouraged by Bing Crosby, who understood the value of recorded sound to his frequent radio broadcasts), created a

---

1   http://www.iaspm.net/iaspm-journal-gender-politics-in-the-music-industry/

leap in the aesthetics of recorded sound (discussed by Théberge 1997; Milner 2009; Katz 2010; Frith and Zagorski-Thomas 2012; Schmidt Horning 2013, who give different accounts of the development of sound technology and the history of recording). Competition between artists on the continents of the USA and Europe (including Britain) such as that between the Beatles and the Beach Boys, to create better and better musical innovations, kept new technological developments at the centre of popular music recording. This firmly sited records as a commodity, and also started to define the roles of studio staff. During the 1960s, the role of the producer as auteur became acknowledged: this was the time of high-profile producers such as Phil Spector and his stable of artists, George Martin and his influence on the more experimental sonic landscapes of the Beatles' pop music, Joe Meek's electronic experimentation in pop, and Berry Gordy and the "Motown Sound". Studios grew to be large, technically daunting (needing teams of specific recording engineers to run and maintain the machinery) and expensive to hire.

The fortunes of popular music have always been closely tied to economics as well as technological developments, and at notable points in its history the record industry has become top heavy and close to collapse. The panic induced by online file-sharing mimics that of the 1970s when cassette tapes allowed people to copy music at home and bypass the purchase of music from the major labels that released it. The downsizing of the industry that resulted from the upsurge in street-generated music in the late 1970s (punk music) changed not only the aesthetics of music but also the working practices of those who recorded it: power in the studio became more about conversation than domination, and even in those areas where auteur producers such as Stock, Aitken and Waterman (a production team who came to prominence in the mid-1980s in the United Kingdom) operated, there was a strong sense of independence: Pete Waterman's label was an independent label and his releases used to chart in the Independent charts as well as the mainstream ones. It was only a few years later when self-producers working in electronic music became successful, building on the experimentation of artists such as Stevie Wonder and Kraftwerk. The team of personnel needed to create a successful track began to shrink: many artists no longer needed session players, especially not orchestras, because their sounds could be created by machines. A studio could be quite a small room, filled with machines that processed sounds, "driven" by a sole producer who might work with a vocalist, for instance. This could lead to some odd situations: Paul Hardcastle's 1986 single 'Don't Waste My Time', for instance, was voiced by the session singer Carol Kenyon, yet promoted under his name. By the 1990s, digital recording technology had driven a move to miniaturization that had arguably started with the manufacture and marketing of Portastudios and the like in the very early 1980s. These were four-track multi-track machines that used tape cassettes and a system of "bouncing" one track to another to create further space for recording, were relatively cheap for a committed songwriter or band member to acquire, and allowed the recording of demos that demonstrated songwriting, arrangements, and in spite of the low sound quality, sonic signatures – the established territory of the producer. Just as Rabelais' release of battle sounds from melting ice conceptualized recording and playback, these machines drove the idea of small-scale recording environments set up in the home (often a bedroom), and crucially, a do-it-yourself approach to making recorded music (Théberge 1997).

The 1990s, as well as being the era of Britpop, had a thriving underground dance music scene driven by cheaper home recording technology and incorporating and developing the introduction of digital music generation driven by MIDI keyboards. Andrew Goodwin expressed surprise that this move to keyboards did not automatically mean that more women became involved in music production at this point (Goodwin in Lull 1992, discussed later in this work) but roles in music production remained resolutely stratified along gender lines, reinforced not just by the gendered structure of the music industry but also by the technical music press.

There has been a marked increase in the number of female self-producers during the first two decades of the 21st century, often facilitated by the inclusion of the software package Garageband on Apple Mac computers. As an educator in HE, I started to observe this process in around 2008; female students apparently had more confidence in "working up" their ideas on their laptops before presenting them in class, than they would have done in a formal studio setting. The move of women into self-production has, however, been gradual and remains largely marginal (see Wolfe 2019), despite some high-profile names (notably Kate Bush, Alicia Keys, Missy Elliott and Björk). It often involves the insertion of men into the process as the profile of an artist increases. Wolfe's account of a resigned Isabella ("Isa") Summers, who was replaced by a male producer after creating the "*sound*" of Florence and the Machine with Florence Welch, and then had to battle for an "Additional Production" credit so that at least her name appeared on the final release, is a sobering (but all too familiar) story to read (Wolfe 2019: 72). As I discuss in the next section and will become apparent throughout this book, the design of this research study aimed to address these central issues and to build upon related debates within academia and industry.

Key Aims of the Book

As you may have already surmised from the introductory discussion provided above, there are two major issues at the heart of this book: one of them is the stereotyping of the creative use of music technology as male; and the other is the much more insidious issue of gender ventriloquism, in which male producers use women artists as mouthpieces for their own versions of girlhood and womanhood. Through examination of the construction of careers in sound engineering and/or music production, specialization, and maintaining a career in the recording industry, this unique set of interviews challenges the orthodoxy of past music industry expectations.

The first part of this book presents these interviews with women producers and engineers, followed by a historical contextualization that includes discussions on women and technology, the role of women in different popular music genres, and the ways in which women's roles are defined through various different channels. The focus, here, is on audio production and engineering, predominantly in popular music genres, by female mediators. In this it challenges the assumption that women are visual signifiers of youth culture, and looks behind the scenes of the recording industry. Where there are women artists in the record industry, both media and academic voices have tended, especially since the advent of MTV (and further entrenched by YouTube and so on), to focus on female appearance in popular music forms (see, for example, Kaplan 1990; Lewis 1990; Roberts 1996; Vernallis 2004; Sharpley-Whiting 2007; Tannenbaum and Marks 2012; Lieb 2013; Hawkins 2019). It is sometimes difficult to separate the sound from the image; the contextualization in this book has been undertaken against a backdrop of constant "loud noise" from the media about the *appearance* of women in pop and rock music and the implications of that appearance for feminism, modern morality, and so on. Robert Walser has noted the complexity of disentangling visual messages and musical content in music that is heavily promoted through video (Walser 2000: 157). This has been further exacerbated by the #MeToo movement and an upsurge in interest in female producers that occasionally seems superficial, the "latest trend".

Producers and engineers most often work behind the scenes of the music industry. I wanted to discover whether there were really as few women engaged in this profession as it appeared at first, and why the gender balance in recording studios – which must have an effect on the *sound* of the music we hear – is so skewed in favour of men and against women. Simon Frith remarked that "Pop is a classical case of alienation: something is taken from us and returned in the form of a commodity" (1983: 12) and it is in the space between creativity and commodification that the implications for the relationship between gender politics and the aesthetics and practices of technological mediation become important. There is much to discover even in the mainstream in the "space between the notes" (a term originally used by Claude Débussy and, later, Miles Davis).

Despite gradual changes in attitudes to women's roles in other walks of life, pop and rock not only continue to preserve the stereotypical roles for men and women that have been challenged regularly since the 1970s (this has been theorized by researchers such as McRobbie and Frith 1978; Cohen 1991; Negus 1999; Wolfe 2012, 2016, 2019; Leonard 2016; Born and Devine 2016) but they also provide retrogressive havens within which those made uncomfortable by social change and challenges to traditional gender roles can take cover. No matter how much women attempt to accelerate change, effective results of research and campaigning for equality materialize painfully slowly. Wolfe's recent research (2019) demonstrates the will for change within the more independent parts of the music industry: she describes the actions taken by the British organization Association of Independent Music (AIM), for instance, to provide platforms for discussion on gender issues not only in production but also the industry in general. Sadly, as Wolfe remarks, awareness does not solve inequality (2019: 51).

I will also discuss the processes of songwriting, where the implications of emotional direction being given to teenage audiences by male songwriters and producers through the vehicle of young male and female pop stars' voices are an issue, and where this informs the contextualization and discussion of the gender of music producers. Songwriting is often closely embedded in the creative processes of production, and this symbiotic relationship is an important factor in the gendering of professional roles within the music industry.

Women Producers and Participant Voice

Between 2009 and 2018, I interviewed (either face-to-face or by email) more than 30 women working in various roles in the recording of music. These interviews centred on the life trajectories of the interviewees, the development of their skills, the opportunities they had, the disappointments they experienced, and the adaptability and resilience they needed in their professional lives. They mostly covered producers and engineers who work as manipulators of sound, rather than creators of sonic brands ("auteur" producers): most (but not all) of the women that I interviewed are mediators of other artists' sounds, rather than self-producers. In this respect, this work complements Wolfe's research (2012, 2016, 2019), presenting a different perspective on careers in the British recording industry, although there are overlapping areas of practice that are discussed where they occur, as well as many common issues to do with gender and work. Occasionally, I had the opportunity to interview a self-producer with such a unique or pioneering approach that I felt it would enrich my research. Janet Beat, a pioneering electronic composer; Chantal Epp, a producer of cheer music; and the pop artist Sandie Shaw (who provided a brief email interview), are examples of self-producers whose practice falls outside the norm. In the main, my interviews illuminate the working practices of women whose roles are focused on the mediation of other artists' output. My research includes women who work in R'n'B, grime, gospel music and reggae, all music genres that are particularly rooted in black culture, as well as mainstream pop and songwriter genres. In this respect it builds upon Wolfe's (2019) study which mainly focused on white middle-class women, educated to University level. My research in the first part of the book follows what Angela McRobbie defines as "identity ethnography" (McRobbie 1992) that prioritizes the active making of meaning (Butler 1990) of women in the creative industries.

I discovered that there is not a typical producer role, which is interesting, because of course in this emerging female profession, there is not yet a woman producer *stereotype*. My interviews in many cases paint a much more positive picture of the working environment for female studio professionals than that revealed by the historical contextualization that follows it in this book. Their careers often have a strong independently entrepreneurial trajectory and, with very few exceptions, their individual approaches to their profession are generally positive and confident despite problems they may have had to overcome. The women I interviewed had a strong sense of self-belief; it is given, however, that I have interviewed survivors, rather than those who may have abandoned their careers due to the many setbacks that the historical section of the book describes. Nevertheless, a feeling of positive change continues in the younger generation of producers, and it is to be hoped that this is an effective and permanent change of ethos.

The spread of ages of the women interviewed (from early twenties to late sixties) results in varying degrees of reflection upon their careers. Most of them had not been interviewed before, but they were all positive about participating in the study. The interviews took place over nine years (between 2009 and 2018) and naturally the industry evolved during this period, so consequently some of the interview questions were adapted during the study in order to take these changes, which mostly involved media visibility, into account. In general though, a chronological process was followed in the questions in order to follow the career trajectories of the participants, and the first four chapters are constructed in such a way as to allow the reader to compare and contrast the different accounts. Additional information was often volunteered at the conclusion of the interviews, and where relevant this has been fed into the discourse, especially where it has affected its trajectory. Sometimes, a request was made that this material should be unattributed, and this request has been respected. In some cases, I made the decision myself to anonymize what I felt was sensitive material. As part of our conversations I was also party to other confidential information which I have chosen to exclude and which has affected my approach, quite often making me angry: this has occasionally been an obstacle and has undoubtedly had an impact on my objectivity as an author.

The women whose accounts are presented here are predominantly based in the UK, although some of them were born and brought up elsewhere. London is a city that was acknowledged by many of the interviewees as "the place to be". It is a large urban area that presents continual new developments in culture and the arts, combined with a financial and commercial ethos that facilitates a professional trajectory for those seeking to make a living as, or from, musicians and artists. For a female practitioner, cities like London also provide a progressive and inclusive environment that may encourage and nurture them in a career that is still very much male dominated. Others are based, or have been, in urban areas in other parts of Britain where they may move between careers in music technology education and freelance work, for instance. The exceptions to this are the two women who are from the USA, both of whom have worked with artists who have had a strong response from British audiences. I had the opportunity to interview Tina Weymouth in the context of her playing bass with the band Talking Heads, and asked about her production work with the Happy Mondays, and I met Susan Rogers at the ARP conference in Oslo in 2015 and arranged to do an email interview with her after a conversation about her sound engineering work with Prince. In most cases, the women that I interviewed agreed to do so on the basis that they should be named. This is a deliberate decision on my part, and there are several reasons behind this. Firstly, as "back-room" workers, I wanted to bring them to the forefront of music industry activity because I regard their contribution to the end product of music to be of such importance. Male producers and engineers often attain auteur status and/or have the privilege of choosing anonymity in some genres of music, for instance dance music. Being recognized for their work has been important for some women in this book. My choice to name the participants has a disadvantage in that they may feel inclined to present only the more positive side to their careers. It is worth the reader considering that part of the survival strategy of anyone in the creative industries is positivity that can appear at times to be a "Polyanna-ish" approach – an optimistic veneer that disguises some of the more unpalatable realities of life in such a gendered profession – and that this is particularly necessary for women in the creative industry. As an example of this, I have considered my experience of writing *The Lost Women of Rock Music* (2012). During the initial process of researching the PhD that later became the book, I became extremely distressed at the number of incidents of assault that had been reported to me. At this point, one of my supervisors underlined the fact that I was writing about survivors and not victims, and suggested that I should write about these experiences under the heading "Industrial Hazards".[2] I have made the decision here to focus mainly on the professional experience and activities of the women that I interviewed, but the reader may assume that there have been additional incidences of assault and disruption that may not have been reported to me. Sadly, the music industry is rife with offensive sexual behaviour, racial stereotyping and general bullying by male colleagues, and it is true that in some cases, these men express sympathy for feminism. Women are all too often defined by their gender instead of their skills and their positive contribution to the arts. Choosing to focus on the latter is not an attempt to gaslight the range of professional setbacks experienced by the women that I have interviewed: rather, it is to respect and consolidate the value of their roles in collaborative music making and, by acknowledging their achievements, to provide positive role models for female producers and engineers that follow them into the industry.

I did not ask direct questions about age, ethnicity, sexual orientation, marital status or parenthood, although information about these issues was volunteered in some cases. This is because they are questions that I would not wish to respond to myself in an interview situation, and more importantly they are questions that are not generally asked of male professionals. Issues of intersectionality are therefore not directly focused on in this book, although at the time of writing they are very much in the forefront of discussions on diversity. Because such discussions are fluid and very fast moving, I did not wish to risk further date stamping the information here beyond its snapshot quality of early 21st century practice. My concerns with historical misogyny are directly related to my own career as a singer, songwriter and band leader in pop and rock music, and I feel qualified to undertake this secondary research, whereas as a white, straight and privileged woman I do not wish to appear condescending in writing in-depth about women whose backgrounds and experiences are entirely different to mine. This decision has partly come about through some of the rather patronizing (and occasionally racist) texts that I have read

---

2   Five rapes experienced by women I interviewed were reported to me *after* the book was published.

in preparation for writing this book, and has also to do with a personal ethical standpoint. The book's focus also limits its scope in covering issues of diversity such as parallels between the experiences of women and white working-class men, for instance, and the very large area of race-based issues for both men and women in the music industry. I acknowledge that these issues, too, are under-researched. However, in one specific instance I have been able, with permission, to include an account of direct discrimination that gives a sobering perspective on racial prejudice in the early 21st century.

As Helen Davies remarks, the status of women protagonists tends to be as perpetual novelties in the industry, periodically noticed in "breakthroughs" identified by media commentators, a major problem being that "When women are mentioned, they are nearly always represented primarily *as* women, rather than as musicians ... Their very femaleness is deemed to give them something in common" (2001: 297). I am conscious that I may be accused of adding to this ghettoization of female experience, but the intention of this work is to redress a balance of writing that foregrounds male professionalism in the music industry by adding to the growing discourse on women, control and technology, and also to introduce some authentic accounts of professional strategies and experience that add to the history of the British music industry. In the interviews, some of the women I spoke to made the decision not to raise the issue of the effects their gender had on their careers: if they did, some of them defined themselves as feminists, and some did not.[3]

There are various different "worlds" of female production. The self-production phenomenon extensively researched by Wolfe (2012, 2016, 2019) has grown out of a parallel increase in access to relatively cheap home studio technology, and a desire for audio autonomy for women singer-songwriters as feminism has taken effect and we have become more self-assured as artist practitioners. There is also an extensive international "world" of female electronic music composers and DJs, as noted by Hinkle-Turner (2006), Rodgers (2010), Farrugia (2010), Reitsamer (2019) and Gadir (2016), yet this world remains inaudible to mainstream curators and historians. At the Electro exhibition at Philharmonie de Paris in 2019, for example, women were almost completely sidelined, apart from a small ghetto of women producers presented by the international organization female:pressure that was represented in photographic format.[4]

3   There could be many reasons for this; for instance, being "one of the lads", pride in achievement in a male environment, or misgivings about being professionally ostracized (as though colleagues might not have noticed their gender). Sometimes, I think the reason was professional fear.
4   https://philharmoniedeparis.fr/en/electro-exhibition (accessed 5 August 2019).

The first four chapters of this book therefore draw extensively on interviews, which then go on to inform the theoretical discourse that follows. I have chosen on occasion to include large sections of each interview, because I believe the authentic voices of the women that I spoke to should be honoured and presented in such a context that the reader has the opportunity to engage with both their thought processes and their personalities. Without exception, these were energetic and inspiring interview subjects, and I hope this is transmitted in the way I present their words. In these first chapters, practical and "life" issues surrounding the historical and educational aspects of the gendering of recording in popular music will be explored in order to provide a context for the practice, problems and progress of women as they move into studio and live production in the hope of becoming professional equals to their male peers. The inclusion of questions about their early lives illustrates the fact that, in some cases, lack of privilege did not prevent them from achieving a certain status as practitioners.

Because of the mysterious, "magical" nature of production and the lack of a solid definition of what a producer actually *does* (in common with many other music industry roles), for some women the self-definition as producer may come late in their careers. The "job descriptions" of producer and engineer vary from business-based to the aesthetic to the technical, and can involve creating and working to budgets, project management of processes and teams (clients can be major labels, advertising agencies, film companies, or the bands and artists themselves), songwriting, arranging, vocal coaching, construction and repair of studio equipment (sometimes building the studios themselves), and recording, programming and mixing. All these roles are encompassed in the practice of the interview sample, and we shall see that they continue to be affected in different ways by male-dominated hierarchies in recording studios. The contrast between the positive attitudes of the women who were interviewed, and the historical and economic obstacles that the music industry and society in general puts in the way of the advancement of women's skilled employment in this area, seems like an anomaly at first until it becomes apparent that resilience in the face of opposition is an important survival tactic in this field. It was when the academic Victoria Armstrong introduced her research paper on the teaching of music technology in schools at the 2015 University of East London Femusetech event with the words "It's rather depressing, really", that I realized the lack of opportunities for women engineers and producers to move into more mainstream work *is* rather depressing; this makes it all the more extraordinary that the women interviewed here have managed to create and sustain their careers in the UK music industry and thrive within it.

Summary of Chapters

Chapter 1 examines the stimuli and motivation behind the focused interest in sound and music that led these women to see themselves as part of the process of audio recording. We will see that, for some, the presence of tape recorders, pianos or other creative technology in the home encouraged an affinity with technology and machinery; with others, it was sound itself, often simple, everyday stimuli, that led them to prioritize hearing and listening over other senses. Family members, often the father, encouraged some of the interviewees, sometimes simply as an exemplar of who and how to be as an adult. With many of them, there was a trigger: as Mandy Parnell describes it, a "moment" of realization that the studio was the environment that they wanted to work in. This could be part of a school project, as Isobel Campbell describes, or attending a concert (Laura B), or accompanying an elder sibling to a recording studio (Felix Mackintosh). Learning the skills needed to become a professional in the field before specialist higher education courses were available was difficult for some; considerable ingenuity and concealment of ambition so as not to appear to be a competitor were often a necessity. Good fortune and the ability to capitalize on unexpected opportunities also played a role at this stage of their careers.

Chapter 2 describes their entry into the profession in greater detail and demonstrates different motivations for becoming producers and engineers. For instance, some women (such as Helen Atkinson and Eleonora Romano) were fascinated by the music industry, but knew they did not want to face audiences directly as artists; others (such as Katia Isakoff, Isobel Campbell and Lauren Deakin Davies) were artists frustrated by the lack of control over their own work, who decided to empower other artists by being more responsive to their needs, in effect operating in the opposite way to those mediators who they felt had not listened to, or delivered, what they wanted. We see that a willingness to undertake even mundane tasks in the studio (literally making the tea) allows potential engineers and producers to engage with artists and technical and creative studio processes from the inside, and crucially, work out which additional skills they need in order to make professional progress, and take steps to learn these skills either formally or informally, something that men have to do too.

Chapter 3 examines the actual practice engaged in by the producers that I interviewed, demonstrating the ways in which they have made themselves indispensible to certain clients through specialization, and the ways that they use their ingenuity to obtain and sustain work. This can be within an organization (Janet Beat setting up a musique concrète course for Laban dance students at Worcester College of Education in the 1960s, or Dot Allen setting up a music technology suite at the Elizabeth Garrett Anderson girls' secondary school, for instance), or by finding a niche in other areas: advertising (Adrienne Aitken), reggae (Cathy Cuvelier), cheer music (Chantal Epp), high-end listening (Colleen Murphy), live music monitor engineering (Eleonora Romano), or rap/grime music (JPL and Ms Melody). Engineers such as Isabel Gracefield Grundy and Lauren Deakin Davies specialize in working with singer-songwriters; Helen Atkinson, Olga Fitzroy, Laura Leitch and Terrie Harris work mainly with bands. Yvonne Shelton specializes in maintaining the authentic sound of gospel choirs on pop records, working alongside other producers, and Karina Townsend and Rasha Shaheen have worked in unusual environments (the Swiss mountains and the Algerian desert, respectively), where they had to adapt their skills in order to make recordings in unsophisticated and extraordinary circumstances.

In Chapter 4 the relationships between the women and their colleagues and clients are examined. The music industry is competitive, like other creative industries, and it is also extremely gender segregated. Work can be deliberately disrupted by male colleagues in order to prove that the studio is no place for a woman; through the experience of Janet Beat, we see the different "pranks" that might be played on female studio workers by even some quite senior colleagues. Janet's experiences occurred 50 years ago, but we hear that there is still a stigma attached to a woman "being in the wrong place" in terms of her gender, despite sometimes working in environments supposed to demonstrate women's empowerment, such as the experience of Lilith Fair described by Eleonora Romano. Clients in "boys' music" need aural proof that their engineers know what they are doing, as Mandy Parnell discovered, and there is still an assumption that "the girl" is there to make tea (Lauren Deakin Davies) or that the engineer must be a man (Laura B). Working with women clients can also be difficult; stereotyping is not just a male problem, and the most difficult issue to come to terms with is often that of hidden bias from women as well as men. For some women, their gender was a positive advantage, perhaps unexpectedly: JPL, Felix Mackintosh and Ms Melody have all worked with rappers, and after initial informal negotiations, these working relationships have often been fruitful and positive. However, Susan Rogers reports a difficulty with authority over some of her male clients. Unpleasant sexual harassment was reported by some of the women; the difficulty with this basic and threatening way of keeping women out of studios is that there is no possibility of reporting it without damaging their own reputation. As Wolfe notes, not many businesses have diversity policies, and they do not act on them when they do (2019: 43). At the time of writing, there is no #MeToo movement for people behind the scenes in the music industry.

Chapter 5 contextualizes women and audio recording within an historical narrative, starting with a general overview of women's engagement with developing technologies and applying this to music recording. The concept of "genius" is explained, and its relationship with the creation of music recordings versus listening to them; the hierarchies of studio work are discussed, and the roles assigned to musicians according to their gender are noted and examined. The concepts behind controlling the sound of music and their social implications are considered, following the deeply embedded maleness of the music industry through the creation of a popular music recording.

In Chapter 6, the concept of gender ventriloquism is introduced; the fake empowerment discussed in the previous chapter is elaborated further, and "power" is compared to power. In other words, the impression of female power, or empowerment, is compared with the *actual* power of male mediators who control not only the sound but often also the lyrical content of popular music, often invisibly. The power of even global superstars, such as Madonna, is challenged, although her true story in terms of production is a difficult tale to unravel. An historic narrative is presented, in order to demonstrate the different ways that male producers act as ventriloquists, through lyric-writing, sampling and vocal processing, using often much younger female artists as mouthpieces not only through lyrics but also through sound. The almost romanticized concept of the Svengali producer is criticized, alongside the assumption that women artists should be subject to the control of their male producers, even if they are supposedly demonstrating female power and agency. This chapter is focused on the implications of male mediation for female artists and builds on my article for the "Gender" issue of the *IASPM Journal* published in 2018, mentioned earlier. In this chapter, the focus is further diverted away from the women practitioners and their working contexts described earlier in the book, into a discussion about the hidden gender politics in popular music and the concealment of control over the power balance between men and women in the recording sector of the music industry.

The power imbalance explored in Chapter 6 underpins Chapter 7, in which I discuss strategies that women audio practitioners have developed to fight back against stereotyping, using the electronic dance music scene as a case study to demonstrate the ways that the press mediate music made by women. A critique of academic writing is introduced into my discourse, and I explore the ways in which the music industry is attempting to rectify the gender imbalance in recording practice. Although EDM producers are not generally mediators of other artists, exploring this area allows us to step back from the overt gender stereotyping in mainstream pop and look at an area of popular music making that replicates gender divisions despite the focus on the sound of the music within that scene rather than the visual appearance of the practitioners. The undercurrent of sexism behind this music genre reinforces the need for change.

In Chapter 8, I discuss music technology education in schools and universities, focusing on more formal learning and attempts to address sexism in teaching. Music and technology education are areas in which traditional gender delineations are rife, and this chapter gives an overview of research in predominantly secondary music education, including music technology education, that might affect the aspirations and attitudes of young women hoping to enter the music industry as studio professionals. Internalized sexism and learned helplessness are examined alongside the idea of using female instructors in order to give female students positive role models. The challenges of male culture in learning environments are noted, and the difficulties of continually starting from scratch in terms of students' expectations and professional ambitions are also described. The importance of making changes in the behind-the-scenes world of sound engineering and production is underlined, and a summary of the landscape in terms of female producers and engineers in popular music at the time of writing is presented. New audio spaces, cheaper equipment and new methods of distribution are providing entry-level opportunities for women professionals; however, the challenge for these new producers is to sustain their careers and build reputations in a world of perceived shrinking opportunities for audio professionals in general. DIY production introduces further competition into the world of popular music production, and the fragmentation of the record industry makes finding budgets for producers more difficult; however, times of social and commercial change and unrest often provide opportunities for new working practices that have previously excluded particular communities from agency, and this is where women and non-binary engineers and producers who have skills and entrepreneurial abilities may find the potential to thrive.

In the concluding chapter of the book I describe the ways in which initiatives to address gender imbalances in the recording industry have had an impact at the time of writing. Ultimately, I have prioritized finding an answer to the question "Why are there so few female producers?". In common with other fields of research, I conclude that there are many factors that affect the current state of affairs regarding gender and music technology, sometimes apparently conflicting reasons delivered with equal authority by different sources. Hindsight makes it easier to imagine a resolution to the slow process of rearticulating gender issues in the workplace and beyond, and as contemporary feminist Chimamanda Ngozi Adichie remarks:

> I was once talking about gender and a man said to me: "Why does it have to be you as a woman? Why not you as a human being?" This type of question is a way of silencing a person's specific experiences. Of course I am a human being, but there are particular things that happen to me in the world because I am a woman. (Adichie 2014)

1 Starting Out: Early Engagements with Sound, Music and Technology

In the first four chapters of this book, I will foreground the stories told by the women that I interviewed, beginning with their early engagement with sound, music and technology, and moving on through their entry into the music industry. Following this, I will demonstrate the ways in which they manage their professional portfolios through entrepreneurial approaches and specialization based on their acquired skills, and going on to explore their relationships with their clients and employers, and their crucial professional engagements. The chapters have been organized in this way because no matter how much experience, how many skills or how many imagined scenarios a music professional has developed, the industry networks that they create and maintain are absolutely crucial to their ability to continue their practice. The lived experiences of these women producers told through their own accounts of engagement with the music industry and its values thus come to the forefront in the first part of my narrative. Later in the book, the historical, cultural and social contexts in which they practise will be examined to demonstrate the constraints that still apply to female practitioners in a professional world that is still gendered as male.

Within this chapter, we are introduced to a sample of the interviewees, tracing their trajectories from their early years to the start of their professional careers. Their first engagements with listening, often at home, may have influenced their later deeper engagement with sound and music; I was curious about what might have started their relationship with listening. Significant experiences in their lives then stimulated their desire to pursue this interest further, and they identify key moments that consolidated their decision to work in recording music. Each of them then had to find routes into the industry, starting to build up their skills in order to achieve what they saw as their destiny, beginning to take proactive steps towards becoming career engineers or producers. Relevant sections of the conversations have been chosen to illustrate different issues that were given particular emphasis at the time of interview.

These women have followed many different paths into their industry, hindered, and occasionally facilitated, by a combination of social and cultural conditions, their own personalities and skillsets, and the windows of opportunity that for any successful musician are simply defined as "good luck". Breaking away from the traditional female role in popular music as vocalists (see, for instance, McRobbie 2000; Warwick 2004; Stras 2010), or as in the first case discussed in this chapter, trying to break into the world of electronic composition, often followed on from an early obsession with sound, music or technology, and sometimes a combination of the three.

We shall see that the broad spectrum of cultural backgrounds represented by the interviewees reflects not only the multicultural nature of the music community in Britain (especially its main cultural centre, London), but also a variety of different routes into an interest in, or an obsession with, sound production and consumption. The types of production and engineering practice that I will examine in this book are not entirely dependent on privileged upbringing or traditional education. In this respect my research differs from that of Paula Wolfe's (2019), which is focused primarily on self-production (a very different vocation that requires not only the means to purchase recording hardware and digital software; it also requires the time and the determination to learn how to use these in order to create high quality music, and strong motivation and vision). Through their own stories, we will see the variety of different upbringings that my interview sample experienced, and the ways that they negotiated the inevitable setbacks that not just being an audio professional, but being a *female* audio professional, threw in their paths.

First Engagements with Listening: The Home Environment and Parental Influence

Following Mavis Bayton's lead in her influential book *Frock Rock* in which her interview sample was asked about early years and family influences (1998: 55–58), I began by enquiring about the first connections my own interviewees had made with sound and with technology. Given the drive and resilience necessary to sustain any career in the music industry, I felt that an early engagement with these things must have been an important factor in their later choice of career. Sometimes encouraged by parents and contemporaries, sometimes challenged by them, everyone was immediately able to pinpoint significant factors in their childhood that had influenced their later career choices. I began with the Scottish electronic composer Janet Beat (who was in her late sixties at the time of our conversation, and the oldest of the group of women that I interviewed), who recounted that her home environment was not encouraging of her curiosity and desire to experiment with sound and music:

> We had an old wind-up gramophone ... I spoilt it in the end because I fiddled with it and made the turntable go backwards to see what it sounded like. The piano was a big tall upright piano and I used to climb up on the armchair that was next to it, put a stool on top of the armchair and I used to drop spoons and things to see what effect it had on the sound. And I used to sit right under the piano and listen to the overtones, the harmonic partials, ... what I called rainbow sounds, which would be harmonics.

Janet found these sounds in other, everyday household objects, too:

> ... there was a chrome-plated tea tray my mother had but it was tooled, so it had a surface like a tam-tam, and I found if I hit it and put it next to my ear I could hear the harmonic partials. I found if I hit it in different places you got different pitches. My parents were worried, they thought there was something mentally wrong with me, because I called it the rainbow tray, and of course to them it was colourless: it just looked silver.

Janet's family continued to misunderstand and disrupt her musical activities, sometimes in a distressingly disrespectful way. For example, Janet's father later found a box of tapes of her music that had been damaged in a flood at their house:

> He'd cut all the tapes up to tie up his sweet peas and the raspberries and the blackcurrants in the huge kitchen garden we had. So they've all disappeared. They would have dried out, but it was "Janet's old junk".

A fascination with everyday sounds was also noted by the producer Adrienne Aitken, who was based in the English town of Aylesbury, and whose familial musical tradition included a grandmother who played piano for silent movies. From being a baby in her cot, she recalled:

> hearing ladies' shoes walking by; ladies' feet going "chk, chk". I heard that and I loved that sound, and I loved the sound of keys. I just loved the jangle ... I just loved the way things sounded from a stupidly early age.

Her home environment provided further inspiration; because there was a reel-to-reel tape recorder belonging to her father in her childhood home, experimentation with sound and manipulation of technology began to feel as though it came naturally to her:

> It wasn't a mystery and it wasn't the unknown. The reel-to-reel tape recorder was always around our house – a very old-fashioned one – so there was never this thing where you walk into something and feel out of your depth or alien to it. I always felt quite comfortable around that kind of technology to the point that for my first demos, I used his tape recorder, which had a two-way left and right type of record, so that you could record both ways. You could record backwards; in other words, instead of turning the tape over, you could record the other way with the other side buttons. And you could bounce from side to side, and that's how I did my first demos, recording on one track, bouncing that track with the next track and bouncing that back again. Most of them were vocal harmonies but that's how I first started experimenting, because technology was around and it didn't faze me.

Fortunately, not all fathers were as dismissive as Janet Beat's, who belonged to a different, older generation. Although her family was not musical, the Scottish electronic musician and music production tutor Karina Townsend picked up on technical influences when she also was very young from unusual sources:

> I was very wee, in a high chair, my dad was an art lecturer and my mum was at home with me and I think my dad had ideas about hothousing me or something, so he used to put me in a high chair in front of the Open University and leave me. One day Dad asked, "What have you been watching today, dear?" and I apparently came out with, "Massachusetts Institute of Technology!"

Karina's family included recording technology as part of their family practice, as had Adrienne's. Just as in Adrienne's household, a reel-to-reel tape recorder was used frequently by the family:

> My Dad had a Stellaphone, a lovely, chunky, clunky reel-to-reel and he would use it to record family events. Before they got married my mum worked out in Sri Lanka and Pakistan, and so they used to send each other tape letters. He also used a tape recorder in schools; he taught in teacher training college. I suppose this would be one of my youngest memories of recorded sound: he worked with the science teacher, Dr James Richie, and they recorded schoolchildren's singing games and rhymes. And because he also made films, they recorded soundtracks for films with tape.

The positive influence of fathers on their daughters' interest in technology has been noted by Bayton (1998: 56–57) and was reiterated by many of the women in my research. Sometimes, this was due to the encouragement and expectations of fathers based upon their own professional experiences, as in the case of the US musician and producer Tina Weymouth, whose father expected his daughters to be just as good at technical activities (if not better) than his sons, because of what he had experienced in his wartime career:

> My Dad was in World War Two. They had all the men out in the field fighting, so they had a team of women mechanics. And he said they were fantastic. Never was the operation tidier, with more attention to detail. They were superb mechanics. So that just gave him faith, and all his daughters are mechanical. His mother was the one who taught him how to fix electrical things. And I'm the "handyman" in our house.

Ease with machinery was also attributed to paternal influence by the producer and music technology educator Samantha Bennett, whose father's enthusiasm affected her because he repaired electronic devices at home (and was also an ardent music fan):

> My dad, who I was like this with as I grew up [holds hands close together], ... was an obsessive record collector for a start, so all I remember is just records and records, an insatiable appetite for records, an insatiable appetite for live music. He was a guitar player himself in a band in the '60s, and in the daytime he was an audio-visual engineer for a television and radio company. And so as I was growing up, every night after school when he got home from work there was a broken piece of equipment on the dining-room table, whether it be a VHS recorder or a microphone, or an early camcorder in bits on the floor, and a soldering iron, and records on. He'd come home, we'd have dinner, and then whatever broken piece of equipment he hadn't quite managed to fix at work, he would fix. So I remember this Multihands on the dining-room table, over a broken video machine, or some piece of equipment and my dad there with his glasses on just going, "Now, this wire there, that needs sticking there, you got to solder that bit there", and anything he was doing, I wanted to do; anything he did, anywhere he was, I wanted to be.

Similarly, Alison Ward, who went on to become a live sound engineer at London's Vortex jazz venue, was brought up in a gender-neutral way and received the same encouragement from her parents as her brother. As in Tina's household, she was simply expected to be able to engage comfortably with technology, and not to fit the female stereotype of being uninterested in mechanical or electronic gadgets and toys:

> My dad's quite into gadgets, and I had a very lovely relationship with my dad because my brother and sister were older than me so I was almost like an only child, and by the time I came along Dad wasn't working. He had more time; he wasn't travelling so much. I mean, I don't know what it is; maybe he just likes the buttons or the lights. I was given Scalextric for Christmas when I was six. I was into Action Men, I was a real tomboy, and it was encouraged.

Sometimes this paternal influence was accidental; Cathy Cuvelier, who is a reggae producer, was brought up in the south of France, and her early memories come from her father's workplace:

> I would say machinery gave me a sense of rhythm; my father worked in a factory after he left the Army and I used to go to work with him a lot, and I remember moving my head to the sound of the machinery and just starting to tap around with the metal and whatever was around. I think that was my first introduction to sound.

Cathy spent much of her upbringing in a children's home, where she later would become known for her interest in the communal record player, and in electronics in general:

> I didn't remember it for a long time until I saw some footage, getting in a lot of fights if somebody else was going to the turntable. That was my property! I was still very young and my family gave me this name; I was called Electrician, the Mechanic. I remember those dolls where you had a little recorder in the back. I only needed a screwdriver and I would just take the box out of it, and touch the wires to find out how they record, and actually could make it work. I didn't like anything girly; everything was, "If there's a screw there, that means there's a wire behind it, if there's wire I want to see the wire." So, that's the nickname they gave me.

It was the producer and music technology instructor Saran Headman's mother who was the role model for her eventual career. Saran found inspiration in her mother's hands-on approach to her job:

> My mother is a sound engineer for film and TV, so I would see her making her own cables, often getting her tools ready to go to the studio to splice tape. I would get told off for using her Chinagraph

> pencil! She gave me one of the cables she made in those days when I graduated from SAE[1] as a present. It still works!

The influence of her mother was a driving force behind the career of Masol, a DJ and producer who was in her twenties at the time of the interview. She had come to London as a teenager with her mother, after being brought up in the Republic of Cameroon. Her whole family was inventive and musical:

> I came from a very, very musical family. My Grandad used to have this small record player with the little vinyl, the baby vinyls [sic], and he always used to play old school rhythms, like from the 40s, cool jazz, he was really into jazz and blues. My grandma always had her Nigerian gospel music, and she was a singer; she used to be in a gospel choir back in Nigeria.

Speaking of her mother, who currently helps her to organize music panels and events for young women in south London, Masol continues:

> ... she was actually an artist back in Cameroon, she did a couple of albums, a couple of tours, and had videos, and I would run outside and be like, "My mum's on TV everyone! Turn the channels round." So it was always a thing; we always used to meet for Christmas and New Year, and it would be like a musical cavalry, everybody had something to show off and talk about. And my mum had a restaurant where she had a jazz quartet, and where lots of the national Cameroon artists, top celebrities, used to come down and perform every Saturday night. So music was a thing where I really couldn't try to escape from it because it was always around me, front and centre.

In her community in Cameroon, recycling and repair of broken and damaged articles was part of life. There was no option to claim for broken equipment on insurance, and little money to buy replacements. Scrap materials were recycled in creative ways to craft little machines that worked perfectly:

> My brother used to build little portable radio tape [players] with wooden boxes. We never had a boom-box, but we had a wooden one, with speakers inside, that was our own boom-box. And my sister used to do musical bicycles, where she had like lights, she had a strong wire, and she would bend them into a bicycle and then connect some tiny speakers, I don't know how she used to make them;

---

1   The SAE institute provides music industry training, including training in audio engineering.

> minute, miniature speakers, and put them into a plug and you have lights [going on and off] you know?

The musician and producer Katia Isakoff described a different sort of embeddedness of music in family life. She came from a musical family, with a mother who had been a singer and a father who had been a professional drummer, who played the Darbuka (the Arabic tabla) and who had composed and performed music for the James Bond film, *The Man with the Golden Gun*:

> At that time all the kids shared a bedroom, and my brother had this wardrobe and you'd open it and all these records were stacked in the first one, and then in another built-in cupboard he had his decks; he'd taken over the whole space with records everywhere, and turntables. Then that moved to having a shed where he and his friends would go and play music till 2 in the morning, blasting dub bass, toasting away, writing it all down.

When she was a child, Katia's parents had owned a cabinet sound centre with a record player in it that informed her ability to listen deeply. Three records had been supplied with the unit: a Rolling Stones double album, Tammy Wynette's 'Stand By Your Man' and Benny Hill's 'Ernie':

> Being a kid, there was no snobbery around it, there were three records and I learned all the lyrics back to back, and so I can do a brilliant Tammy Wynette, and I memorized all the words to the Ernie song. Every single night, for ages, I would sit religiously in the living room cross-legged in front of the stereo with some headphones, lights all off, listening to the double album of the Stones, and crying to 'As Tears Go By' and 'Ruby Tuesday', all the sad lyrics. I was obsessed with the lyrics and the stories because I actually thought they were about real people.

Listening to vinyl recordings was also a formative experience for the mastering engineer Mandy Parnell. Her first remembered engagement with sound was with 7" singles, when she was very young:

> My parents had a greasy [spoon] cafe in Wickford in Essex and the jukebox guy used to come round and change them, and he used to give me all the ones he took out. And I was obsessed; I didn't play with dolls: in fact, I hated dolls.

This fascination continued into her boarding-school days, when institutional rules could not prevent her from continuing her obsession with records: "I wasn't allowed to play my records. I'd get up in the middle of the night and sneak down to the hall where the gramophone was to play 'em, and listen to Radio Luxembourg under my sheets." Later, we will consider further the historical gendering of listening to music, another myth that is debunked by the women in these interviews.

Finally, the interest in storytelling through lyrics and sound mentioned earlier by Katia Isakoff was reiterated by the London-based R'n'B producer Jacqueline Pelham-Leigh, who had ambitions from very early on to be a songwriter:

> Every Sunday in my house when they used to cook they would play music, so from a very young age, five, six, the first things I read were the song lyrics to songs. That's how I started, I learned to read, you'd open [the sleeve] up and you'd have the lyrics there. I remember listening to Stevie Wonder, Diana Ross's 'Love Hangover', and at six, loving the records. And funnily enough my father says that about five or six years ago he found a piece of paper where they had asked "What do you want to do when you grow up?" And it seems I wrote: "I want to write songs". And I thought, what six-year-old thinks about writing songs? [Because] I was so interested in the credits on the album sleeves, probably.

The "Calling": Engaging with the Professional World

The next stage in Mandy Parnell's journey towards being a sound engineer was an "epiphany" that came about by accident, as a result of absconding from the school where she had had such trouble listening to music. Earlier, we learned about her obsession with music. A chance meeting in the street granted her access to an inspirational moment that decided her future career:

> I ended up being a runaway from boarding school, and ended up on the streets in London, [and] met this girl Junie who was a housekeeper at The Manor, Virgin's residential studio in Oxfordshire. This was at the time when Queen and Rush and all these beige rock bands were going in there and recording, so it was a very high-profile studio. And she invited me to go down there one weekend to hang out. So the assistant engineer took me into the recording studio 'cos there was no-one there, and it was a clicking moment: I've got a picture of her and this assistant engineer behind the desk that I took of them; I walked in there and I thought "what *is* this?" I mean it was just a slight "moment".

"Moments" like this were described in many other interviews. For the dance music producer Laura B, a "calling" to sound engineering came after other employment options were forbidden when her parents vetoed the original army career that she had planned. Like Mandy Parnell, her decision was spontaneous and linked to the idea of escape. Laura had been born and raised in Corsica; her interest in music technology happened almost by accident:

> I wanted to be an airline pilot, and to do that I had to leave home at age 15 and join the army, or go to army school. In France, that's how it works. My parents wouldn't let me. I was very disappointed because I was quite gifted in maths. A few months later I was having a coffee in my hometown in Corsica where I grew up, watching a whole show being set up on the main square; they were putting up stages and things. There was somebody at the concert, at the mixer, who seemed to be orchestrating various people and doing something that I thought was quite interesting and I thought, "Oh, I'll do that". And that was it: I was 16.

Later, Laura had the opportunity to attend a concert by punk band the Clash in France, and ended up touring with them entirely spontaneously, and learning the ropes of live sound engineering. Here, she demonstrates commitment and ambition, taking a sound engineer at his word, rising early and being prepared to travel at a moment's notice:

> They came to play in Paris and I was just completely blown away. I discovered everything at once, you know, life, music, rock, punk: the Clash were a fantastic band and I listened to them all the time. I was so taken by the whole thing that I went to see their engineer at the end of the night and said "I want to do that, I want to learn about engineering, what can I do?" And he said, "Well if you come here at seven in the morning, tomorrow morning, we're going on tour, you come with us". And I did; the following morning I was there at 7 o'clock and I went on a big European tour with the Clash. The engineer showed me how to wire up his rack; he had this huge rack, full of compressors and gates and equalizers and stuff, so I was in charge of doing that. Then really quickly I got in charge of doing the sound for the support band, which I was doing entirely on my own. So I did the sound for bands like The Beat, which was just really, really good fun; and Theatre of Hate was a band that was produced by Mick Jones at the time, so they were the support band for the Clash.

Laura did not feel out of place with the all-male crew and the all-male line-up:

> I was a complete tomboy, I've always been; I was working quite hard; no stress, no heavy lifting, but doing whatever I could and being treated really well by everybody. I made great friends with the band, made great friends with the engineer, of course.

The experiences of Laura and Mandy of seeing recording equipment for the first time and finding it fascinating and inspiring are echoed by Felix Mackintosh, who now owns a recording and mixing studio in north London, and who had a similar formative experience at an early age:

> The first studio I went to was Abbey Road when I was about 12 or 13. I got to bunk off school and I spent two days watching my older sister's boyfriend recording, and it was just absolutely exciting. I hadn't realized till quite recently that it was actually one of the major things that made me want to do it, because it took a very long time from then to actually recording [myself]. I got to shout on a track and I remember the smell of it: it was kind of tape and polystyrene cups, and people being incredibly funny, and adults being ridiculous and [me] thinking, "Wow this is brilliant".

Later, Felix wanted more control over what happened to her recorded performances. The seeds of her desire to become an engineer were sown at this point:

> As a female bass player, I got really fed up of not understanding what was going on, and being slightly marginalized in the studios. But I didn't ever see any female engineers the whole time I was going to studios or booking them.

The romantic "feel" of the studio described by Felix also had an immediate impact on the studio engineer Natalie (pseudonym used) in the northeast of England, who was shown around a recording studio on a school visit for her Media A-level course, and found the enthusiasm of the studio owner completely infectious. She later worked for him in the same studio, an analogue studio situated on the Lambton Estate in County Durham; like other women in my research, she felt a sense of belonging when she entered the studio for the first time:

> I think it was a mixture between the way he described stuff – because I remember asking whether or not he got much money out of it and I was severely reprimanded for that [laughter] and I think it was the setting in the studio and the feeling in the studio. It was really comfortable to be in and it was quite inspiring, and it was a really unique place and I think it just stuck in my mind that it was somewhere special that I wanted to go back to. I didn't get into sound engineering because it was a deliberate choice, do you know what I mean? It kind of fell out of other things, but I felt like that was somewhere that I wanted to be.

An affinity for the studio atmosphere had also captured the imagination of Isobel Campbell, formerly of the Glasgow band Belle and Sebastian; she had been musically inspired by the cello playing of Maggie Graeber, who had come into her primary school at Jordanhill on the outskirts of Glasgow to discover whether any of the pupils would like to learn cello. Graeber played 'The Swan' from *Le Carnaval Des Animaux* by Saint-Saens to the children, and Isobel found herself drawn to the instrument. When Isobel was 13, a new music teacher started at her school; although the two did not see eye-to-eye, he did organize a recording session for the children:

> 'Sounds Of Jordanhill School', it was imaginatively called. And I was, luckily enough, asked to record a cello solo for that record. The piece I was asked to play was 'The Swan' from *Carnaval Des Animaux*. The same very piece that Maggie Graeber played when she first came into my class to demonstrate cello! On the day I went to record my solo, it was another one of those life-changing, awakening, epiphany moments. I had such a great day that day. I loved everything about the studio. I loved the big room and all the buttons and lights and glass and the lounge with MTV playing all day in the big TV room. I felt so comfortable and instantly at home. It's funny because years later this is where Belle and Sebastian recorded our debut album, *Tigermilk* and I remember being in there working that week with everyone, feeling the magic, having a wonderful time, knowing something very special was taking place and all the while remembering my cello solo for 'Sounds Of Jordanhill School'. It felt meaningful.

Finally, one of the youngest producers that I interviewed, Lauren Deakin Davies, articulated exactly the same feeling:

> My main awakening when I was about 15 was going into Universal Studios with my band, and I was just the person looking over the shoulder of the engineer going "What does that do? What does that do? What does that do? This is what I want to do with my life!"

From a different inspirational perspective, an enthusiasm for radio led to the development of transferable skills for two of the women that I interviewed. The demystification of knobs and faders, matched with an enthusiasm for music, triggered a technically-focused engagement with music production. Colleen Murphy, the director of Classic Album Sundays and a producer of music, now resident in London but born and raised in the USA, said:

> I was around seven or eight when I got my first transistor radio, and radio was the thing that pulled me in; I was obsessed with listening to the radio to get turned on to music. Luckily, I grew up near Boston so we had college radio stations and more progressive stations than the rest of the United States, so I could discover new music that way, and I think I came into it from that perspective of, "I want to turn people on to music". And so I had a radio show at the age of 14; we had a ten watt radio station in my high school, so I was already starting to get a little bit technical then on that side of operating my own radio show with the microphones and running a very rudimentary radio board with about four pots, probably, not even faders.

Eleonora Romano, a live sound engineer who was brought up in Sicily and who later moved to London to live and work because of its central focus as a music city, described a DIY ethos at home:

> My father was a scientist, a geologist, volcanologist: he made his own television, he made his own radio, portable radio, this kind of stuff, and he would buy the latest technology, like the first Walkman, or the first hi-fi, so from that point of view I guess I got the scientific part from my dad. My mum is just more arty.

Like Colleen, Eleonora Romano had her own radio show in her home country of Sicily following from her enthusiasm for music:

> One day myself and a friend of mine, it was August and there was not a lot to do (at least for me, I'm not a very summery person), we saw some kind of ad in the paper and we were trained for about a month in the recording part of the studio, and then I was the one who ended up doing the programme: my friend wasn't that much into it ... my [radio] programme was specific, it was rockabilly, psychobilly, kind of punk, and my slot was on a Sunday. So I was always into music.

Out There: First Steps towards Entering the Profession

Despite the increase in sound engineering courses both at vocational and academic institutions over the last 20 years, which will be discussed later, it was interesting to hear the variety of different routes taken into the music industry. These often followed the assembly of skills, resources and networks from an imaginative range of sources. Before music technology started to be taught in schools and before access to relatively cheap digital music technology was available (particularly to girls), a learn-it-yourself process was in operation driven by highly motivated women (see also Wolfe 2019). For example, Janet

Beat had to wait until she was at Worcester College of Education, where she was training to be a teacher, before she could fully develop her music technology skills:

> I had to take music appreciation classes for the Laban dance group led by Joan Russell; I would improvise and they would dance and improvise when I was improvising and I'd say to the tutor, "Look, he's responding to harmonic rhythm which is the next thing I'm going to go on to". So, they asked me to write a piece of electronic music for them for one of their shows.

Janet had to think laterally in order to be able to collaborate with artists with similar mind-sets to her own, eventually finding encouragement from an established female electronic artist:

> I found that as far as education institutions are concerned, the music departments were always more conservative. If you worked for drama, or with the dancers, they were far more adventurous because their attitudes hadn't been conventionalized as far as music's concerned. I bought my own synthesizer from Peter Zinovieff's EMS studio in Putney. I'd met Daphne Oram too who was very encouraging. She was so delighted to find another woman interested in musique concrète and electronic music!

For some of the younger producers, an interest in music technology started at school, where they sometimes had to assert their right to learn, especially at single-sex schools. For example, Chantal Epp first became interested in music technology at Surbiton High School, where she had an inspirational music teacher whose instruction she still recalls. She had been doing well in the school choir and reached Grade 8 on piano and Grade 7 on violin:

> We used to have a free period at school and you could choose what you wanted to do so I did music production, using Cubase. I did that for probably two or three years, and then in my final two years at school I took over the class, and helped out with the teachers, teaching all the younger students.

Helen Atkinson, studio manager and engineer at RAK Studios in London, attended Lady Eleanor Holles School in Hampton. She was the only student there who wanted to learn music technology; "It was just me and the teacher". She continues:

> When I looked at the music syllabus for A-level there was a little thing that said "Music Tech" at the bottom and I thought, "Ah, that's

the one that I want to do". I didn't want to do straight music, I knew that I wanted to be in the creative industries but not actually be the artist, or be the actor, that side of things. And I thought, oh yeah, that sounds really good, so I took that on, and I think actually my school were very instrumental in helping to nurture that, because I was the only person.

Her formal education was augmented by a community music project at the local youth centre, Heatham House in Twickenham:

They had a studio and you'd go in and learn Pro-Tools and they'd help you out and help you record your mates' bands and all that kind of stuff. So that was really instrumental in actually helping me to know that I wanted to be in a studio environment, rather than go on to university or do something like that.

"Soft" experiences of recording, such as those provided by the community studio described above, give aspiring studio professionals a grounding in skills that help them to feel confident about progressing further in the profession. Entering the music industry as a studio or live sound engineer is notoriously competitive, even for male engineers; the ability to network is essential, but sometimes networking happens serendipitously. The comparative ease of networking in the music industry for men in contrast to women should never be underestimated (see, for instance, Leonard 2016; Hooper 2020: 131). Occasionally, the women I spoke to had not realized their position in their choice of profession was a sought-after one. Despite the moments of inspiration experienced by some women, the pathway into the profession for most was often gradual, and involved informal (often unconscious) mentoring and "being present" with a degree of invisibility, during which studio skills were almost surreptitiously learned. Cathy Cuvelier describes this mode of learning:

I learned by watching people. I was in the music scene a lot; because I grew up in a children's home I was out a lot, going to live events all the time. I have a bigger cousin who loved reggae music at that time, so she used to take me with her. And I met Joseph "Culture" Hill back in the day when he came to my grandmother's house; he was part of a programme at the time where a promo tour would bring you in from Jamaica, so he finished up at my grandmother's house. He was in Burning Spear, you know. So I was introduced to the music through family members, sitting there quietly and just watching, and I loved the studio time because I could sit next to the engineer, and just watch what he was doing.

Owning home recording equipment was a major factor in Felix Mackintosh's learning. She had been playing in a band with session bass-player Guy Pratt, who later went on to work with a series of well-known artists including David Bowie and Madonna. Felix managed to acquire her recording equipment after the band split up:

> We got a deal and we were bought a Portastudio, with one of the guitarists from his band who I was going out with. It was a four-track cassette player; I have got no idea what make it was. I took it over and when we split I kept it, and then I started making crazy tracks using space echo and bass, using whatever I could. It was so crude, so crude. I loved it though. After the band broke up and I lost that deal I got left with the kit, which was great.

Felix became aware that she needed to learn more, and casting around for something to do with her unexpected spare time, she found a music technology course that eventually led to her being able to make a small income from recording other artists:

> I was just trying desperately to find what to do and I heard an advert for a course at Sound Kitchen, which was a women's studio below the Rio [cinema in Dalston, London]. God knows when this was: '95, '96, I don't know. So I went and did a six week course, and then after the course if you were really crazy on [recording], you could stay on and do little sessions and you got paid a fiver a day or something like that.

Laura B's route into recording through being a trusted pair of ears at live gigs, described in the previous section, was also followed by Sally Smith. This happens because studios can be daunting for musicians, and they sometimes want to bring in an advocate to protect their aesthetic identity. This person may end up working for them permanently. Sally, who later became a studio recording engineer, learned how to work with live music by attending her brothers' gigs:

> ... my brothers were in a band, and their sound engineer was the sort of archetypal sound engineer of the time who used to forget to turn up to gigs, or if he did turn up he was completely wasted, so I used to step in. I didn't like stepping in and not really knowing what I was doing, so I made it my business to learn what I was doing, and I really enjoyed it.

Debbie Dickinson took on a similar role after realizing that she needed to safeguard the live sound of the band she was managing, to the point where she became as much a part of the band as those who were on stage:

> I didn't really have an awareness of the importance of sound to live music until I was working with an all-women jazz group (the Guest Stars) in the mid-80s and became aware of how bad the sound was at the live gigs when we were being mixed by the inevitable male sound engineers who were at the venues. We put so much work into the music and organizing the gigs, only for it to often be ruined by some guy on the mixing desk with cloth ears, and this got me interested in understanding sound and ultimately becoming a live sound engineer. I very much relate to sound as an integral part of the music.

However, not everyone that I spoke to actively *chose* to become technically proficient; Terrie Harris was driven to create her own studio because of the prohibitive costs of paying for studio time for her own music:

> ... this is a weird one – I never thought in my life I would end up doing engineering at all. I was always a girly-girl at school, was always in my high heels, short skirts, big hair, different colours. And it was just a whim. One day I decided I wanted a studio, because we were using other people's studios, we were going all over the place and, I think because it was a man's world back a good odd 20 years ago, there weren't female engineers. So you'd go to these people and it would cost you a bomb because you're a female, a struggling artist with their own music, I used to always write my own music, and then it was a case of: I'd had enough!

Of a similar age to Terrie, Adrienne Aitken's initial ambition was to be a singer-songwriter with keyboards as her main instrument. After early interest from record labels, she started to use recording studios and became frustrated by the fact that the engineers and producers in those studios did not appear to take her seriously at first, which she attributes to her youth (she was 18 or 19 at the time), then:

> Suddenly, people started listening, and then more and more things got listened to, and that evolved into me making decisions as opposed to suggestions, and that evolved into me producing. It was a real organic thing because I never set out to be a producer but I found I was fascinated by the ability to come up with ideas and have them actually manifest into the tracks. And not just that, but when

> they worked and people went "I like that", then I thought "I actually can do this".

Adrienne had the same hunger as Lauren Deakin Davies. She was working at the time with a male colleague who didn't want to be involved in the technical side of things (a phenomenon also reported by Wolfe 2019: 82):

> It was a completely natural evolution of processes, plus the guy that I was working with was a complete technophobe and I took to it like a duck to water. First time in the studio I was looking at everything and going "How do you know what everything does?" and would be asking engineers "What does that do?" and being a complete pest, but I wanted to know and I was hungry for that information. I loved the idea of how to make things work and how'd you get that sound. So everything I evolved into as a producer came from hunger, passion and the need to know. And I suppose to a great extent, without sounding arrogant, the skill to be able to hear.

In the following chapter, I will return to this idea of "growing" studio skills as a result of disappointment in existing male-dominated set-ups, which was often a matter of aesthetics as much as a feeling of disempowerment.

There were other situations through which the women I interviewed suddenly became more proactive in their own career decisions. For the Manchester producer Yvonne Shelton, who has made a career out of arranging gospel choirs for pop music recordings and "minding" authentic gospel vocal blending alongside existing producers, this happened when she was excluded from her church choir:

> When the choir found out I was singing for non-religious people, "the devil's music", I got kicked out of the choir and I just carried on doing lead and background vocals and arranging vocals; if you're in a gospel type choir you learn how to arrange. You're always asked for different arrangements of things, so I ended up getting a lot of vocal arrangement work.

London producer Chantal Epp described another example of a negative event that instigated a career in music. A cheerleading injury led to her developing a unique business as a producer of cheer music, a niche activity that we will return to later. Her injury coincided with her final year at university and, when a promised opportunity was withdrawn, this led her to focus on setting up on her own:

> I was the captain of my squad at the time, and my coach was like, "Oh, why don't you do the music for the team, for the competition", so I thought I'd have a go and get the lecturers at university to help me ... He owns a uniform company that sells cheerleading uniforms, and he said, "Why don't you work for us, and develop your skills – and maybe we can develop this area with you?". And I was like, that sounds great. And then I worked over summer, developing my skills in cheerleading music and come January, I had to have surgery on my ankle, and he came round to my house to choreograph a routine, and he asked, "So what are your plans for next year?" and I said, "Oh you know, finishing Uni, you know, maybe look for a job, and hoping to develop this music side of cheerleading more". And he didn't really say anything about it; he didn't really want me to come over and train anymore, and I just felt like he'd lost interest in expanding his business in that area, so I thought "Screw you, I'm not going to wait around, waste my time".

Rejection from the team because of physical constraints drove Chantal's ambition. The very idea of creating original music for the sporting activity from which she felt she was being excluded had been suggested by the same coach who had rejected her from the team.

In summary, many of the women that were interviewed had an early interest in sound, music and/or technology and combined this with an ambition to enter the music industry either in order to record their own music, or to make sure that musicians that they knew had their sound mediated by a trusted person. "Priming" by family and school experiences, and fascination with the environment of the studio itself, played an influential part in the determination of these women to work as engineers or producers. For some, a familiarity with sound technology, augmented by influences and expectations of family members (often fathers), normalized the place of that technology as part of life within the home, leading to an expectation within themselves that it should be normal to fully engage with such technology in the workplace. For others, their childhood environment in general provided the stimulation for out-of-the ordinary engagements with music. In the cases of Janet Beat and Chantal Epp, however, sheer anger at the injustice of their situations (family contempt in the former case, an accident in the latter) motivated them to move beyond what seemed to be expected of them and to create scenarios of self-determination in their careers. "Lightbulb" moments that inspired a desire to work in a professional recording studio context were described by Laura B, Mandy Parnell, "Natalie" and Isobel Campbell. Often, the word "obsession" has been used as a driver towards moving into the profession. Finally, the variety of learning methods, often self-initiated, are described by the interview sample, from practice-based learning, through to opportunities at school, surreptitiously watching professionals, a formal course, learning live sound, financial necessity, or turning around negative events.

Building on the interview material used in this chapter, and introducing other "voices" that add additional perspectives to the narratives of the women that I spoke to, the following chapter explores experiences of professionalizing skills, further shadowing, and early unsupervised sessions.

2 Becoming Professional: Entering the Music Industry

In this chapter, I have selected examples from my interviews that have highlighted routes into the professional side of music production, moving on from their first engagements with the industry. We have seen that entry-level opportunities for women producers and engineers often had the sense of accidental good fortune about them, yet the women themselves were driven by a combination of an innate confidence and enthusiasm in their use of music technology, and a strongly focused sense of ambition that often took on the appearance of a "calling". Consolidating their skills to a professional standard and working as mediators for other people rather than as self-producers, or working outside their circle of friends, involved taking a step into the professional world by whatever means they could.

Training, Apprenticeships and Mentoring: Routes into the Studio

Paying one's dues at an entry level in recording studios is an experience that both male and female studio professionals undertake. We will see varying degrees of formality in the practical training and experience that was undertaken by the selection of women that I interviewed. One of the interesting issues to emerge has been the way that they have dipped in and out of vocational training courses to augment their skills, networks, determination and patience.

Only one of the women interviewed, Mandy Parnell, had gone through a formal interview process. She had trained at SAE as a sound engineer in the 1980s, and at that time was one of only two women on the course. She had not originally been aware of an advertisement that the studio The Exchange had placed in the business publication *Music Week*; it had been there for a while:

> I was just on the phone and flipped [when I] saw the ad and they said "The cut-off is tomorrow for the CVs". So this is pre-computer times, and I didn't have a typed CV anywhere, so I hand-wrote a letter with spelling mistakes that I scribbled out (Graham at The Exchange has still got it), and all like squiggly on a bit of paper. I was

the "joke" interview; they couldn't believe somebody would send this in as a CV. If it had been nicely typed I probably wouldn't have got the interview, to be honest with you, because their criteria was that they didn't like to take people on who'd had any formal training. They liked to train them in-house, [in] very old school apprenticeships. 'Cos this was the '80s I think they *were* looking for a token woman in a sense.

There was intense competition for the job:

> They kept me waiting two hours for the interview. So by the time I got in there I was so wound up I don't think they could have *not* given me the job, I came across that forceful. They had a hundred applicants and they ended up taking three of us on.

This was in the 1980s, just as working practices were about to change with the introduction of digital music technology. Mandy's training experience at The Exchange followed an "old-school" trajectory:

> We'd spend two weeks in the copy room, doing production parts. Production parts were still on reel-to-reel then. Bin masters, the masters that went to the factory for the cassettes, so that was very long, real time. We had two copy rooms going. A lot of work came through the copy rooms. You started off in the copy room and you'd have one-week training where you'd sit behind an engineer. And I sat behind Ray Staff, who was a Trident[1] engineer who's over at AIR [studios] now.

Ray had one of the first Sonic Solutions digital workstations, which cost £100,000, and Mandy found it very difficult to understand how the computer worked, because her initial training had been in the use of analogue recording technology:

> So I asked him whether I could take the manual home on Friday; they all laughed and took the mickey out of me as they always did, you know, typical male mentality, try to figure it out without the manual. You don't find many men that will open a package and look at the manual. I took the manual home, read it, wrote down loads and loads of questions, went back in on the Monday and went "I've got questions". I think I won his heart forever on that, to be honest.

1 Trident Studios, which opened in London in 1968, was one of London's most famous studios. They pioneered the use of Dolby sound and eight-track recording, later developing a mixing desk marketed under that name.

Like Mandy Parnell, an awareness of the need for strategic planning after her first spontaneous decision to join the Clash on tour had led to Laura B's move to London from Paris. Returning there afterwards, Laura B continued to develop her career, finding work in the Studio de Champs-Elysees, recording the mainstream artist Daniel Guichard and appearing with him on French TV as his engineer:

> Guichard is really uncool when you're 20 and you're listening to music coming from London and you're listening to the Clash and all these bands, and you're doing Daniel "boring" Guichard. And I went on television with him, as his engineer, because he obviously had TV following him everywhere, so TV came into the studio, so I got on the TV as the engineer for Guichard and I thought, this is really rubbish.

Feeling trapped by the role, she made a spontaneous decision because of the speed at which her skills were developing:

> I thought if I stayed in Paris now, I would never progress, I would never do the great stuff I wanted to do: I'd never work with the great artists I wanted to work with, I'll just stay here and that'll be it. So, I came home that evening, and the next morning I was on the first train to London. Literally just like that, no plan, not knowing anyone, nothing at all.

Later, after the move to London, Laura used her experience of live engineering with the Clash as a bargaining tool when she searched for studio opportunities:

> The sound engineer from the Clash said he knew the girl who was managing Utopia Studios, little place, a really good studio in Primrose Hill. So he said "Just go and see her, just say you've worked with me". So I went to see her, I said, "Hi, it's me, I'm looking for a job in a studio, do you have anything?" and she said "No we don't need anyone, but next door are looking for someone". And next door happened to be Mayfair Studios. So, I strolled up the road, went to Mayfair Studios, knocked on the door, saying "Do you need an assistant engineer?"

A similar sense of determination and invincibility to that reported by Mandy Parnell focused her performance at the interview:

> And I was just so fired up about everything and I really wanted to be the best engineer in the world. I had done the Clash; I had been

> working only for two years [and] I was really excited. And I think they just couldn't knock me. A few days later I had an interview with [the owner] John, who asked me some technical questions and I replied to everything, and he kept saying "Ooh, I'm impressed, ooh, I'm impressed". And I got a job.

Once she had a foot in the door, however, she had a similar back-room experience to Mandy; aspiring engineers had to go through a test of their commitment and fortitude before being allowed into the control room:

> Mayfair is where I got my main base in engineering, it wasn't with the Clash, it wasn't in Paris, it wasn't Guichard. [It was at] Mayfair; I was stuck in a copying suite for three months. No fresh air, no daylight, no nothing, just loads of cassette machines and just like a half-inch machine and I would get masters, or copies of masters and run the cassettes through like a copyist. And I was doing that, day in, day out and I had to hack it. Mayfair wasn't going to play sweet. Training was just about as hard as it gets. And everything would be as disheartening as possible, just to filter people out.

Sally Smith followed a different pathway, by bartering skills with a studio owner. She moved from live engineering into studio work in the 1980s by negotiating an exchange of administrative work and book-keeping for studio training in Nick Sykes's north London "Rooster" studio. Most of the time she worked as a tape-op because the artists coming into the studio were quite well known (Billy Bragg used the studio, for instance): "I didn't really have the nerve to say, 'Let me take over, let me do stuff'". She carried on working as a live sound engineer while in training, and eventually by 1985 she had enough confidence to move on to freelance engineering at Triple X Studios in Harlesden with her then partner, recording smaller bands who eventually used their skills for their live gigs, too:

> We did a lot of sessions there, the two of us, or sometimes one or other of us, depending on who was available, so that was the first kind of commercial studio stuff I'd done. There were no big, big names, but there were bands that had small record deals that came in a lot. It was quite a big variety of stuff, we had some really nice very melodic singers, and some really heavy, thrashy type stuff. It was all sorts of stuff. And from that we got quite a lot of live work as well, because they were all gigging bands that came in. So quite often we'd go and do their live sound as well as the studio sound.

An Alternative Route: From Artist to Engineer

Several of the women that were interviewed became producers and engineers through the route of being recording artists first of all, and this mostly happened with vocalists. Sometimes, frustration at the cost of recording, and sometimes frustration at the inability of producers in the studios where they were working to capture the sounds they heard in their own heads, was a motivator. Someone who had previously regarded themselves as purely a musician would find it necessary to learn the technical skills they needed to become autonomous and set up on their own, as described here by Isobel Campbell:

> The main reason I learnt recording skills was to obtain the ability to execute my ideas as accurately as possible. More knowledge of equipment and recording terminologies meant I could get closer to the sounds I was imagining, hearing in my head and dreaming about. Over the years the more and more time spent in studios it just seemed natural and right to be involved in pushing buttons and twiddling knobs.

Isobel spent long working days in Cava Studios in Kelvingrove, Glasgow from 1996 to 2009, recording with her band Belle and Sebastian. She describes it as "my second home". Their schedule was intense, and during this time she began to realize that she needed to have more control over the studio hardware herself in order to achieve the sound she wanted as a client, which did not always match the aesthetic decisions made by the studio engineer:

> Most days we'd start at around 10am or 11am and leave around 4am or later at times. During this time with the band I remember feeling a little frustrated because I could often hear specific sounds in my head and I'd try and convey them to the studio engineer and often he wouldn't quite understand or capture what I was getting at. For example, Evie Sands came into the studio whilst she was in Glasgow to sing 'Landslide', a song I had written. I remember Chris [Geddes, aka Beans] and I begging one particular engineer to distort a vocal we were recording to tape and the engineer was getting flustered and uncomfortable.

Isobel had an idea in her head about the sort of sonic palette she wanted, but this was not facilitated by the engineer, who could not bring himself to tailor his aesthetic approach to that of his clients:

> Both Chris and I are big soul, Motown, Stax and Northern Soul fans and quite often on these great classic 45s the vocal was recorded hot

> to tape. It may have been a mistake but it sounded GREAT! Back in those days a lot of these records were made with a very production-line approach. They ploughed through stuff. Motown and Stax were hit factories. Nonetheless, regardless of whether the distortion was a mistake or not, these vocals recorded hot to tape were very pleasing to the ear. At least that was in our opinion. Chris and I knew technically what we were looking for in the studio but the engineer was visibly squirming and really did not want to do this and in the end he never did distort that vocal.

Experiences like this led Isobel to make the decision to become a producer herself and learn what she calls "the language of the studio", making creative capital out of the negative experiences that she had had when the aesthetics of her work were controlled by people with more advanced technical knowledge:

> I feel like that time in my life was like an apprenticeship for me. I learnt so much. The barrier came down. You can read books and attend lectures on sound recording, but for me nothing compared to the actual real, physical, practical time spent in the studio. Audio equipment becomes less and less intimidating the more time spent around it.

Frustration with other people's working practices also drove Jacqueline Pelham-Leigh (JPL) to set up and run her own studio in Wood Green, London. Originally a rapper, she:

> got fed up of waiting for people to give me tracks to write to. It's as simple as that. So I thought, how hard can it be? And then in 1999 I got my first piece of equipment, the Yamaha EX7. I still use that keyboard, and when I bought that, Yamaha used to do this sort of mini-disc mixing desk, an MD4, so I bought that and I started that way. And when I started I didn't know the difference between a snare drum and a side stick, I didn't know the difference, but you know I was just programming and giving it a try. From a very young age in my music career from the production point of view, I kind of understood it was great to get musicians in; I think that's what helps me with my sound. I have a great way of recording musicians because now I've been doing it for 15 years.

JPL was not afraid to simply ask questions to find out what she needed to know, and this implies a real sense of confidence:

> I was thrown in the deep end. And you know I always believe a lot of things are a necessity or need, and I was quite fortunate enough to be around engineers who liked me enough to teach me as I had sessions with them; they'd teach me the quick reach around things, and I'm a believer in "If you're lost, ask for directions".

Adrienne Aitken had originally wanted to be vocalist, but set up her production company after seeing that a friend was making money from writing music for commercials. Her then partner and herself, driven by ambition, started amassing equipment to realize their potential as producers:

> We said "Well, we can do that". So we set up a production company and started sending demos in. It was a different game then, we didn't really have any real equipment. We had a reel-to-reel tape machine, he had a guitar, I had my Juno 6 and that was it. So we borrowed, hired and scraped equipment to do some demos with, and any time we got any money it went straight back into buying another piece of equipment. My partner wouldn't let me buy anything until we had the money from a job to buy it, which was very wise because I would have got us into debt pretty quickly.

Adrienne had to learn very quickly while they amassed the equipment they needed:

> As I bought the equipment it was for the next job, which meant I had to learn [how to use] it on the spot. So whether it was an Emax sampler, an Akai sampler, or we'd got a desk that's got more than treble and bass on it, you need to know how those buttons work. I was in there learning how it worked, and what I couldn't learn I'd go and find someone that had one, and ask them. And everything was totally done by what my ears heard, and if that sounded all right.

An experience of recording as a vocal session singer was the route taken into engineering by Samantha Bennett, in the 1990s. Through a friend's network, she was invited to add vocals to a track in Colossus Studios in London, working alongside engineer Paul Barton: "And then I ended up just turning up at the studio, and that turned into doing a bit of programming for them, then it turned into engineering, so I just literally fell into that job". She learned how to "drive" the studio herself as an engineer within six months:

> One of the guys, who was a partner [in the studio] thought he was in the market with girl bands and boy bands, so we'd have a lot of these kind of stage school types. I remember that band Blue, who lived not very far up the road from there, sort of north-west-ish

London, coming down and recording something once: it was all demo-y stuff. Sometimes people just literally wanted to pay to come in to use the studio to record their voice on a backing track, just to have it; or a publisher wanted to send a songwriter down with a singer to record a track for an ad or something like that. It was all that sort of stuff, it was nothing like somewhere like Townhouse or even Abbey Road, or AIR, where you have big name artists coming in and recording a big album. I was never a producer, I was an engineer and I'd run sessions or I'd assist on sessions a lot of the time too.

Katia Isakoff's route into the production of other artists than herself came about through disappointment with the quality of the recordings that she, as a client, had left the studio with after a long recording session.

I walked out with nine songs that were so far removed from what I heard in my head; what I was hearing was a finished song, and what was on the cassette was so far away from that, and I just didn't know how to get there. I thought if I just got better at presenting something that's more developed, then I might get understood and someone might hear what I was hearing. So I bought myself a Fostex 4 track,[2] a CS1000 AKG microphone, and a little effects box, because a couple of people that I knew were Scandinavian pop musicians and worked in music shops that sold equipment, so they could at least advise me on equipment.

At a gig at The Troubadour in Earl's Court in the 1990s she got to know an older acoustic songwriter whose lyrics she really engaged with, and she offered to record his songs for him:

"Please come over to my place, I'll record you, you've got to have a cassette, you've got to record, these songs matter too much". And so he came over and I recorded his songs over a couple of days, and they just sounded fabulous because the songs were so good, and it didn't sound anything like what *I'd* ended up with, the sort of speeded-up vocal that just sounded odd to me. I didn't understand the processing that had been done to mine. And so that gave me some confidence.

---

2   Tascam, Fostex and Teac were all companies that manufactured four-track cassette recording machines that facilitated home recording of demo tapes in the 1980s before digital recording equipment became available.

Lauren Deakin Davies began her career as a producer at a Hertfordshire studio, The Cream Room, while she was still a teenager. She had the drive to put together her own bands from the age of 15 and she was determined to "play out" as much as possible. Her own route into production came about through being a client:

> I got hired at 17 as a producer. Like, who *does* that? It happened because I was busking in the street, and someone came up to us and said I think you're really good, here's my card, I think you should come and record in my studio. So we were like "Oh my God!" So we went to that studio and I got on really well with the person that owned it. And then as I got slightly older I started doing my own music production using Audacity and my laptop speakers in my own house, and he knew that I was doing that, he knew I could play guitar, and he knew I could write songs and everything.

Lauren's first job in the studio was as a musical chaperone, employed by the enlightened male studio owner, Martin Lumsden, to facilitate a recording by a young female artist who might otherwise have felt intimidated in a studio environment populated by older men.

> He'd got this 14-year-old girl coming into the session and he had an engineer there who was a guy and who was slightly older. He said "I think you would be really good in the session; I think you should produce this because I think you'd get on with her". That was Alexa Mullins, and we're still really close friends. And that's how I ended up getting hired; I worked on a lot of projects at that studio, and then improving my own studio as well. It's a shed at the bottom of the garden – it's called The Den.

In a similar way to Lauren, the live sound engineer Alison Ward had felt driven to put together her own bands from an early age; she had been a talented young bass player, mentored by Alison Rayner, the jazz musician who had been a founder member of the all-women band The Guest Stars. She started working behind the bar at The Vortex, a well-respected jazz venue in Dalston, London, so she could enjoy the gigs while working at the same time:

> Ally [sic] said to me, "Look, we need an engineer, please can you do it?" And I said, "I don't know", although I'd been looking at the set-up there thinking it was great, you know I was drawn to it ... I was basically dying to get into a sound-booth but I lacked confidence. Then Alejandro, the guy who's now working at the Union Chapel was on, and he invited me to come and shadow him. And as soon as I started I was like a duck to water: I'm in that sound-booth

> night after night, with the most amazing music and with people saying things like "We have played at The Vortex for ten years and I don't know what you're doing, but we've never sounded so good here". And I don't know what I'm doing that's different to what anybody else is doing, but I think as a musician and a sound engineer, that's a really important combination, I think having an understanding of structure through playing in a band and understanding that whole side, that is really important. But I also have technical know-how *and* creative know-how with it, and I'm certainly doing something right because time and time again everybody is saying "This has just been fantastic".

Eleonora Romano started working professionally as a live engineer in 2002 after the experience of shadowing professional live sound engineers, whom she actively engaged with at gigs that she attended:

> I used to go to a lot of gigs, and at the same time started giving my CV to people, or handing them my card and saying, you know, if you need somebody [contact me]. And I went to see an MC5 gig at The Astoria, a friend of mine put me on the guest list ... and when he left I kind of tapped on one of the engineer's shoulders, and I said, "Hi, are you the house engineer or the visiting engineer?" I knew he was the house engineer, because I could tell, so I gave him my card, and actually he did call me and I started working there, training for about three months as a stage/patch engineer and then after that I started working on proper shifts first as a FOH [front of house], then monitor engineer.

She had observed the hierarchy at The Astoria before she started working there formally as an engineer, and worked out the most useful knowledge that she could acquire:

> We used to have three engineers because there are three positions, one is front of house, one is monitors, and the other one would be the person who does all the patching. So, on very busy gigs, I think from three bands onwards we would have a third person ... I started doing front of house; actually, when I was training I was doing the patch, because if you don't know how to patch (lots of engineers don't know how to patch, perhaps I shouldn't say this), but yeah, it's fundamental, and then from that I did front of house and then, probably the last job that I did was monitors. Because in a way that was the most difficult one, it's more senior.

2 Becoming Professional 49

After experimenting informally on her "inherited" Portastudio, as described in the previous chapter, Felix Mackintosh cut her professional teeth as an assistant engineer at a post-production studio working for a producer who recorded orchestras for film scores. Constantly sent off to make tea or to the photocopier just when it seemed things were getting interesting in the studio, she found the work really frustrating at first:

> I remember one time (at that point he had an ADAT Studio), being sent upstairs with the third ADAT machine that had gone down while he had an orchestra at huge expense, because they were on 150 quid each an hour or whatever, so I took the third machine upstairs and was on the phone for ages to find out how to fix it.

She became adept at mending equipment, but had a difficult preliminary experience in sole control of the studio:

> And the first time I actually got to go on the desk was when he fell asleep at about 3 in the morning and his client said "No no, you get on", because he wanted to finish off the project. It was great fun till I kicked the machine; again it was stuff we just don't have any more. All the automation was on a hardwire and I kicked it and it went off, so we had to wake up the producer because all the automation had gone down.

Later, Felix started work at the community studio Ovatones, an Arts Council funded project whose policy was to further the careers of minority communities and women in London (Women's Liberation Music Archive n.d.).[3] The positive approach of the studio to hiring female personnel meant that for a short period the studio had *only* women engineers, which was unusual in the 1980s:

> What was so great about it was that there was a really golden period for about five or six years, where we had three female engineers. We had Libby Elliott, me, and a woman called Sushi. The guys used to come in and the third time they came in they'd say "Well I worked with this woman called Libby, then I worked with a woman called Sushi, now I'm working with you: are all the engineers women?" And we'd go "Yeah". People used to come because they liked it, and it was Arts Council and [gender] stopped being an issue. And then Ovatones started using male engineers and that whole thing kind of just stopped.

3   https://womensliberationmusicarchive.co.uk/

Sometimes, and unusually, the simplest routes into studio sessions worked successfully. Isabel Gracefield Grundy, who originally studied sound engineering on the Commercial Music BA at the University of Westminster, had been combining some freelance recording sessions with her studies. She started to work on electronic dance music with James Reynolds, who was at the time mixing tracks by Tinchy Stryder and Tinie Tempah. She advanced her career through the greatly under-rated and sometimes mythologized technique of making people tea:

> He was in the same building as a really good music accountancy firm; I used to go and make him cups of tea, and then make all the accountants cups of tea, and one of the ladies there was doing accounts for a producer called Fraser T. Smith. She knew that they had an opening there, so she put me forward for that job. My official job title was junior engineer, so I was engineering all the songwriting demos for artists, and then increasingly towards the end doing some bigger sessions, and I mixed a couple of records for him as well. And in my time there, we did Cee-Lo Green's *The Lady Killer* and Adele's *21*.

Isabel moved on to work at RAK Studios in London's St. John's Wood, and there began to develop her own strengths as a producer/engineer:

> I'm really good [at] working with songwriters, and I'm really strong with arrangements and that sort of thing. So I do a lot of work with rock bands, not heavy rock, but experimental stuff, I do a lot of work with singer-songwriters. I've just finished producing a record that is pure folk, which is quite unusual for me because I tend to come from an electronica/dance background. And it's all really vintage sounds as well. So when I'm producing it's much more about finding out what the artist's influences and wants are, and then you patch them together, rather than necessarily having a specialism. So I'd say my specialism is – or I try and make it be about – facilitating what the artist wants rather than imposing any sort of signature sound. But because I tend to contribute to arrangements I'll just have note choices and suggestions that are just what I tend to go for, so through that you can tell it's mine; but not necessarily through the sonics of it.

It was a sense of injustice that drove Cathy Cuvelier to open her own reggae production studio, because she had spent so much time working uncredited for other artists on an informal basis that she felt she had become invisible. At first, because of her gender, she was encouraged to be a singer; she did, however, find one engineer who encouraged her to do what she wanted:

> And yes, that was interesting because he showed me how he did his job, and I think he was the only one who took me seriously when I said: "I want to do *that*". He was like, "Yeah, if you want to do it, you can do it", you know when everybody's like, "Naah, just sing", and I was like: "I can't sing!" It's like, "Everybody can sing", but that's not me, I'm not feeling it: I'm feeling the machine.

She had sat in on family members' recording sessions in Jamaica, quietly observing what went on, and picking up tips about both sound and studio etiquette. The feeling of invisibility that had worked to her advantage while she was learning skills in male-dominated studios in Jamaica, eventually began to undermine her confidence as an engineer. A member of her family had married one of the musicians from reggae band Burning Spear; she moved to England with them and registered at Cornell College for a BTEC in Music Technology, where praise from her fellow students about her existing studio skills raised her confidence again:

> Then I had the chance to work with Gregory Zack, Sugar Minott, and I travelled to Jamaica to do my production where I'd hire the best musicians and play back my productions in [a] live [situation]. I wanted to make it different by using digital with analogue and mixing the two together; obviously, a real bass will sound better than playing bass on a keyboard, a plug-in, but I still use the plug-in and keep the natural instrument, the reverberation. So I used to experience those kinds of sounds, and I worked with some great musicians. The reggae scene is really versatile. I was always sitting in with someone who had a piece of equipment, and as soon as they left it, "Can I have a look, can I have a go?" When I decided to build my own studio was when I realized I had to ask too much from people and wasn't gaining anything. I worked in a lot of studios and I wasn't credited on the production of so much stuff. It wasn't about the money, it was about the work I did, and the recognition of what I did, and I was wiped out like I never existed, and I suffered a lot with that.

Looking for Opportunities

An ability to imagine themselves in a professional role, and being able to persuade potential employers that there was a need for that role in their studio, was a strategic approach that secured employment for Helen Atkinson, studio manager and engineer at RAK at the time of the interview (and a colleague of Isabel Gracefield Grundy). Helen originally started working at RAK: she could see that there was a gap in the support structure of the studio that she could fill, because RAK was relying completely on freelance engineers at the time:

> I was doing a lot of pick-up work of things that just needed to be done all of the time, like keeping all the stores tidy and making sure the microphones had clips and that the screens were cleaned and the pianos were back in the right places, and all that kind of stuff; the in-between jobs that when you've got four studios and a bunch of freelancers just tend not to get done so frequently. So I spoke to the management team here and I said "I'm here a lot of the time, and I'm picking up a lot of the work that your in-house people would have done five years ago but now you don't have any in-house, and maybe you should redress that balance". We came to an arrangement where I was on a part-time retainer so I could still go off and do freelance work and keep things fresh and interesting but then, at the same time, I've got a steady income and I know where I'm coming to work most of the time.

A similar enterprising approach to entering the recording industry was echoed in an entirely different music genre by one-time rapper Ms Melody. Like some of the women interviewed at the beginning of the chapter, she had started out as a performer, and had achieved a level of success before deciding that she didn't want to be subjected to the control of corporate labels as her independent career became more successful:

> By the time I was 21, I got headhunted to be part of an MC-ing girls' group. Got signed to it, a small independent production company, released a few songs and we were up with a bidding war against a few big major record companies including Virgin and Columbia Records for a couple of million pounds, and I decided to walk away from it and the whole group fell apart. It didn't sit right. I knew that I definitely was not driven by money; I knew that I was driven by wanting to be creatively free and be able very much to have a say in my creative expression, and I didn't feel that I had that, in that particular situation.

Feeling that she was not being taken seriously, she enrolled on a City and Guilds course in Sound Engineering at the Institute of Music Technology in Deptford, south London, where she passed the course. In this respect she demonstrates an understanding of the need for formal training that has also been reported by Felix Mackintosh and Cathy Cuvelier. It was the respect of other students in her cohort that encouraged her to set up on her own:

> I didn't know what I was doing, but it was during that course I thought of starting my own business, where I wanted to open up a place like an Internet café where people come in and hire a workstation by the hour, with music software and a little music keyboard

and headphones. I said it as a joke in class, and another student said that's a bloody good idea, and 18 months later I'd opened it, funded by the Prince's Trust. I started in a place about two minutes from London Bridge, a place that was formerly called The Hit Factory that was owned by Pete Waterman. In 2004 I had a room in there. And I was around renowned engineers, so I had a very fortunate start. When I look back on it now, I smile because of the level of my naivety. But I was riding high on passion, and luckily for me they took me under their wing after a while.

Ms Melody found herself at the heart of the burgeoning grime (and later funky house) scene from the early 2000s onwards, picking up tips from successful artists in the genre who shared the same workspace and who were working in cutting-edge music genres:

> Skillz had a really successful group at the time that was called Big Brovaz and they were actually doing some chart-topping music, which was quite rare for an urban act back in 2004; he was good to me, I was very inspired by him. And then a funky house producer moved in about 6 months after me, and he was actually one of the originators of funky house music; he was mashing up and breaking up beats, and being quite experimental with grime or different types of sounds until he kind of created his own, which then got classified as funky house; his name was Fingaprint and me and him still remain good friends to this day. He's had a lot of chart success.

My final example illustrates a fact highlighted by the self-defined recording engineer Steve Albini at the ARP conference at Leeds Metropolitan University in 2010, with his response to a question from the floor about the best routes into the industry. "Learn to repair studio equipment", he replied, "and you'll never be out of work". This was exactly the experience of one of the most successful engineers that I interviewed, albeit from the USA. Susan Rogers had discovered when she was young that she preferred listening to music to making her own music, and gave up piano lessons after two years: "I realized that I loved records *way* more than I loved music in its raw form". Stimulated by overhearing the disappointment expressed by a friend who had failed to become a recording engineer, she took extraordinary lengths to gain the skills to enter the recording profession through a lateral route:

> I was too timid or humble to *admit* to wanting to be a recording engineer but prodded by nascent ambition I landed a position as receptionist at a two-room Hollywood trade school called University of Sound Arts. I couldn't afford the tuition to be a student so I learned

> by reading the textbooks: *Modern Recording Techniques*, *Sound System Engineering* and *The Theory of Sound*. My life changed when I overheard a perhaps bitter, underemployed teacher telling an audio student, "If you want to always have a job, become a maintenance engineer". I put myself on the maintenance engineer track that day.

Just as Mandy Parnell had swotted up on theory, Susan was determined to learn everything she could by reading manuals:

> I followed a friend's advice and persuaded the United States government (over the phone) to send me the US Army's electronics training manuals. They sent me 10 paper-bound volumes covering principles of direct current through microwave technology, just for the cost of postage. I studied these books and about the same time responded to a help-wanted ad in the *Los Angeles Times*.

Through being an audio service technician, servicing many of the 500 very varied studio environments in Los Angeles, she became in-house maintenance technician for Rudy Records in 1981, a studio in Hollywood that was owned by Graham Nash and David Crosby, and where she occasionally assisted on recording sessions. She observed: "I didn't realize it at the time, but getting to observe a range of record makers from veterans to the clueless presented the perfect smorgasbord of correct and incorrect studio behaviors [sic]!" It was in 1983 that Susan joined Prince's studio in Minneapolis:

> He assumed that the person who installed and repaired his equipment could also operate it (and why wouldn't he?) and so expected me to fulfil the engineer's role on his records. He didn't know or care about the artistry of the audio engineer. He had his own sound and was very hands-on in the studio; he basically engineered himself with the assistance of someone who knew signal flow. In time I developed my own sound and he trusted me with more artistic decisions. I was his employee until 1988, working on *Purple Rain*, *Around the World in a Day*, *Parade*, *Sign o' the Times*, *The Black Album*, and the records we made for other artists during that period.

I have described in this chapter a variety of different routes into studio work: formal application, less formal apprenticeships, often combined with back-up vocational training, disappointment with commercial studios leading to self-production and from there leading to production of other clients, lack of acknowledgement of the role in collaborative studio processes, and the use of ingenuity to create roles and activities that lead to income generation. Often, there is an overlap between these different factors, and this chapter has further illustrated the atypicality of a career as a producer/engineer. In the next chapter, the value of self-determination will be explored in greater detail, moving on from the idea of being enterprising to entrepreneurship itself, from portfolio working (in particular, being involved in adult education) to niche specialization, and being the "go-to" person for particular skills, knowledge and experience.

3 Specialization and Entrepreneurship

This chapter will discuss the value of specialization, beginning with work in the higher education sector, which can often complement a freelance career and can provide a stable income while still allowing for creative and freelance opportunities. We will then move on to live sound engineering, genre specialization (expertise in the genres of reggae, rap music, singer/songwriter, gospel and rock), work focused on advertising, laptop production, and listening events, before ending with two specific unusual field recording projects that required resilience and a sense of adventure. The development of a niche as a producer or engineer, together with recognition of opportunities that might not at first appear obvious, encouraged several of the women interviewed to translate a gap that they perceived in the studio landscape, into a sustainable career. As Wolfe notes with the self-producers in her research, self-determination is a key current concept in the music industry (2019: 23), and I will show that in terms of music mediators, an ability to conceptualize their essential role and build their skills and networks accordingly is a vital strategy for their survival in their respective professional spheres. Servicing a niche genre is not without its risks (for instance, invisibility to the mainstream which might lead to lack of opportunity to branch out and develop), but it can provide a secure income and respect for specialist expertise by a client or client base that is good for both the morale and the professional standing of the producer or engineer. From the extracts in this chapter, it is clear that each woman has a deep understanding of the area in which they operate and its particular demands and aesthetic values.

Working in Education

For some studio professionals, undertaking educational activities, in particular adult education, allows them to develop not only their teaching and mentoring skills, but also their creative work. Returning firstly to Janet Beat, she was able to develop her experimentation in music with the encouragement of male colleagues at an institution where she was completing her Diploma in Education:

> I had marvellous support from my head of department at my college of education, Dr Watkin Shaw. And people were surprised because he was a musicologist, specializing in John Blow, Purcell and Handel. He was the first one who supported me in electronic music. He was the only head of department I've ever had who said "The thing about having a young person, is you bring young person's ideas in and I want to encourage that". Because I was writing my thesis he knew that I understood music, and he encouraged me and I started a little electronic music course there, [focusing on] musique concrète. With a physics lecturer who was interested we built a little ring modulator; you know Stockhausen had some piece [that included a part for a] ring modulator. We built that with some little filters. And I started a little musique concrète course; we bought a signal generator so the students could get the basic sine waves there and with a little filter and ring modulator circuit we had a little course going; this was some time around 1965.

Dot Allen, who now works at Edinburgh College in the Music department, was inspired by the enthusiasm of John Stevens, who set up Community Music in Islington, London in 1983, to train musicians to work in non-traditional settings; she created a portfolio of music technology teaching work in different educational settings, while continuing to work as a session keyboard player.

> I was involved in [the organization] Community Music; I did a music course there for a year, and we did a lot of technology. John Stevens actually started it; he unfortunately passed away just as we finished our qualification. He was a drummer, but they had technology courses there. I was also teaching in this all girls secondary school, Elizabeth Garrett Anderson School, part-time, doing music technology and I set up their music technology suite.[1] I was also teaching in FE colleges, doing night classes in Cubase and music tech.
>
> *Whose idea was it to set up the music technology suite at Elizabeth Garrett Anderson?*
>
> It was the head of music; originally there were a few PCs that were set up by a previous tutor, Sheila Maloney, who went on to work at Westminster Kingsway College. She left and the head of music phoned me; Sheila put her in touch with me and she asked me to set up a music technology suite.
>
> *And was there quite a lot of interest from the girls?*

---

1   The Elizabeth Garrett Anderson School is one of the schools that formed part of Victoria Armstrong's research, which will be referred to in a later chapter.

> Yes, it was part of their GCSE music; they had to use music tech but they were actually very musical and good at songwriting, so it was a natural thing for them really. But at the time it was those old iMacs, which were quite clunky, using Cubase. It's obviously just females there so there's no intimidation from guys. They've never felt uncomfortable. Quite often I've found when girls are in the studio with guys they let the blokes do everything.

Karina Townsend, also an alumnus of Community Music, ran the music technology courses at the City Lit in London for 13 years before they were closed down in 2015. Her clientele was from a varied demographic, and Karina was inspired by teaching studio skills to a wide variety of people, from 19 to 75 years of age:

> One of my oldest students in recent times has been a lady who was a singer-songwriter, guitarist, flamenco singer, flamenco guitarist as well, who suffered physical issues with her hands that affected what she could do, so she took up music technology in her late sixties, and at the age of 75, when her first computer died, she was given a computer by her sons, turned it on with a new version of Cubase, and thought, "Ah, it doesn't look anything like before", so she came to update her Cubase skills with me. And she's fantastic, and she was in a class with a 19-year-old guy, and a young woman with cerebral palsy, so it's a real mish-mash of everyone. So the lovely thing for me was that I taught music technology subjects to a wide variety of adult learners, some with no experience of technology, some with no experience of music.

Personal experience has driven Karina to become a facilitator and trainer in music technology:

> I've set out to share my absolute conviction that technology has allowed me to participate in music-making events and activities way above and beyond what I'd ever imagined I'd be able to do, and I want to share that with other people.

Live Sound Engineering

Eleonora Romano's skills as a live sound engineer led to her becoming a specialist monitor engineer, eventually leading to her broadening out from rock music and hip hop into entirely different genres of music. She learned to become flexible by working in many different situations that might have been challenging. On one occasion, she mixed The Fall : "You know, Mark E. Smith made me put all the mikes everywhere, in the kick drum, and then at some point I just gave up, 'cos you just think, 'what is this?'". Discussing another memorable occasion, Eleonora recalled:

> I did monitors for Jerry Lee Lewis once, at The Forum, and I did not really sound-check them because he was very frail and he just turned up for the gig. His sister was prepping everything for him, and that was really nice; I was told that he was some kind of monster, but he wasn't. He did not complain, but I guess he's quite deaf by now, but nevertheless he did a brilliant show, but it was very short. I did just one gig, but I enjoyed it because I'm also a massive fan. I think I do enjoy working for people that know what they want, and so when they know what they want, whether they're older or younger, it's all very easy, and very professional.

After her original interview for this book, Eleonora went back on the road:

> In July 2014 I was asked to join Yann Tiersen (who produced the film soundtrack for *Amélie* and *Goodbye Lenin*) and his band as their monitor engineer on their "Infinity" album tour. The tour finished at the beginning of August 2015. I have also been working at the Linbury Theatre within the Royal Opera House since June 2014, where I mainly do sound for contemporary operas and ballet. I have to say that I enjoy immensely working in theatre, it makes such a nice and interesting change from my usual rock'n'roll environment!

Willingness to travel and the stamina to survive under sometimes gruelling touring conditions are essential to sustaining the career of a live sound engineer. "Normal" life has to be put to one side; enthusiasm about change, the stimulation of constant learning, and adaptation to different conditions, mean that the job requires a particular sort of commitment, as touring sound engineer Debbie Dickinson observed:

> I built up my actual technical knowledge on a "needs must" basis. I was lucky because a lot of that early work was in Germany and the engineers there were very happy to talk to me about sound, and actually in general sound engineers (the good ones) are extremely generous about sharing their knowledge and love talking about technical matters. After the Guest Stars disbanded in the late '80s I have continued to be a tour manager/sound engineer with some amazing American and UK based jazz musicians for over 25 years. I still very much learn on the job. I am a sound engineer who works with musicians so I travel with musicians and mix on the equipment that is provided. It is an amazing way of learning.

In a more static position, working in-house at The Vortex allows Alison Ward to develop a side-line in live recording at the venue:

> I've been doing loads of live recordings here; it's changing my perception of music ... because I'm getting this most amazing diet of world-class musicians that are playing here. I'm not interested in doing any studio work, I love the energy of this and what interests me is getting good quality recordings of the gigs. Although there again, to have a good recording that you know represents the gig, captures the essence of the gig, it doesn't have to be top-notch quality to still achieve that. But I'm still a perfectionist!

A proactive personality while at school is something that Alison had in common with Helen Atkinson of RAK Studios, as mentioned in Chapter 1. Alison's journey into live engineering had been supported by her entrepreneurial activities while she was still at school, where she discovered that she had the ability to make things happen. As Alison remarks:

> I started lots of bands and told the school it was sexual discrimination that they didn't have a drum kit and the boys' school did, so they got a drum kit. And then I left school when I was 17, I left early and it wasn't the done thing to do because it was quite a well-thought-of posh girls' school. I was just really touched because we'd played at SW1, this club in Victoria, at 16, 17-years-old, and I got this 12-piece soul band together and sorted out people that could probably play the drums and got people who had brothers with guitars, just get it all in, and we were all right in the end, you know.

Her almost anarchic approach to the scenarios that she could create at a young age evidently fed into her later ability to say yes to opportunities in the music industry that could have been challenging; her live engineering work at The Vortex in London is a high-profile role but support from informal mentoring meant she was able to overcome any sense of being daunted, and thus take on her role while accepting that it might be challenging.

Genre Specialization

Specialization is a strategy that contributes to the longevity of a studio engineer or producer's career; becoming embedded in a genre or scene is often a successful way of focusing skills in a particular area, and becoming a "go-to" sound person in that field.

3 Specialization and Entrepreneurship   61

Katia Isakoff worked in electronic music in the 1990s, developing skills in analogue synth recording in a studio complex in West London and working with Mute Records before changing tack:

> We started working with a band called Add N to (X) who were just being signed by Mute. Through various musicians who we were working with at Unit 20, our studio, we got the contract to produce the album *Avant Hard*, and engineer it there. I became friends with Ann Shenton from the band. They were offered a record deal with Mute, they wanted to go into a studio and it made sense to come [to us] because we were up the road from Mute. We were an analogue-synth studio, we weren't expensive, and we were essentially mates: we just connected, and so it was a no-brainer. The whole thing worked brilliantly because when we needed to bring in more musicians or expand, we had a great relationship with Philip from Eastcote [studio] so we could take the project into there. Alison Goldfrapp came and sang on that record, their first album, and through that relationship and through that network, that's how Goldfrapp got signed to Mute.

The Add N to (X) third album (for Mute) *Loud Like Nature* was significant for Katia as a composer, performer and producer, consolidating her skills, and leading to syncs in a Stephen Spielberg TV series and 2018 Grand Prix highlights. For a while afterwards, she and her partner Steve D'Agostino became technical advisors for record labels who were setting up small demo studios on their premises:

> We had the studio for 12 years, developing bands and so on, so you can imagine a lot of people came through. Any time something crashed it was me who was on the phone to the companies, it was me who was on the phone because a plug-in wasn't doing what it was supposed to be doing, so I had to get my head around all that technology because that's how I earned a living.

Isakoff and D'Agostino worked in partnership, with Isakoff demonstrating the same determination to learn and excel as other women producers:

> If we met a manager or a company and they said, "We're going to set up a studio in our building for the bands that we sign, will you come and set it up for us?" I was there with Steve, making all the cables. So it was like, how do you solder? I'd be on the phone to some of these companies, to the guy who makes their cables and he would talk me through how to do a better job of it. I would be going, "Yeah but how would I normalize it if I did this?" and just learning

that way. So, everything was just about, "Show me and I'll learn. I'll read up on it too, but show me and I'll learn".

Later on, Katia developed her skills as a co-producer, in a sense coming full circle to what she had originally begun as an engineer:

> I did this master-class with a young punky band in Wales, hosted by a University in conjunction with the Music Producer's Guild (I am a professional member of the MPG) where the singer was the least experienced person and the whole band was there; I could see he was really struggling in terms of peer pressure because everyone else could knock it out a lot quicker than he could, and by the end of it I was outside the vocal booth conducting and lip-synching. I was like a personal trainer; we both exercised to get that energy going until we got there.

In other cases, operating within a particular music culture inspired confidence from that community, when the producer chose to branch out. Cathy Cuvelier's upbringing near Marseilles, with its unique music scene, gave her a unique perspective into the production of reggae music. She had worked in a live capacity to begin with, meeting a network of people who were later to respect her extensive knowledge of reggae:

> I was one of the engineers of [sic] Josie Wells, so he introduced me to different people in the business. I was a selector[2] as well and you didn't have a lot of selector females in the business; at the time there weren't usually that many in the reggae scene, the women would do the backing vocals or sing but stop there. So I was more on the other scene and coming from France; I would say that France keeps the reggae turning, gives a new life to reggae when it starts to die in other places because of dance hall taking over and other rubbish, but the cultural reggae that was kind of left abandoned in Europe [I was involved in] bringing that back to life.

Working in public as a DJ allowed her to network with vocalists and invite them to record with her. She built her own studio after interest grew in what she was doing, and she realized that it would be less expensive to record the artists herself:

> A lot of little sound systems started to grow, and I was able to send out [to ask if they would] invite an artist as a guest for the sound system to be on the microphones, and I was extending those links,

2   A selector is a specialist reggae DJ.

and in exchange I would ask the artist to come to my studio and record for me. And every time they did, they would say, "You should go to Jamaica; you should meet people". And that's what I did, from one artist to the other; they would drive you around then you met people and when they came to Europe, they would give you a call and that's the way I started my network, really.

Returning to the studio environment, Jacqueline Pelham Leigh and Ms Melody have both specialized in working with rappers, and their attention to detail has become a "go-to" skill in their productions. JPL has confidence in her skills as part of a chain of production that includes the ability to create mixes that are ready for mastering, which means that she not only negotiates the aesthetic relationships between what the artist wants, what the label wants, and what she can do in the studio but also once the recording is complete, she bridges the audio gap between mixing and mastering. She thus has an overview of the whole "journey" of a song from initial writing all the way through to its release:

> I remember I was in a session with John Moon, who's a well-known engineer-producer, and he was listening to my stuff and he [commented on] "The intricacies of your production". He doesn't think a man would think about it like that; he can hear where I've left all the spaces and that's a very deliberate thing. He was like, "It's the attention to detail". Someone that's really into sonics can hear my attention to detail, whereas someone who's probably not into it just wants the kick drum to be – like they have a term in this day and age – we need the drums to bang – what they mean is they want it to be really hot and they want it to distort. Well, when you send it off to the mix engineer you have to take all of that effort, over-compression, off again anyway. And sometimes I try and explain this, because there's a difference between digital distortion and valve distortion – valve is sweet and it's beautiful, digital hurts your ears.

As we saw earlier, Ms Melody was at the forefront of the development of different styles of British black music in the early 2000s. She has prided herself on creating tracks that reflected the artists she was working with, rather than imposing a sonic aesthetic on them; she is able to clearly identify what makes her mixes unique:

> I could definitely say that I helped with the early growth of grime music as a whole. I was definitely one of the first engineers nurturing and manipulating the sound of that: funky house as well, and I'd say garage music too. I'd say I was definitely one of the go-to

engineers for that style of music. I definitely developed an identity for it in relation to the way the music was translated for the listener.

The idea of being a "translator" of the artists' meaning has also been posited in an unlikely parallel genre of music, that of country music. The country music producer Paul Worley describes himself as being a "facilitator and translator" of the artist's work (interview in Frith and Zagorski-Thomas 2012: 132). Another producer who emphasized the issue of building a bridge between the artist and the listener was Lauren Deakin Davies, who specializes in working with singer-songwriters; like both Ms Melody and Katia Isakoff, she uses her experience as an artist to create an atmosphere in the studio that is encouraging and enabling, so she can get the best out of her clients:

> When I've recorded in the past and I've been the artist on the other side of the screen, there's nothing worse than the feeling of you finishing the take and the producers are not paying attention; the song's ended or something like that and they haven't even responded; they're just sitting on the phone or laughing. The literal worst thing is when you're in a session and you're singing a vocal take and the people are talking in the other room and they start laughing; you're so vulnerable at that point.

Lauren's youth appeals particularly to younger women artists who have previously felt intimidated by the older male producers they have worked with. She described some of the methods that help these musicians to work better in the studio, developed as a result of her own previously unhappy studio experience:

> I think the default is bonding in the first place ... I like to feel that everyone's comfortable, that they are enjoying themselves and that they feel safe; I think that is the first thing that might make a big difference. The second thing is the musical directional choice, because I've spoken to other, usually younger women, who have been in the studio with men. They are never happy with the recordings; [they say] "I just don't feel like it's me. They just went off on one and I didn't feel like I could say I didn't like the direction in which it was heading or anything like that". Sometimes I'll have girls who can play guitar and they'll say they didn't play guitar on any of their records because the guy just said "You're taking too long – let me do it!" I always say if a person can play an instrument, even if it's not that well, I want them to play on it, get them to practice and have pride in the fact that they have played on their song other than just sang. I think that's a sort of attitude: of valuing what the person is bringing.

In her studio, she has made the deliberate decision not to have a separate vocal booth, so the artist and producer are in the same space. Again, she underlined the negative aspects of her own experience and the respect she feels that artists need, praising them at the end of the take or supporting them if they are having difficulties. Isabel Gracefield Grundy, like Lauren, finds that women artists often find her easy to work with:

> I was working with a songwriter recently and she was saying that when she goes into a session with men there's always an initial period where she has to prove that she can do what she's doing, and that she has a right to be there. She said that working with me, it was just totally different from that, that's when she really noticed it. There was no need to prove anything.

This relaxed feeling of confidence instilled by working with a woman producer or engineer will be returned to later.

In another specialized area, Yvonne Shelton "minds" the gospel aesthetic of choirs on pop records, bringing in contemporary (and future) sounds and styles as they appear from the streets:

> I'll put whatever is the new flavour of the gospel scene into the session; it depends what style of music it is, and usually I've got it covered. I work with young people all the time, I do lots of singing workshops across the country. I can tell you in the next five or ten years, what the "sound" of voices is going to be. When the Amy Winehouses and the Adeles and the Duffys and the Jessie Js came out, we knew because we were working with singers like that when they were 15 or 14. We knew that the bigger voices, after a lot of years of breathy, Lily Allen, singy-talky type vocalists, the next wave of singers were going to be "blow the house down", and they did. It's gone a bit like this again and there are going to be, the 14 or 15-year-olds, a lot of guitarists, singer-songwriters going to come through, in the next four or five years and some more medium-belts, quite lyrical voices. That's where it's going to go.

She makes sure that the producers that she works alongside delete the takes that don't sound true to the gospel sound, or those takes which contain mistakes that the producer might not recognize due to their unfamiliarity with gospel choir aesthetics, are omitted:

> Sometimes when they're "comp-ing" vocals they leave a couple of mistakes in that a singer would not be happy with or would think, "That was one of the things you said you've got to delete". So before they master it, [the producer] will say "Do you want to hear it before

> we master it?", and I might say, "The low harmonies are not there, and the high ones don't make sense without them", or "You've got too many hard vocals in, raise up some of the soft vocals to give it that nice crisp sound", because that's what that song requires.

In a completely different genre, at the time of her interview Terrie Harris was specializing in working with British punk-era bands; this came about after Poly Styrene noticed her when she was engineering a live concert:

> She came along [to a gig] and she saw this girl on the desk and she looked at me and she smiled, and I was quite young, and she was like, "Whoah, you don't see girls on desks, are you an engineer?" And I was like, "I'm learning". I used to call myself the caretaker, I still do; I never, ever say I'm an engineer, and she thought that was quite comical, and we got to know each other. "Have you got a studio?" "No, what I do is, I've got a set up at home, I do stuff at home, I've got a little recording booth". "Oh, I've got some poems; can I come down?" And she turned up at my home. I wasn't sure who Poly was at the time; I just knew her as Marianne, and probably that's how our friendship started. I did the engineering for the early demo tapes [for Poly's final album] before, when she was writing the songs. A lot of the songs were demoed within the studio, and I've still got all the demos, of the original first tape demos; I've still got those and they ought to be kept.

Despite the fact that Terrie and her partner ran the studio in the daytime and used electronic drums so that the noise levels were kept to a minimum, a policeman neighbour complained:

> So we decided one afternoon to see if we could get a studio (that must have been in '93), and we came across a place down in Rye Harbour; it was like an air hangar. We built like a shelter inside it, so it wasn't echo-ey, soundproofed it with (believe it or not) egg boxes and we started doing very well. We'd have lots of different people in from TV asking for so many different things: Shalamar, Kev the Witch, who's now on Boomtown. I remember I even got a Christmas email (a spoken one) from Michael Jackson in 1997 and I still have it on hard drive somewhere. It was wishing Little London Studios a Happy Christmas, and I thought that was so nice to wake up to on a Christmas morning!

Eventually even that studio became too small and they moved to Hastings, and consequently became very busy recording a diverse range of artists who liked their analogue sound:

> Ultravox came in, the Bay City Rollers, Sham 69, Poly Styrene, UK Subs; Steve Furst had to come, he's on *Little Britain*. He's come in a few times because they used to use Little London Studios as their comedian rehearsal studios; it was quite a lock-in sometimes. We've done Joss Stone, Pigeon Detectives, Arctic Monkeys, Hard-Fi, Kaiser Chiefs, Clash, Specials, The Alarm, Babyshambles, The Libertines, Keith Levene ... and Mitch Mitchell.

Mitch Mitchell, who had drummed for Jimi Hendrix, approached them to record a session for him, which was part of a live US interview with the comedian Dan Ackroyd:

> He's gone on for over two hours, and we're still thinking, oh my God, have we got enough hard drive space because it's a big file that we're taking up. We ended up with the whole life story of Mitch Mitchell that I've still got in a vault, that says everything about him and the band and how he got on with Jimi himself, and also with Noel.

Although the Mitch Mitchell recording will have great historical value, it was actually an unexpected side-line that brought the studio their most commercial success, demonstrating that regardless of specialization, flexibility of outlook is still one of the major survival techniques for a studio professional. Terrie continued:

> The most successful commercial project we ever did was a thing for children, deprived kids under the age of 18 that were being thrown out of schools. They were having bad times, it might have been drug abuse, sexual abuse, so many things happened to these children all over the country. And we'd pick them up and teach them how to do engineering. So we'd go across the country to different colleges and schools, and we picked up this little crowd of kids, altogether about 54 children across the country, just getting them up, learning, back on their feet and a few of them became success stories.

Perhaps ironically, given the subject of this book, the award that they were given for their project had to be renamed to reflect the diversity of the practitioners who were active in that field:

> From doing that, I got awarded an Entrepreneur Award in 2006. It used to be called the Men of the Year Award, it's now called the People of the Year Award, and there are eight in Europe every year.

Other Specializations: Laptop Production, Advertising, Listening Events and Field Recording

In my next two examples, the use of a laptop computer is crucial to the work being done. The portability of the laptop and access to the Internet while "on the move" have allowed some producers to adapt very quickly to changes in practice. The small size of the technology allows it to be used discreetly and in small spaces, often allowing progress to be made in private. Jennifer Brown describes the use of bedrooms as recording studios (identified by McRobbie and Frith [1978] as girls' primary social space) as "electronic cottage[s]" where small music businesses can privately thrive and consolidate before venturing into the mainstream, a work practice that can greatly facilitate women producers (Brown 1996: 41; see also Wolfe 2012). As an example of this, Chantal Epp's cheer-music business grew out of her in-depth knowledge of the genre, underpinned by the technical knowledge she had acquired at school (see Chapter 1) and later at university. Having been a cheerleader herself, she was deeply embedded in the culture, understanding the different global contexts of cheerleading to the point that she was able to try to anticipate future trends:

> *What's the actual sound of cheerleading music? How would you describe it?*
>
> It's highly energetic, dance-y, tons of sound effects. The current trend is for voice-overs of the team all over the music. It's very, very unusual. And after a long time you do get a headache listening to it. It's 145 bpm and sometimes a bit faster, sometimes a bit slower, but it's quite strict in terms of what it consists of.
>
> *Do you play the instruments on the track yourself?*
>
> The trend in cheerleading music is to get songs that are already in the charts, and then put them together, but I like to add my own personal touch to them because otherwise every mixture sounds the same. So I like to mix different instrumentals together, underneath different acapellas of songs if I can find them, and just blend it all together, so it's like a mash-up or a remix of a song, essentially. But it's eight to ten songs in one two-and-a half-minute track, so it's really, really particular; each song has to be in each different section of the routine. I try to add my own beats, and I'm trying to get guitar and piano and stuff in there but I'm still developing it in that area. It's kind of new to the cheerleading teams; I'm not really sure if they're going to like it, so I'm holding back on it but I'll develop it a bit more.

Chantal Epps's awareness of the value of social capital (a term coined by Pierre Bourdieu), her network of potential users, and her understanding of her role in the sport as a supplier and facilitator, allow her to capitalize not only on her technical skills, but also her story: she is embedded in the culture that she provides a service for. In the niche area where she works, she is using what Keith Negus describes as a "collective-synthetic" approach between the worlds of art and entrepreneurship (1999: 88). Because she attends live events and live-Tweets them, she can offer her services to a captive audience, or market. This proactive approach to garnering business opportunities is one noted by Dafna Kariv (2013) of female entrepreneurs in general.

This ability to use a network of contacts contributes to the sustainability of a freelance career for producers and engineers. Helen Atkinson's people skills led to a specialism in live recording from TV shows; after consolidating her reputation as a sound engineer for live bands at RAK, she developed a side-line as an "in the box" mix engineer for iTunes, when she was asked:

> "I don't really know if it's your sort of bag, you're in a proper studio with nice equipment and stuff, and this is more like working in the box, and doing mixes for iTunes". So Saturday nights we'd do the live shows, as the live shows are being broadcast, mixing the audio that comes back, because everything goes on sale at midnight the night after. That's quite a different sort of work environment to the usual "studio, making an album" sort of environment that I'm used to working in, but it's all good work. And then also I work with Abbey Road Live now, doing some of their freelance work for them; things like recording festivals, or we recorded the One Direction shows that they did at the O2 for their movie, so my first ever film credit happens to be on One Direction, which my family thought was quite funny.

Helen credits her stamina and her ability to remain patient to the variety of different activities that she becomes involved in, and working to her strengths:

> Just finding that fit, or where your niche is, and then sort of exploiting that because people don't want to work with you every day if you're going to turn up and be miserable, or not be happy about the job, or not be willing to get in there and get stuck in and do it. I think people are always a bit more happy to overlook some of the technical things that you might not be able to do initially, people can build their technical skills but what you can't build is the ability to want to spend time in a room in a high pressure situation with somebody. So you definitely have to be prepared to be flexible, and even where I'm in-house I like to keep what I'm doing different. When you're

working in a creative environment it's quite important not to get stuck in the same rut doing the same sorts of things all the time.

Adrienne Aitken's decision to specialize in commercials led to 15 years of work in the advertising industry, with some high profile and lucrative work:

> Probably the two biggest I'd say [were] the Cup-a-Soup one, because everyone knows that (sings) "You only get a hug, from a Bachelor's mug". That was us. And I did Kit-Kat, McDonalds, General Electric: we did a massive global campaign for GE. That was probably financially our biggest ad because it was huge and it was an "in perpetuity" buy; they used it on everything, they still do. We've done hundreds, thousands of ads.

With her partner, she developed an advertising jingle into what was to become a chart hit:

> I had an idea based on a commercial and we did a song around that commercial. It's very cheesy: do you remember the Budweiser "Wazzup?". Everyone was going "Wazzup" and all that and I said we should do a track; it was one of those ideas moments and we spent a day and a night in the studio, and wrote and recorded a track, with Phil, myself and the engineer we were working with who wrote most of the lyrics. We put a band together, called it a fictitious name, The True Party, and I called myself Trudy, and we licensed it to Positiva. They put it out in the UK and Ireland, and we charted at number 13 and got on *Top of the Pops*. So I'm really happy to have been a part of that, just have that in the little tick box, one of the things you want to do. Cheesy as you like, but it was fun to do and it was fun to see it turn around so quickly because everything else takes so long. And even the commercials which are completely soulless from a perspective of, "I've written this because I feel it or because that artist feels it" and stuff, there's no satisfaction from that point of view, but you write something and you record it and it's on the telly, that's nice.

Working on commercials raised her profile to the point that she was able to record her childhood heroes:

> I worked with Slade, and I absolutely loved that because I grew up listening to Slade as a kid, the Christmas song and 'Cum on Feel the Noize'. And they came to me wanting to record a new version of 'Cum on Feel the Noize' and I thought, "Oh my God, it's Slade!", Slade as in Dave Hill and Don Powell, not Noddy [Holder] because

obviously he left years and years ago. And to be recording a song of my childhood was just wonderful for me. I loved it.

Other Niche Occupations and Projects

A completely different niche practice has been devised and developed by Colleen Murphy, who started Classic Album Sundays in 2010. After training in radio in the USA, and on moving to the UK to work as a DJ, she saw the opportunity to start listening events for small groups of people to give them the opportunity to listen in to high-quality vinyl albums on top-end speakers. Her concept has now been franchised across the world, and she has also found time to create remixes; I asked her how this came about:

> Just through my DJ career, really. I started my own label in 2002 first, called Bitches Brew with another woman, so for the first production she and I produced the first song. And then we started commissioning [artists] ourselves, doing remixes ourselves, and producing stuff for our own label. The first time I actually did a remix was for a label called Suburban in New York City, which was run by Tommy Musto who was a really cool guy, a very good producer. He used to come into Dance Tracks where I worked, and he asked me to do a remix, and do something for them. I didn't really push that side of my career until we started the label. And since then I've done remixes for DFA, I just did one for Fat Freddy's Drop which is coming out soon.

> *So is it still a case of people coming to you?*

> I used to solicit for remixes, but Classic Album Sundays is really what I'm building, and the remix and DJ side is almost like a side thing, because the kind of stuff I'm into is never going to be hugely commercial and I don't really want to change it. I couldn't just become Pete Tong, like you start out cool and then you just sell out because you want to make money, I couldn't do that with music.

Two of the most unusual music production and engineering projects were relayed to me by field recording engineers, both of whom double up as music technology instructors; these two examples show how varied specialization can be, and how resilience and a can-do approach are vital tools for building a career as a sound engineer. Karina Townsend was invited to record location sound in Bavaria for the sound artist and instrument-builder Limpe Fuchs who had been asked by Dr Anne Robinson to contribute improvised sound to a reflective film she was making called *Wakeful*, the name of a British ship that was sent to the Baltic to quash the Bolsheviks in World War I.[3] Fuchs lives in seclusion in a converted stable with homemade furniture, and sleeps outside wrapped in sheepskin. It was difficult for Townsend to plan in advance:

> Because it was really the first time I'd done anything like this, I knew that pre-planning would be key and so I'd tried out various microphones and recording equipment, setting up template sessions that could be called up quickly and easily without stemming the flow of creativity on the day. Quite apart from anything else our luggage limitations meant that I couldn't take mic stands and so I'd made various microphone holders and adjustable clips and clamps that could fit onto furniture. I had a bag full of bungee cord and every imaginable kind of tape just in case. It was all very Heath Robinson but ... it worked!

The project took three days, and eventually included another of Townsend's skills:

> Finally, and somewhat unexpectedly, I ended up doing the voice over for the film. Anne knew she wanted a Scottish voice and a woman but knew she didn't want to use her own voice for this particular project. Many years back I'd been the voice of the Scottish *Daily Record*'s lonely hearts phoneline (yes really!!) and had won an English Diction prize at school – plus I had access to a very nice Coles ribbon mic – the kind used by the BBC ... It was a harrowing read – much of the text was from the personal diaries of two of the sailors on board the ship and some of it was very graphic although much of it was also very mundane.

Reflecting on the project, she notes: "I guess that it was very much my range of skills, technical and interpersonal, that got me the job and from that first role, I ended up playing more of a part in the whole project".

The other unusual specialist standalone project was undertaken by Rasha Shaheen:

> I was asked to travel to South Algeria and work on a project in the refugee camps of the Western Saharawis with a charity called Sandblast. I had two roles in this project, one was to record and mix the work of a singer-songwriter called Pia DeKeyser. She is an English musician whose aim was to travel to the camps to record her songs via collaborations with the Saharawi musicians, the aim being to spread the word about the camps' existence with any profit from

---

3   https://wakefulproject.org/about-the-project/

the music being put into the refugee camp studio (the only recording studio in a refugee camp).

As part of the project, she had to train an engineer to take over once she left, on a one-to-one basis:

> Susu (the trainee) and I worked 6 days on a 3 track EP in a studio that had power cuts once or twice a day. The studio had not been used for 8 months and so when we arrived, we had to clean the hill of sand that had blown in through the gaps in the doors. The equipment was tightly locked up in sand-proof containers and essentially we had to wire the control room with the live room. There were no shops that had any supplies (mics, strings, anything really), and there was no Internet if we needed to upgrade or find out how any of the equipment worked. I went there not being able to fully find out what system I would be using. We spent the first day cleaning and testing for line connections. Harsh conditions overall, but I think limitations bring out the best creations.

The project was successful: "We managed to record three songs, and invited seven Saharawi musicians to collaborate and overdub their parts on the songs. When I returned to the UK, I helped arrange the songs with the artist, and at present they are being mixed and mastered".

This chapter has presented a variety of areas of music production and sound engineering that the women in my interview sample have engaged in during their careers so far. I have shown that adaptability, resilience, managing a portfolio of clients and updating and developing professional skills are important parts of their work ethos. It should be noted, at this point, that these are skills that a male audio practitioner would also be required to possess. The difference is that there have been fewer examples of female role models for the women in my research to look up to and feel inspired by. In the following chapter, the implications of this will be examined further.

4 The Workplace Experience and Relationships with Clients and Colleagues

This chapter will detail some of the challenging scenarios created by clients and colleagues (whether male or female) in recording situations run by the engineers and producers that I spoke to, and strategies that the women working on their sessions had to develop in order to complete their work. As I noted in the previous chapter, some of these scenarios could also be experienced by men working in the same situation. For instance, a few years ago in my own career as an educator, I came across a young male music student who walked out of a session where he was working as an assistant engineer, because of the sexism he encountered from some male clients. This was a remarkably brave act, considering the lack of employment opportunities available in the recording industry. We will see that an ability to understand and tolerate a working environment where sexist and racist banter is normalized can prolong the career of a woman in the music industry (see also Leonard 2016). Problems do not always come from male colleagues and artists; women artists who are unused to seeing a woman behind the desk sometimes also find the experience unnerving, and in one instance, one of the engineers I interviewed told me about a female studio manager who would not employ female engineers as a matter of policy. However, we will also see that in some cases, both male and female clients prefer to work with a female engineer or producer. Some information in this and later chapters has been anonymized in order to protect the identities of the interviewees.

Using a selection of examples from the interviews, I will start with a discussion about harassment from aggressive colleagues, followed by a discussion about working relationships with clients. After that, the strategies that have been developed in order to manage misogynistic behaviour from both co-workers and clients will be presented. Some women claimed to have had no trouble with overt harassment, but an awareness of covert exclusion from opportunities because of their gender was mentioned in several interviews; undoubtedly, reporting or acknowledging harassment can affect the perception of a woman studio engineer and lead to a reputation of being "difficult".

4 The Workplace Experience and Relationships with Clients and Colleagues

Despite that studio pranks are also played on male engineers, the degree of determined disruption revealed by the interviews was sometimes quite surprising. For example, one engineer reported being employed by a London studio and on her first day being deliberately given so much wrong technical information (she was much more skilled than her male colleague realized), she decided simply not to go back to work there again.

Relationships with Aggressive Colleagues

Janet Beat described several instances in which her work was undermined by her male workmates. Janet, a pioneering electronic musician and educator in the 1960s, tried to share her enthusiasm for sound synthesis and computer music wherever she worked. Some colleagues were supportive, as noted in the previous chapter; however, others resented her enthusiasm. She describes her preparations for a concert being deliberately disrupted by a colleague:

> When it came to the day of the concert this so-and-so had taken this tape recorder home: "I'm not having that sort of music in my building". The concert went ahead because I went to the Drama School and borrowed a tape recorder from them. That particular tape recorder had a detachable power cord and on another occasion in between the rehearsal and me going off to have an early lunch before the lunchtime concert, somebody had been in and taken away the power cord. So I just went into the staffroom and took the cord off the electric kettle! You know, [facing] spite like that, I just dig my toes in.

Extreme behaviour begat extreme remedies:

> On another occasion somebody had gone in and deliberately set the tape on record and was wiping the tape clean but I always took a back-up, I always had a back-up. So what I had to do was I had to have an early lunch, and then I had to sit in the concert hall guarding the tape recorder.
>
> Eventually it got accepted.

The sabotage could be quite challenging:

> Then there was trouble with a technician [who] just used to move all the wires around in the electronic music studio. There was one time when I had to give a harmony class and I wanted to show a student how to use the music typesetting programme, and then it wouldn't work. I looked, but the plugs were labelled right. What he'd done is take the labels off the plugs, put them on other cables

so it looked like they were all in the right place but they weren't. I soon twigged what was going on, and I marked all the cables with a security pen. When he wasn't around, I'd get the old ultraviolet light and I could get all the plugs the right way round, but didn't change the labels. In the end he had to re-label everything.

The aggression Janet experienced was not just from technicians; some of her academic colleagues were prejudiced about her because of her gender and articulated this quite clearly:

One principal told me, "We want you to train another member of staff to run the electronic music studio because it won't look right round the schools to have a woman in charge", and I said, "First, you're in breach of the Sex Discrimination Act, equal opportunities", and then he said, "Oh, and you're English", and I said, "That's racism". And he just looked at me and said "You can't do anything about it, there are no witnesses, I'm the principal, you're a junior member of staff, who do you think is going to be believed?"

So I've had to fight. Somebody once said to me, "I suppose you're pleased now there is an Equal Opportunities Act", and I said "Not really", and he looked shattered and I said, "Because it's driven the anti-woman [feelings] underground, I want it above ground where I can see it and deal with it".

Other problems could occur when a young and vulnerable woman engineer worked in close proximity with a much older male studio owner. "Natalie" (pseudonym) found that proximity to her mentor in the studio developed into a romantic relationship; there was a considerable age difference between them that led to him preventing her from working with younger male bands, although there had not been a problem with her working with older clients:

There've been sessions that I've been excluded from, like being told "I can't have a girl in the studio because it'll distract the band", was one thing that I really didn't like. It wasn't a session that I didn't like, it was something I was excluded from.

Was that the band that said that, or was that the studio owner?

That was him that said that, which was really annoying.

Why would you have been a distraction?

> I really don't know, I think it was just his mind-set because me and the studio owner ended up seeing each other at the end, and I don't know whether he was just a little bit worried that the band were good looking or something, and I was going to spend all my time wondering about what they were doing, rather than worrying about what he was doing. It was just something that he said once, that stuck with me.

In another case, Eleonora Romano talked about engineering live sound at festivals around the world. On being questioned about the attitudes of colleagues to women sound engineers in other countries, Romano remarked that she accepted the challenges that she faced, as part of her job. She trained in the UK because she encountered less prejudice there than in other European countries. I found it surprising when she remarked that some of her worst experiences of misogyny occurred in the USA. For example:

> I was working at this women of the world festival called Lilith Fair. It should be a celebration of women, but actually all the people that work there, they're all men, and I only saw women in catering. I didn't see any female engineers or lighting engineers. I did seven days with Kate Nash, and the very first day I was treated really badly by a really big stage manager, you know they're all very tall or whatever, and we were the only band with stage monitors, because in the States mostly they use in-ear monitoring nowadays. Anyway, we were upgraded from a small stage to the main stage, and we were the only band with monitors and they didn't like that. And that guy from the very moment I walked on stage just unloaded on me with verbal abuse and all sorts of stuff, and I didn't say anything, I just carried on with what I was doing, because otherwise I wouldn't have had a show; there were really tight deadlines and sound-checks and stuff, so I finished doing that, and then I went to catering.

The eventual apology came privately, where the stage manager could deliver it without the humiliation of being seen to capitulate in front of his crew:

> ... and in a very dark corner of catering this guy comes and says to me, "I apologize", saying he had a lot on his plate and this and that. I said: "I'm sorry, I don't accept your apology because you're apologising now, while nobody can hear what you are saying to me, whilst before you had an audience and I don't think it was right, what you did". So, I had a lot of that, not [always] as bad as that, but I had a lot of that in venues.

Working Relationships with Clients

In addition to problems with sexism from male studio colleagues, a woman producer may have to work with both male and female clients who believe that women do not have the same technical ability as men. Sometimes, support from colleagues resolves the situation. Twenty years later than Janet Beat's experience, Mandy Parnell had support from her male studio manager when she came up against gender issues from clients who tried to undermine her at The Exchange studio where she worked:

> I've had people refuse to work with me on the grounds that I was female. I did have problems at The Exchange; I had funny problems, but I was lucky because my boss was supportive and gave me free rein to tell anyone to fuck off if I wanted to, and to show them the door if they were any way underhand. He totally supported me on that level. But you know, I'd get the normal banter: you'd get these breakbeat guys or drum'n'bass guys, these little geezers seeing me sitting there and they'd go "D'you *know* how to cut a loud record?" and I'd just laugh at them and go, "Well, where am I working? I work at The Exchange, you know: we're known for loud records. Do you think they'd have me here if I couldn't cut a loud record?" That'd be it, job done. So you would get that where they'd be a bit shocked.
>
> *After you'd worked with them, did they change their attitude?*
>
> God, yeah, they'd come back.

Laura B became so frustrated by the belittling remarks of a star client that she resorted to physical means to express her feelings:

> I was working with a famous drummer who ran a record label as a side project. [He had an] ego the size of a planet, of course. But that's normal. But he walked into a studio I was working in and he had no face for me at all, from the start. I started working and the rug was being pulled from under my feet minute by minute through the session. I could feel that my grip on everything was going; he was taking it away from me. And I thought "This really is not on. I'm not spending the day at the mercy of this guy".

Laura remedied the problem with direct physical action:

> I was dropping in and we were working on some stupid time signature, it was really complicated and at one point I asked him to count me in. He said "one, two, three, punch" and I swear, it was stronger than me, I punched him. I didn't drop in: I punched him. But he had

4 The Workplace Experience and Relationships with Clients and Colleagues

> a smile on his face and he had a troop of personal assistants who were on the sofa in the back of the studio, all of them with glasses, telephones, clipboards, blah, blah, blah, and they all went [stifled laughter] because they all probably wished they did it. And I don't know why, I didn't do it very hard of course, but it was from the heart, and he kind of knew it.

Felix Mackintosh underlined the need for engineers and producers to have calm personalities because stressed clients can sometimes be difficult to work with for many different reasons:

> It's very easy for even very good people to get panicked in the studio and say things like their headphones aren't working, or interfere with a mix, for instance. Once somebody starts interfering with it: "Put the guitar up, put the guitar up, put the guitar up, turn the vocal down, turn the vocal down, oh no, the vocal's too low": they can very quickly ruin something that's very nearly right. So that's about breathing, holding your horses, or stopping and explaining that this is where *you* think it should be if they want to do their thing, and not taking responsibility completely for something, if it's somebody else's. The best engineers are just very calm people.

Felix noted the need to retain the confidence of clients in her skills, during moments when normal and unforeseeable equipment breakdowns happened:

> Kit just *does* go down. I really, really try to stay away from the gender thing, but there is a problem that it can be that somebody then loses their faith and they think it's because you don't know what you're doing that a piece of kit has gone down.

She developed a robust way of dealing with the "maleness" of some sessions, especially with advertising clients:

> They used to make the most disgusting jokes in the advertising sessions, and they'd look at me. Some of them were offensive, some of them weren't. But it's what happens; it's the *real* world where people actually *do* make nasty jokes. And just by being flipping female and you go well "Yeah that was offensive", but you don't walk off, and you don't stop talking to them, I think *that* changes attitudes. I think it's not being po-faced that changes attitudes. God knows, women can be po-faced with each other and other groups can be po-faced with each other, and it's great when people aren't. You can say to someone, "I don't like that" and it's better to have the conversation than not have the conversation about all of those things.

One of the things that women studio professionals often have to get used to is being mistaken for an assistant. Terrie Harris weathered the assumption that she was there to make tea by remembering that this was how she started her career, so she became magnanimous about it and appreciative of her professional journey:

> But also with the bands, they'd look at you because you're a woman on the desk and it's like, what's she doing there? So they'd always think you're the tea girl, which didn't bother me, and if it wasn't for being the tea girl and a runner, and starting from way down at the bottom and learning how to put cables together and being a technician and just working your way through, I'd probably never have been an engineer. So it just shows you how you just fall into a job. I went from singing and dancing, to making the cups of tea, doing the sweeping up, just learning off the back, whereas people now to get that trade have to go to university.

Lauren Deakin Davies expressed amusement at being mistaken for the intern; a young producer at the time of the interview, she has experienced a different and more open approach to her gender from her younger clients that highlights the out-dated attitudes of some of the older musicians that she has worked with:

> I was recording this "dad band", and I think they were doing covers and I was sitting there with the desk behind me, sitting in the engineer's chair, and the guy started giving me his tea order, assuming I was the assistant. And I was like, I'm not against making you a tea, but I'm clearly the engineer and the producer here; and he thought that the other guy, who was the assistant, was the engineer.
>
> I was like: "This is tragic".
>
> *Was he embarrassed when he found out?*
>
> No, not really.

Laura B also found assumptions about her role amusing rather than upsetting, using humour to cope with the assumptions made by male clients:

> I have some odd stories ... I was working at a studio [as an engineer] and one day somebody walked in and didn't say anything for five minutes and then I said something like "What's up?" and he said "Oh I'm waiting for the engineer". That happened once, made me laugh.

Later, we will see how Colleen Murphy's use of a gender-neutral name whilst working as a DJ led to the assumption that it would be a man entering the club with a box of records, not a woman. These assumptions cross all activities and genres in the music industry.

Working with female clients, too, can present difficulties. Whilst being at the centre of creativity is exciting, studios are also places where there can be a great deal of stress. There are high expectations from the client and often their record label. Studio time is expensive and a musician who has difficulties in working to a set timetable because of limited skills or anxiety, for instance, may become agitated. It can also be difficult to build a good working relationship with an engineer or a producer who feels like a stranger, both personally and professionally, even if they have a good reputation, and this may be exacerbated if they are a woman. This is Laura B's description of such a session:

> It happened once that a female singer walked into the studio, a familiar singer who came with her own band and stuff and I had to mike up the whole band. And within 15 minutes or something she started sort of pulling at me, like "Aren't you ready yet?" I said to her it takes time to mike up the whole kit and stuff, I was dead quick and I knew exactly what I was doing. It still takes about half an hour to get the whole session going which is already going fast. Within ten minutes she was on my case.

Laura decided not to humiliate her client in front of the band:

> I took her aside; this is the only time it's happened, I took her outside the session so no one could hear what was said. I said that if she stopped me from doing my job, I could not do my job, and therefore I could go home, but if she wanted me to do my job she had to leave me alone. And once I had miked up everything and could listen to things, I was open to her criticism, but not before then. I can't remember exactly how I spoke to her but it's the first time I've pretty much said to someone, sort of "fuck off my camp" sort of thing.
>
> *Do you think it's because she was inexperienced?*
>
> No, it's because she was really stressed. Because what happened is that she completely changed once she heard that. We did some brilliant, brilliant, brilliant recordings. She absolutely adored working with me. She's the one who called me the fantastic Laura B, when before I was just Laura B; and to this date we are working together, we did a show together last week. And we are like that. That is the only time a woman has been like that with me.

Mandy Parnell tells a similar story about a well-known female artist; even when a good working relationship had been established during the mastering of several EP releases, there was still an awkward atmosphere, until:

> When we went on to do her album I realized what was happening. She would tell her manager what she wanted and then her manager would tell me. We were in the album, it was quite intense and I really wasn't understanding what she was looking for, and I was getting quite frustrated and in the end I turned round and said "Well why can't you just talk to *me* about what you want? Why do you need to keep talking to him about it? Why can't *you* just tell me what you want?". And she just looked at me and you could see she was like "Yeah, why can't I?" and it was like she just wasn't used to it. "I've been in that many studios where they don't take my opinion when I'm working with the engineers, they're so rude with me that I just find it easier if I tell my manager and then he tells the engineer. And then there's no bullshit". But that's the only story I've ever really heard that's like that.

Lauren Deakin Davies described one of her worst sessions as being one where the (female) artist's manager insisted on being present throughout the session, dictating the song that the artist should record and then "tut-ting" and swearing when the artist found it difficult to play because this was new and under-rehearsed material. Disturbed by the bad atmosphere he had created in the studio, Lauren persuaded him to leave and discovered that the artist was being pressured to lose weight by the manager and her PR. Later, the manager attempted to bully Lauren, expressing shock that he would be expected to pay for the series of writing and recording sessions he had arranged with her. This was quite possibly because he felt that Lauren's relative youth and gender meant he could get away with it.

The suppression of a woman's studio skills by male collaborators is common. When asked to describe any times that she felt her gender caused a producer to underestimate her skills, one producer that I spoke to (anonymized here) related the following story about the production of a song where she had contributed the vocals:

> I did a song for a guy, for a campaign song against female genital mutilation, and he was happy for me to come in and sing it, but when it was me talking about how I wanted the vocals placed, or how I wanted them comp-ing, his interest just went. I just said, "I find it really interesting how you want me to sing on this song for women about women, but after 32 years' experience as a singer, you find it funny that I'm saying 'Can you listen to me about which

harmonies need to be up'". He wanted all high harmonies, but the high one didn't make sense without the low ones. I just thought, "You fool. You're delivering the song to a women's organization, about a women's issue, with a woman singing it, and now you're fobbing me off when I'm trying to get mildly technical with you". Then when he put the song out, he just put his name up there, he didn't even credit me. He will [credit me] on the official release, he'll have to. His ego is just ridiculous.

Both Susan Rogers and Adrienne Aitken acknowledged the possibility of a hidden bias against them because of their gender. Sometimes, this could work in their favour, as Susan notes:

> We don't know how often we were dismissed before being considered for a job, or what kinds of assumptions were made about us. I've been told that I've been hired because of my gender on occasion. I've never been told that I wasn't considered due to my gender.

Adrienne was heartened when work came to her studio because of her production skills:

> Before, when I was running the studio, some people came to the studio because they wanted a studio, some people found me through MPG or through my interviews online and say "I want a producer" and maybe I just haven't noticed all the ones that haven't because I'm a girl, I don't know. And before that the work came through word of mouth: "Oh, actually this sounded really good so therefore we want to go there". Perhaps there's a thousand others that would have come to me if I wasn't a girl, I've no idea because I haven't noticed it. But perhaps there are some amazing acts that I've missed because I'm a girl, I don't know.

In a genre of music normally assumed to be quite sexist, Ms Melody found her gender to be a positive advantage in the grime scene in London:

> I think the advantage that I had, and a lot of people always said the same thing: "Don't you sometimes feel a bit vulnerable in the studio with all this equipment and you're there by yourself with all these guys?". And I'd get asked that all the time. And I said "You know what? It's worked to my advantage. I'm no threat. And because of that I can honestly say, I've had three different locations and been there for a number of years, and not once has anyone attempted to not pay me, not once has anyone tried to take anything from me, or steal from me, and not once have I been broken into". And I think

> that says a lot, because I know a lot of other studios that are male-run and those kinds of things have taken place.

Ironically, Laura B found that it was a *woman* manager who finally ended her career as an in-house engineer at a large, well-established studio when its ownership changed and a female manager was appointed:

> ... and three months later she announced that I was sacked. I said "What do you mean I'm sacked, you know this is my family, it's been four years or something I've been working with these people, what's going on?". You know, you're the one that's new on the block. She couldn't give me a reason, but she said that when she took her position she put me on a three-month trial and three months had expired today. I really think she got rid of me because I was a woman and she wanted to be the only woman who was working there and I was way too smart, way too clever, way too dedicated. And so she got rid of me. Something like four years later or something, I was talking to some guys from Florida, and we were talking about unfair dismissals. And I was like "Oh yeah, once I got unfairly dismissed by my studio and I was sacked by a female manager" and before I could say anything the guy I was talking to said, "it wasn't XXX was it? She's done that wherever she's been".

Finally, Helen Atkinson describes having very few problems with clients in the studio:

> I think in all honesty, I've only ever worked with one client in 14 years that has ever made me feel uncomfortable and I don't think that had anything to do with me as a woman, it was just because he was genuinely not a nice person in the slightest, and not at all fit to be in any sort of work environment, let alone the studio. I used to find that when I worked with bands it would take two or three days for them to figure out that I wasn't their mum or their girlfriend, and for them to kind of relax and just to treat you as one of the rest of the gang.

Negotiating Potential Misogyny by Artists and Co-Workers

Certain subgenres of hip hop and rock music have in common a history of misogynistic words and attitudes; the feminist response to this was led by Tricia Rose in her book *The Hip Hop Wars* (2008) in which she debunked many of the myths surrounding the seeming inevitability of the association of early 21st century hip hop with pornography and violence. Some of the women that I interviewed worked in genres of music with young male artists whose public personae might have been perceived to be difficult for women to work with in the studio, especially as mediators of particular lyrics. Wolfe discusses the fact that Isabella Summers, original producer of Florence Welch's material, and the "Machine" in the title Florence and the Machine, was put off by the "hypermasculine" environment of rap music (2019: 82). However, for women with experience themselves of creating this music – or who were raised in communities in which this music originated (as we saw with Cathy Cuvelier) – this may not be such a problem. JPL advises the more "foul-mouthed" rappers: "Save that for live, let's keep it clean for your record". Asked if they take her advice, she replied:

> They do. I think it's because I was a rapper; the rappers I work with like me to cut them because I can say to them, "That syncopation isn't quite right, swing it back this way, or slow down the rhythm there and speed it up there, you can't have it all like coming at people like a machine gun; you know when you do your triple time or double time it's supposed to be more like a feature, or an accent to show that you can do it".

Her expertise as a rapper and the way she uses a computer as a musical instrument means that she is deeply embedded in black music culture and has a deep understanding of its aesthetics:

> It's all about the musicality for me, and I remember saying to people that sometimes it's harder to rap than it is to sing because you've got to really make sure the rhythms and syncopations are just about right for people to actually want to listen to what you're saying, otherwise it becomes noise and no-one wants to hear a din. Sometimes it's easier to talk to somebody who understands where you're coming from, that has done it; if you tell me it can't be done I can show it *can* be done and this is *how*, you know.

Felix Mackintosh was working at Ovatones studio with an all-female engineering crew when she came across rappers as clients. The studio had a community music remit and much of the work that came through it was from young urban Londoners, which brought up a conversation, as she relates:

> Through a certain period it was sort of coming and going; the n-word was used a lot which, because of my generation, is a word I'm not going to say out loud because I find it a really, really offensive word. But obviously it was a reclaimed word at one point. So to say to some young black man that he wasn't allowed to use that word, which I was having to do quite a bit in schools, seemed very strange.

> And obviously we were having artists like Eminem coming up. It was very ambiguous because in one way it seemed very misogynist, and then in some ways it seemed quite funny. A lot of it was funny; a lot of it was OK.

Like Mandy Parnell's clients (mentioned previously), once Felix had proven herself to them, her male clients believed in her: "What I used to get was people looking really doubtful when they walked into the room, and then being really happy to come back". As she found out through this experience, "A huge number of men love to work in mixed working environments. They find it fabulously liberating. At the same time they like male things. It's good for people to have both things, very good for people". Ms Melody made a similar observation. Asked if she had ever reversed the situation where a male engineer records a female artist, and if she felt that she "heard" male voices differently to male engineers, she replied:

> A hundred percent! Because I look out for different things: tonations, diction, believability. There's certain things I want this recording [to be] like: certain attention to detail. The reason why I personally believe that I became so popular is because of what other males told me, and they said that there's just a level of care, a level of nurturing that I give to the vocal that they just don't see with other engineers that they've worked with. It's like ... I will analyse the hell out of what they are saying and I'll take every single tiny syllable and if I just want to emphasize the smallest little point I'll do it by either dropping out the beat, or just echoing slightly into the background maybe a word or the end of something that they've said, or elongate or stretch something; and those are the kind of lengths that I would go to that other people would just kind of pass that by. I would say that 85% of my clients are males and they've left their engineers to come to me.

She also feels that because of the dangers and competitive nature of the grime music environment, her clients feel more secure with her as a woman engineer:

> A lot of those guys have said they feel safe with me, and they feel that there is a higher level of understanding for their safety. I think about them; I think about the kind of environment they're in, consideration that they're in my space for a number of hours and sometimes these males can feel vulnerable themselves; maybe it's the particular males that I've engineered and the area that I've been in. A lot of them have said that there is just this safety aspect that they like. They never feel as though I'm patronizing them. They never feel

as though they are having an egotistical clash with me, where I think that they feel that they have that with other male engineers. Even if another male engineer said to them "No, do that take again", they might take offence, where with me they didn't. So it was quite interesting. I always thought that was male pride or something like that.

Susan Rogers reported an entirely different experience, citing male authority as being a "given" in the recording process, even for women artists. This could be because she works much more with mainstream artists:

> The more vague instances of gender playing a role in the studio were the times when I felt I couldn't say what I wanted to a male performer. Believe me, this was not due to shyness. But there have been times, and there are still today with my male students, when I have been cautious to not emasculate men. The risk is that the performance suffers, or confidence is lost, or the lesson isn't learned. I am not saying that I indulge or protect men from candid assessment, because I do not. I am saying that I can't always have the same conversation with a male artist that T Bone Burnett or Tony Berg or Don Was can have. I can never be a father figure or a male role model, and sometimes that is exactly what is called for. I have envied male producers this innate level of authority, which I have to earn. This (real or imagined) male authority is a powerful force with female artists, too.

Industrial Hazards: Negotiating the Gendered Environment

Sometimes the desire to relegate a female audio technician to a sexualized role overcomes professional etiquette. Many of the women that I interviewed claimed not to have been made to feel sexually uncomfortable by male clients; this may be true. It could also be that reasons of professional bravado, or simply not wanting to dwell on unpleasant aspects of the job, made them reluctant to speak. They also may have felt unsure about what I would report in this research. The following passages are anonymized for obvious reasons:

> And then there's a top engineer that is a male, that has worked with a lot of bands, including Status Quo: he's well known. I really needed a job when I first started off and the only way I could get that job is if he touched my tits. But I did it because I needed the money and I needed to feed my family. It wasn't anything sexual, it was just a case of, "Come here, let me touch your tits", still got a T-shirt on, but I just think it's so degrading, when I look back at that, and I was young at the time, I think, do you know what, you arrogant pig. And I wish I could name that person, and he's probably still doing that

now with all the young engineers that are out there, and I'm sure that someone, somewhere that reads this book will turn around and say, "Aha!" Because, yeah there was a lot of innuendos, sexual, if you want something then you have to get it. It was never sexually as in shagging with me, but it was always like, oh I want to feel your boobs. I've always had big boobs.

The lack of professional respect engendered by the above behaviour has resulted in this engineer having to carry the burden of her tormentor's behaviour to every job he passes on to her, and quite possibly beyond this:

It was always a let down because I've got so far, and then suddenly they'll just punch you in the face with the thought of they want to touch you up physically, and you'd done such a good job.

This particular engineer is trapped between the old-style engineering community and the more youthful one:

The music industry is a man's world. I'm over forty and every time I want to try to break into that music industry I get told, "You are too old"; so if I want to go and work with young bands now I'm too old. If I want to work with the older bands, more experienced bands who've still got their top roadies and whatever, then I'm the tart.

In another example, several months after our interview, one of the younger engineers who had previously reported no problems with men's behaviour during recording sessions wrote to me about an incident with older male musicians. She found this distressing, because she had previously thought that she was respected for the work she was doing, and that this respect superseded her gender "availability":

I experienced mild sexual harassment in a session for the first time ever, about a month ago! Weird experience, nothing too bad – "just" some ungentlemanly behaviour from a group of 50-something session players all egging each other on and "having a laugh", including two of them hitting [on] me the moment I was alone (both the same way ... odd): "Ha ha, I expect you have a boyfriend and you think I'm a creepy old man, Ha ha ..."; some hugs hello that couldn't be avoided politely and gave them a chance to cop a feel, and some comments at a level I would overhear, about me. Water off a duck's back really, but I was sad about not having an arsenal of pithy put-downs to offer them for their bad manners, rather than freezing like a rabbit in the headlights and laughing along lamely. Gotta work on that ...

4 The Workplace Experience and Relationships with Clients and Colleagues

In an example from an educational environment, a student on a Music Technology degree, who had been educated at a single-sex school and transferred from a gender-balanced English degree course, described her experience of working in the studio in a mixed team:

> It did come as quite a shock when I came to [the Music Technology course] and saw that I was one of only a small handful of females on my course, especially after spending eight years in education surrounded by only girls in the classroom … For one of our group assignments we had to form a band and write, record and produce a song together. I remember feeling particularly awkward being the only female in the control room with about five other male students, and being ignored when I would make suggestions about the mixing process, but hear one of the guys repeat what I had said later and be listened to. One of the boys in my group seemed to go out of his way to try to make me feel uncomfortable, commenting on my appearance and telling extremely offensive "jokes" about female genital mutilation in front of me.[1]

There were also reports of general bullying: one engineer I spoke to worked in a small studio for a year, cutting her teeth with a producer who was known to be difficult. She described his almost threatening approach, which was hidden from clients:

> You'd be Pro-Tools operating for him and he'd stand over your shoulder and if you weren't fast enough he would just be really abusive to you and that was terrifying. I remember once doing a session where there were some very complicated things that I had to do and I made a mistake very early on in the chain and didn't spot it, and it meant that we recorded some vocals in the wrong key, and I cried after that session. He was so nasty about having made that mistake. But actually I wouldn't put that as the worst thing because I think well, that's the situation, that's what you sign up for, and you learn to be cool and calm and collected and that's part of it, so actually the worst sessions are the boring ones, where no-one cares and the music isn't good.

When asked if she felt that this treatment was meted out to her because of her gender, she replied: "They had tried, I think, between 25 and 30 boys before I came on board, and most of them had lasted two days to a week". And I got through the first month and then it was like, "OK, well, you know, we'll give

---

1 Hopkins and Berkers (2020) also report rape "jokes" in HE music technology sessions where male students outnumbered female students.

you a contract". However, this engineer knew that after being able to tolerate the humiliating behaviour of the studio owner, whose reputation was known in the industry, it would be much easier for her to find work in a larger and more reputable studio later on.

Recording Female (and Male) Vocalists

For some engineers, being "blind" to the gender of clients is an important part of their practice; this approach is in keeping with the producers interviewed by Michael Jarrett, whose working practice is that "absence summons presence" (Jarrett in Frith and Zagorski-Thomas 2012). The "translator" approach taken by Ms Melody, mentioned earlier, brought to the fore the message of her clients:

> That is how I look at myself, as a translator; you bring me something and it's about me interpreting it correctly and bringing it back out to the public exactly the way you want it to be heard. So if for example you want the message to be raw, I'm not going to put on loads of glossy effects to make it be softened; I'm going to position your voice in the speakers at a particular angle so that it sounds really, really hard.

Olga Fitzroy (who won the Music Producer's Guild 2016 Recording Engineer of the Year award) also frequently records male vocalists, though in the genre of rock:

> *Have you ever reversed the normal situation where a male engineer records a female artist, by recording a male vocalist? If so, what led to this decision being made, and do you think you "heard" his voice differently?*

> Quite often – It seems to me that most singers in bands are male, so I've often recorded male vocalists. I think the decision was made because I happened to be the person that had been booked to make the recording, perhaps I'd worked with that artist or someone connected with that artist before. If I'm trusted to record drums, guitars and strings [then] why not vocals? I don't think women in general hear things particularly differently to men ... I've read articles saying that women have better hearing than men on average, but I don't think being a good engineer is about what frequencies are audible to you, it's more about aesthetic choices, and being competent. Most of the biggest records over the years have been mixed by men, but women enjoy the results just as much as male consumers of music, so I don't think there's a significant difference.

4 The Workplace Experience and Relationships with Clients and Colleagues

Opinions about gender essentialism and hearing differ greatly from practitioner to practitioner. One of the sound engineers interviewed by the author was convinced that women's bone structure gave them an advantage as far as aural perception was concerned, and she had discussed this with her male mentor. This opinion was shared by the US engineer Carla Olson in her interview with Howard Massey, who asked if there was a "genetic reason that causes women to hear things differently from men". She responded:

> I don't know, but I do find it to be true, and male engineers tell me that all the time, too. It's not that we hear things totally differently; it's a lot more subtle than that, like the way things sit in a mix. A lot of the times the way I mix a vocal is different from the way a male engineer might do it – they'll actually say to me, "Wow, I wouldn't have thought of doing it that way". I don't know – maybe it's a physical thing. Or maybe it's just a vulnerability thing. (Massey 2009: 129–30)

The remarks by Ms Melody, cited earlier, about her "attention to detail" might also bear this out. However, it is just as likely that the men giving these compliments are "listening out" (Green 1997: 56) for difference, and their own listening activity is thereby gendered.

"Hannah", an additional sound engineer who did not formally participate in my study (referred to by this pseudonym throughout), specializes in vocal recording using ProTools and has also worked with mostly male clients ever since she started sound engineering. She was adamant in an email communication with me that she works with the voice as sound, even though in press interviews with her, it is clear that managing the person producing the sound, as much more than just a sound source, is equally important to her. This she has in common with Lauren Deakin Davies and Katia Isakoff, who express a particular interest in the transmission of authenticity in vocal sound, whether the singer that they are working with is male or female. Katia cited Joe Meek as a Svengali producer of male vocalists as a counterargument to the idea that male Svengali producers only prey on female singers. She feels that many women artists deliberately make a decision to sound girlish, and cites Madonna as an artist whose singing voice belies her years, partly because Madonna works in the field of pop music and has remained in that area, where younger singers challenge her position.

Madonna's mode of work involves a producer/artist relationship that works in a traditional way; she is a powerful artist who does not generally make detailed statements about the roles she and her producers play in the recording of her songs; the hands-on approach is sometimes alluded to but mostly assumed. This is interesting given Björk's tirade on her website in 2008 about male journalists' assumptions. At the time this appeared, it so clearly articulated the frustration of being stereotyped (and, significantly, expressed by a high-profile female artist) that it added impetus to my research. These examples are included here to underline the fact that my interviewees do not exist in a "bubble", but are in fact (often less visible) practitioners who are pioneers against gender stereotyping in the recording studio:

> it feel[s] like still today after all these years people cannot imagine that woman can write, arrange or produce electronic music. i have had this experience many many times that the work i do on the computer gets credited to whatever male was in 10 meter radius during the job. people seem to accept that women can sing and play whatever instrument they are seen playing. but they cannot program, arrange, produce, edit or write electronic music. (Bjork.com 2008)[2]

It is rumoured that Joni Mitchell was obliged to sit with male producers "in the room" in order to be able to release self-produced work in the 1970s, yet in 2008 when Björk made her comments it was still assumed that the man in the room is the person with power. In the USA, a wry observation in a *Billboard* article cited by the artist and producer Missy Elliott notes that if more female artists chose to work with female engineers, the gender balance behind-the-scenes might be corrected, given time (in Newman 2018). In the article the online journalist Melina Newman discusses this phenomenon with producer Alex Hope, who had decided that she wanted to be a producer at the age of 16:

> While many male and female executives have been supportive, several female producers expressed dismay that more female artists don't seek out female producers. "It's interesting that a lot of female artists have this feminist message and they'll make their record with all men. It seems kind of hypocritical", says Hope. "This [woman] will get up to accept an award and be surrounded by straight, white, middle-aged men".

There is evidence that some women artists do seek out female producers: Björk herself has worked with the programmer Leila Arab, and her album *Vespertine* was re-mastered in Iceland by Mandy Parnell in the presence of both Björk and Leila, thus maximizing the female presence in the studio. The British artist Florence Welch started her recording career with Isa Summers, a hip hop beat-maker and producer who has co-production credits on her

---

2   http://bjork.com/news/?id=854;year=2008 (accessed 24 November 2010), posted 22 August 2008. No longer available.

albums. The British hip hop artist Nadia Rose, in an interview on BBC Radio 4's *Women's Hour*, declared "I'm all about my women"; Rose works with the producer Black Obsidian (Tiana Rochelle) and Bamz, both of whom are female friends of hers.[3] The classically trained musician and producer Mica Levi (who works under the name Micachu) produced the 2018 album *Devotion*, by the artist Tirzah, and the artist Bishi secured funding from the Performing Rights Foundation to present a series of sessions focused on "The State of Gender" in creative technology in 2018. In the USA, the artist Grimes has produced Janelle Monae. There does, therefore, seem to be some indication that Newman's lament was premature.

***

In this chapter I have described the complicated working environment for women in recording studios, predominantly articulated through the voices of the interview sample. On the one hand, they have to prove that they have the necessary skills in order to complete the session to the same ability as one of their male colleagues, and on the other they have to "pitch" their gender at a reassuring, non-sexually-threatening and competent level. We have seen the testing mechanisms and "pranks" that are put in place by male colleagues and the strategies developed to overcome these; we have looked at workplace relationships, managing misogyny from artists and co-workers, and awareness of gender issues when recording. The significance and consequences of the historical and current exclusionary tactics used to keep women away from male-defined territory, both in recording studios and live sound environments, will become clear in the following chapters, beginning with a description of the ways that music technology, production and even methods of music consumption have become gendered as male.[4] There is, however, another issue that some women producers have to negotiate that increases

3   https://www.bbc.co.uk/programmes/b086kxpg (accessed 3 August 2018).
4   In the early 1990s, for instance, I was employed by a community organization in the London Borough of Southwark to teach young girls rock music, and train youth workers in programming skills using an early Steinberg program, Pro 24. After about a year the nearby Ministry of Sound approached the organization offering help to run a music technology course aimed at getting young men who carried guns off the streets. This was seen as a more urgent need, the training was offered on a voluntary basis, and my equally vulnerable group of young women lost activities that they valued greatly (and I lost my paid job). The success of the programme run by the Ministry of Sound is debatable: there is still a lot of gun crime in London, and there is also a lot of well-produced music with a lyrical focus on young men killing each other.

their burden: that of racism. Since her first interview for this book, Ms Melody has experienced a setback that is entirely to do with the fact that she is black and female. To develop her music production business, she took on the lease of an old Barclays Bank building in south London at the end of 2017 (in fact, where she used to bank the takings from her work as an engineer and producer). In this building, she is setting up and plans to run a high-specification music studio, a photographic facility, a business centre and a legal advice service. However, after paying out £35,000 in rent over 14 months (comprised of funding raised from savings, her family and two investors), the building was threatened with repossession by the landlord when she fell behind with her rent by four weeks. Despite offering the outstanding rent to the landlord the next day, they refused to allow her back into the building. Responding to her solicitor's query about why this had happened, the managing agent commented that, as Ms Melody reported, "They did not understand how someone like me was able to afford somewhere like that", questioning where her money had come from "because I didn't fit the profile of what I should look like to have that level of property". She was accused of wanting to use the building as an illegal nightclub, or even a cannabis farm. Deciding that giving up and living with the resulting bitterness for the rest of her life was not an option she wanted to consider, Ms Melody took the landlord to court and won back her building, with the help of a new investor who paid the six months of back rent. The accusations of illegal activities were thrown out of court by a judge. However, the validity of the accompanying discrimination case that she brought was not accepted due to the rent arrears, despite her reliability as a tenant for the 14 months preceding the non-payment. This incident shows that racial profiling is an additional burden placed upon black women attempting to forge a successful career as a music producer. Beyond this individual incident, Ms Melody also noted that she is always aware of the double identity of ethnicity and gender that play out through perceptions, assumptions and expectations. She told me:

> I have a very rigid view when it now comes to life. I no longer believe you get what you deserve. Instead I believe you get what you fight for. Being a good person or not isn't a strong enough basis to distinguish what may be the outcome. I also believe that my apprehensions towards unfamiliar territory will make me less likely to want to explore it like I may have done before. Before, I had nothing to lose ... now I do. I've changed a great deal from the point where I first began and although I know that's a natural thing, I think I preferred the old me that naively believed people would look past my skin colour and gender. Both have been the making, then breaking then making of me ...

5 Male Culture and Studio Territory

In this chapter, I will move from primarily interview-based material to an exploration of the social, professional and creative contexts in which the audio professionals I interviewed have been working. A wider historical perspective will be taken that sets out the ways in which men have enculturated this particular part of the music industry and music technology as "male territory". Later in the chapter, my primary sources will be reintroduced in response to the historical and cultural research that forms the main part of the chapter. This will provide a commentary upon the increasing visibility of women producers and engineers in the 21st century, which continues to develop against a backdrop of not only misogyny, but also essentialism in general. We will see examples of the ways in which women's abilities to engage with technology have been explored by feminist writers, and how revisiting the myths around male genius with an awareness of the collaborative context of invention and technological development brings to the forefront important female team members. Later in the chapter, we will look at some of the ways that recording environments are positioned as a masculinized territory, which propagates the myth that music production and engineering are exclusively a male domain.

The definition of men as cerebral creatures and women as their supporters and muses has been in evidence since the Industrial Revolution (see, for instance, Wilson 2000). There is no natural propensity for men to have technological skills and women not to, as we have seen from the interviews conducted by the author. Emerging feminist histories continue to uncover the concealment of women's contributions to developments in different technological areas: for instance, Wajcman (1991) and Shetterly (2017) detail women's contributions to aerospace and military technology in the USA from different perspectives and at different times. More nuanced understandings of gender and various production practices in the music and film industries have emerged, too (see, for example, Steward and Garratt 1984; Bayton 1998; Whiteley 2000; Fleeger 2014; Wolfe 2019; Gaston-Bird 2019). The male-dominated narrative of studio practice is thus slowly being amended, although Tara Rodgers' comments about histories of electronic music summarize the approaches of many histories of music production: "A patrilineal history of electronic music production is normative, and ideologies of sound production circulates unmarked for a particular politics of gender" (2010: 15). Historically, writing about music consumption, too, has often been assumed to be of more interest to men than women (see, for instance, McRobbie 1990; Kruse 2002). This is significant because precedents and role models are influential factors for those women hoping to enter any work environment that has previously appeared to be inaccessible to them. The lack of a "bridge" into the profession exists partly because of a lack of visibility in the form of documentation about existing and past women practitioners. This happens in other areas of the arts, including literature and visual arts practice. In music, as Rodgers remarks: "Just as recording engineers use the processing tool known as *noise gate* to mute audible signals below a defined threshold of volume ... arbitrary thresholds have often silenced women's work in historical accounts" (2010: 11). Elizabeth Hinkle-Turner contributes to this conversation from the parallel musical "world" of electro-acoustic music, in which:

> the electroacoustic research, work and activities of men have been thoroughly acknowledged, chronicled, taught in the classrooms and included in the concert hall. The research, work, and activities of women, however, have not received the same extensive treatment. It is not a difference in *achievement*; it is rather a difference in *reporting*. (2006: 255; original emphasis)

For any woman who wants to enter the recording profession, a lack of historical documentation often exacerbates the lack of representation in the contemporary music technology press. If we follow the chain of activity back towards creative manufacture and recording, the music technology press is firmly targeted at men (and young white men, if the photographs of producers and their kit in almost every music tech magazine are reflective of their target readership and the background of their writers). The contrast between the ways that writers for music technology media, and popular culture media, discuss music is so extreme as to appear to be poles apart. Paul Théberge studied this in-depth (1997: 106–130), and indeed my own survey of the British music technology print press in 2010 revealed that little had changed since Théberge's original research.[1]

---

1 In 2010, I bought a selection of music magazines that reflected different genres of music in order to evaluate the photographs in them that would reflect the readership of the magazines. Overall, the identification of music technology as being "just for men" was overwhelming; in many of the genre-specific publications, for instance, the hip hop magazines, the objectification of women's bodies was

Historical Views of Women and Technology

Gaps in our knowledge about the engagement of women with complex technologies are gradually being filled in. The introduction of manufacturing machinery during the Industrial Revolution is a good starting point if we are to understand the ways that industrialization has exacerbated gender differences. In the 19th century, the operation of machines by male operators after their introduction as replacements for manual tasks consequently led to that work being regarded as being of higher status, and thus more valued, than the work that was being done by women. In cotton producing areas in Britain, for example, when "spinning jennies" were introduced into factories during the Industrial Revolution, this was accompanied by an increase in status and earnings for the men who took over spinning, while weaving passed mostly to women who suffered an equivalent lowering of status and earnings. Phillips and Taylor[2] note that:

> the classification of women's jobs as unskilled and men's jobs as skilled or semi-skilled frequently bears little relation to the actual amount of training or ability required for them. Skill definitions are saturated with sexual bias. The work of women is often deemed inferior because it is women who do it. (1980: 79)

---

a powerful parallel message to the content about music. This underlines the way that the rules of engagement in music production are reinforced by music publications, and in particular those focused on music technology and emerging genres of music.

Even when objectifying photographs of women were not presented in the publications, the lack of representations of female practitioners was marked. In the October 2010 issue of *Future Music* there were only two images of women in the entire issue, both reflecting stereotypes that are recognizable and accepted. One was captioned "Your Mother wouldn't like it". The image of mother-who-doesn't-like-it is an example of mom-ism (Gaines 1992); the woman is bespectacled, in late middle age, grumpy-looking and very frumpily dressed. The other photograph is an image of Rihanna, recognizable as a typical example of hip-hop soft porn imagery.

The hip hop magazines covered the international spread of gangsta rap, which has highlighted gender attitudes and imagery that are directly connected to pornography. This underlines the fact that despite incursions from strong female producers like Missy Elliott, and strong female artists like Queen Latifah and Erykah Badu into hip hop, many parts of the genre are a no-go area for women unless their appearance is sexualized (see Sharpley-Whiting 2007 and Rose 2008). We will see later the ways that sexualization even infects activities that foreground the use of music technology by women, such as DJ-ing.

2 See also Lown (1990: 174), Berg (1984), Liddington and Norris (1978), ch. V.

This is an interesting observation that we can transfer quite easily to the idea that the work of female vocalists is less important than the work of male producers, an issue further explored in the next chapter. It is notable that the skills acquired by female vocalists are simply not regarded as skills that are honed and practised to achieve professional standards, but as natural attributes, according to Angela McRobbie's assertion that "as unskilled rock workers women are a source of cheap labour, a pool of talent from which the successes are chosen more for their appropriate appearance than for their musical talents" (2000: 145). This has a strong resonance with Phillips and Taylor's (1980) equation of women's work with a *lack* of skill, and men's *with* skill.

Feminist writers such as Sadie Plant have rediscovered the mathematical skills of women who had previously been overshadowed by their male counterparts, acknowledging their contribution to technological development (1998: 5). Ada Lovelace, according to Plant, was at the centre of the invention and development of early computing. She was a musician and mathematician who worked alongside the inventor Charles Babbage, writing the first recognized algorithm for Babbage's Analytical Engine. This was an unusual activity for a woman during the 19th century; however, by the 20th century, computing and mathematics were becoming increasingly gendered.

Just as in the cotton industry, skill definitions led to gendered labour divisions with computing and mathematics. Wajcman (1991) documented such a change after the computerization of military navigation systems in the USA in the 1930s and 1940s. Women in wartime America were allowed into previously male occupations; female mathematicians were amongst the first ever computer programmers. The ENIAC (Electronic Numerical Integrator and Calculator) computer started off as their "territory", yet it was

> because programming was initially viewed as tedious clerical work of low status that it was assigned to women. As the complex skills and value of programming were increasingly recognized, it came to be considered creative, intellectual and demanding "men's work". Thus, depending on the circumstances, different cognitive styles may be characterized as "masculine" or "feminine" according to the power and status that attaches. (1991: 158)

The "forgetting" of the important roles that women have played in the development of technology, especially in wartime, is in a continual process of being rectified and documented. Margot Shetterly has recently celebrated the roles of women "computers" who worked on sending John Glenn into space in 1962; they had begun their professional careers as maths teachers before being employed by the US military at the outset of World War II. Later made into a film, *Hidden Figures* (2017) was a ground-breaking book for many readers of African American origin, not only from a perspective of race but also of gender. Throughout the book, Shetterly underlines the fact that although mathematics-based careers have become predominantly male occupations, in the 1950s and 1960s they were seen as women's work. She illustrates how easy it is to gender an occupation according to cultural, social and political convenience, and very much echoes the issues discussed by Wajcman (1991). Occupations have frequently been re-branded according to hegemonic needs, often quite cynically. Claire Evans, whose book *Broad Band* catalogues women's involvement in the development of the Internet, writes that in the early 1940s:

> One member of the National Defense Research Committee that administered a human computing group in the early 1940s, ballparked a unit of "kilogirl" energy as being equivalent to roughly a thousand hours of computing labor. (2018: 24)

In common with the idea that technological skills are exclusive to men, the concept of male genius has also become embedded in social, business and cultural practice, sometimes incorporating the idea of male femininity in order to rationalize a spread of skills that includes creativity. Christine Battersby gives a detailed account of the attribution of "feminine" characteristics to men who were regarded to be geniuses, relegating women's roles to being listeners and supporters, an audience for expositions of male genius (1989: 39). She cites Jung, who inferred that the "inner masculine side of a woman brings forth creative seeds which have the power to fertilize the feminine side of the man" (Jung 1945: 207, cited in Battersby 1989: 7). Throughout the history of creativity, as well as the history of everything else, women have been documented as lacking that special element that makes them capable of displaying signs of genius, or entering the elevated world of the auteur; instead we are muses and providers of emotional succour. This is summarized by George Upton, a music critic for *The Chicago Tribune*, who wrote:

> Man controls his emotions, and can give outward expression of them. In woman they are the dominating element, and so long as they are dominant she absorbs music ... Woman reaches results mainly by intuitions. Her susceptibility to impressions, and her finely tempered organization, enable her to feel and perceive, where man has to reach results by a slow process of reason ... she will always be the recipient and interpreter, but there is little hope she will be the creator. (1880: 21–28)

Worse, perhaps, in the opinion of the artist Ruskin, women existed to support the genius of men: "Her great function is praise" (cited by Parker and Pollock

1991: 10, in Battersby 1989: 39). The positivity of some scholars about women's roles in the music industry reflects Upton's declaration about the purpose of women in their relationship with music: that of absorbers. In her writing about classical music, Marcia Citron assigns an active role to female *listeners*: "What is clear ... is that there is no essentialist female way of processing music. Yet in many cases a woman has become part of an interpretive community of women that has participated in musical reception" (1993: 178). Later, Sheila Whiteley noted that women are "active makers of meaning" by listening to their partners' record and CD collections (2000: 5). Nicola Dibben has an altogether franker and more downbeat interpretation of what happens: "At best, listeners are characterized as passive, even when involved in the kind of 'structural listening' upheld by Adorno ... at worst, listeners are the dupes of an imposed ideology" (1999: 341).

It is interesting to consider these different approaches to listening alongside the gendering of "transportation" through music discussed by Keir Keightley in his article on listening (1996) in which interpretation, making of meaning and structural listening are seen as semi-spiritual concepts. In Keightley's critique, the identification of technical expertise as being a defining feature of maleness is applied to the production and consumption of music. He writes about the fetishization of hi-fi equipment in American homes in the 1950s and 1960s and illuminates the way that the media of the time amplified gender power struggles at home, in spite of the fact that in the early 20th century, home audio equipment was originally heavily marketed to women (see Katz 2010: 62–68). By the 1950s the technical "aura" of the hi-fi had become symbolic of the divisions between a man and his wife. According to contemporary media commentators, territory was marked out by sound and volume, and underpinned by an assumed feminine inability to twiddle knobs. By the mid-1950s in the USA even focused listening had been co-opted as a male prerogative, according to Keightley. The marketing of audio equipment included the territorializing concept that the volume and aural space of the music played by the man of the house on his hi-fi was designed to keep his female spouse out of his masculine zone within the home. The advertisements of the time simultaneously parody the attitudes of the men to whom the equipment is marketed and the women with whom they live, while endorsing the idea that this type of gender division is desirable and normal. The article cites a particularly offensive publication by Edwin C. Buxbaum, which heralded the "gendering of the experience of mental transportation" (in Keightley 1996: 168).[3]

3   Buxbaum's article (Buxbaum 1949) was challenged by Halpern, who demonstrated that she was a detailed and informed listener, and was as much an audiophile as Buxbaum himself.

Buxbaum suggested that women are not even capable of fully understanding the deeper meanings of music in a striking example of "expert" misogyny.

It is only relatively recently in history that women have had a wider opportunity to articulate their own attitudes to their creative activities, whether domestic, professional or recreational. This can be risky, as Helen Davies points out:

> An admission of a feminist viewpoint can be extremely harmful to a female performer's career. This creates the absurd situation whereby performers whose lyrics and images are explicitly feminist have to repeatedly deny this in interviews. This helps to naturalize social relations in music, so that gender is not seen in political terms, but simply as part of human nature. (2001: 304)

The denial of and aversion to feminism is endemic in the music industry, and not just in the visible parts of it. Research published by Marion Leonard in 2016 addresses questions initially raised by Keith Negus in 1999 in which he acknowledged the fact that women in the music industry deny not only feminism, but also often their gender, in order to attempt to operate on equal terms with their male counterparts. Some of the women Leonard interviewed clearly subordinate themselves to their male colleagues and internalize this feeling, infantilizing their self-perception by referring to themselves as "girls" and condoning behaviour they would object to in any other context in order to keep their jobs and make progress in their careers. This was borne out in my interview with Janet Beat, where she spoke of her teaching in mixed-gender education, in an account of her introduction to a class of new students. "What shall I call you?" she asked. "The Lads", replied the young men in the class, which was majority-male. There were some young women at the front of the class. "What shall I call *you*?" she asked. "We're The Lads too", was the reply. Leonard's research shows that women have great difficulty in positioning themselves as female in the "world" of behind-the-scenes music making (2016).[4]

One of the difficulties historians have found when writing of women's experiences has been women's understandable unwillingness to talk about their professional relationships with men who may be their seniors in the studio hierarchy, or to criticize the way the music industry's gender relations

---

4   It is also notable that Isabel Gracefield Grundy, cited by Paula Wolfe, firstly describes herself as "genderless" before going on to say she is a "teenage boy in her head" (2019: 86). Co-option of maleness is an essential tool for survival for some women in studio environments.

stymie their professional progress. The music industry is competitive and thrives on changing personnel because aesthetic and business practices are constantly in flux. For both men and women involved, whether as artists, producers, managers, or within other structures of the business machine, any sort of perceived negativity or "attitude" could result in (or result from) professional practices that could be deemed to be illegal in the public sector.[5] We have seen that disruption, sabotage and sexual assault have been experienced even by the small sample of women interviewed in the preceding chapters. There is an additional environmental aspect in the workplace: any "attitude" emanating from a woman could affirm the underlying belief that youth music is created as a force *against* the perceived controlling nature of women. This is "mom-ism", a term coined by Gaines (1992), and is demonstrated by the surprise expressed by both male and female clients (noted in the interview sections in Chapter 4) that the women they have worked with are able to do the complex and authoritative work that they had assumed only men had the skills to complete. In general, it is still common in the music industry for women artists to be defined as pop stars[6] (deliverers of a message), and men as auteurs (often creators of the text as well as mediators of the message), roles that have become entrenched by the mutual agreement between female singers and male producers. This underlines the importance of studies on the gender activities *behind the scenes* in the music industry as the industry changes and develops. The Art of Record Production conferences and publications in particular provide an interesting potential platform for discussions about contemporary changes, and it is possible that the 2016 MPG awards' lauding of women recording practitioners reflects this concern about encouraging women into roles in the recording studio by providing visible role models for aspiring female engineers and producers.[7]

After Lucy O'Brien's pioneering work on women and the music industry in general (*She-Bop*, first published in 1995), recent writings on women and self-production by Wolfe (2012, 2016, 2019), Gaston-Bird (2019), on digital music and sound art (Born and Devine 2016), and DJ culture (Gadir 2016)

---

5   After the first publication of *The Lost Women of Rock Music* in 2017, five more rapes were reported to me. I had asked about violence, assaults and rapes during the original interviews but the musicians that I spoke to did not wish these to be documented as part of their stories.
6   There are, of course, many male "stars", who in common with female ones, perform over tracks created by male producers. However, this article is concerned with gender gatekeeping as opposed to gatekeeping in general.
7   https://www.mpg.org.uk/news/mpg-awards-2016-winners/   (accessed   30   December 2020).

have documented the growing interest by women in manipulating their own sound, and becoming involved in the mediation of others' musical recordings. As Wolfe has noted, the Association of Independent Music (AIM) regularly focuses on gender imbalances in the British music industry, with AIM's Alison Wenham constantly reaffirming the need for this discussion after revealing that 80 per cent of the member companies were male-led (Wolfe 2019: 29).

Notwithstanding this, in her interview with me, Isabel Gracefield Grundy observed that the music industry is an exciting environment to be part of, regardless of what role is played. It is the assumed reasons for this excitement that divide the genders:

> Part of the industry that I work in is a glamour industry and there's an element of being in it that is about wanting to be near to famous people, wanting to work on things that lots of people hear about, and getting on telly. So you're in it because on some level you've bought into the idea of success, and you're aspirational, or you wouldn't be working 80 hours a week for very little money, if you weren't pretty much prone to believing in that crap anyway. But that's why men get into that as well. I don't know whether it's something that they would deny, I suppose from men's point of view I'm pretty much certain that what's spoken about is liking working with machinery, working with technology, rather than rubbing up with famous people.

Role Models and Male Gatekeeping

At the beginning of this chapter, I underlined the importance of female role models as trailblazers who illuminate routes into studio professions that had previously seemed impossible to navigate. These women depend on media recognition to move from the margins into the mainstream, becoming established as a new normality. In 2008 the journalist Kitty Empire could not identify a "female Timbaland" whose aura was enough to guarantee a clamour of artists wanting to work with them; she observed that although some women artists program, engineer and produce their own material, as far as she was aware, there were not many who did this for other artists. She writes: "Perhaps it will be only when they work for other artists that they can claim any sort of professional kudos from this activity; Anne Dudley [producer of Alison Moyet and Tom Jones] was the only British female producer I could think of" (Empire 2008). Emma Mayhew points out that "globally successful female performers are more likely to take up this role when they have reached a certain commercial longevity" (2004: 149) and this appears to be true in some cases: when a woman artist reaches a certain level of potentially risk-free income generation, she may be allowed to produce (usually herself). There are notable exceptions, especially in the USA; for instance, Linda Perry has a reputation as a songwriter/producer for well-known artists such as Christina Aguilera, for whom she wrote and produced the track 'Beautiful' which got to US no. 2 in the Billboard charts, and Missy Elliott, who has become involved in the "There are no female producers" debate, using Twitter to counter-argue her case.[8] However, this role is still very rare in Britain, as Empire notes in her blog for *The Guardian*, and the lack of female role models along with the lack of a visible entry point to the profession were issues that I encountered throughout the research of this work. Isabella ("Isa") Summers, the "Machine" part of Florence Welch's production team, is one rare British example, although early in her career she felt pressurized to take a secondary role to the male producers involved in the music (see Wolfe 2019: 69–72). When Boden Sandstrom explored the gendering of sound engineering as an occupation in 2000, she identified three areas subject to male authority and control: (1) the issue of power in relation to access to the field; (2) power, gender, and differences in mixing; and (3) sound engineers as sound mediators in relation to the participants, whether performers, business staff, audiences or others (2000: 290). Twenty years later, a male-dominated studio environment is all too often regarded as the status quo; there is a feeling that this state of affairs need not (and therefore cannot) be changed, and it is serviced continually by affirmative comments in the media by industry professionals. The fact that "The androcentric view is ... continuously legitimated by the very practices that it determines" (Bourdieu 2001: 32) underlines the same "natural order" approach to gender roles in the music industry that manifests itself in so many other walks of life. This assertion of natural order is illustrated by an exchange between Paris Askar and the record producer and journalist Howard Massey in 2005:

> *PA*: Do you think there is a "male culture" behind the scenes of record production?
>
> *HM*: This is a clearly male-dominated area of the music business. It always has been. Musicians tend to be predominantly male, and so there tends to be a "locker room" mentality in the recording studio – a lot of dirty jokes, and things like that ... Basically, I think that many male musicians don't feel comfortable having a female in the studio, in any capacity – whether as the producer in charge of things

---

8   https://twitter.com/MissyElliott/status/956349994713436160 commenting on https://www.billboard.com/articles/business/8095107/female-music-producers-industry-grammy-awards?utm_source=twitter (both accessed 31 May 2018).

or the assistant engineer who's making the tea. Sometimes they feel a bit constrained when there's a woman in the control room with them. (Askar 2005)

These comments are notable because they ignore the feelings of *female* musicians and assume that they don't have an opinion about the atmosphere in the studio in which they are working (and his comments are also, of course, disproved by the women engineers that I have interviewed). In fact, employing male engineers and producers can be regarded as constraining by *women* artists and has been for many years. In an historical example from 1984, Sue Steward and Sheryl Garratt noted violinist Vicky Aspinall's comments about working with a male engineer when The Raincoats were recording the song 'Animal Rhapsody', whose lyrics dealt with female sexuality. The engineer:

> took exception to the words, started to make remarks about them, and seemed to be quite threatened, I think ... [Gina Birch, guitarist/vocalist] felt it rather off-putting. Especially when you're recording a vocal, you feel exposed to the engineer: he can hear every word. She would have felt more comfortable with a woman. It was quite funny, actually, to watch his reactions; but we were aware of him as a stage between us and the music. (Steward and Garratt 1984: 77)

This issue of proactive gatekeeping by male engineers and producers was also a concern of Mavis Bayton, whose study of women musicians from the 1970s to the 1990s included a number of women artists who did not want to engage with men at all in the production of their music, unless there was no alternative. For these women, controlling every part of their "sound" was a politically positive act that asserted their gender power. She wrote that for those women who do not want a male "stamp" on their musical product: "a feminist all-women band with a male producer cannot claim that all the creativity that went into the record was female" (1998: 7).

In reality the recording studio environment can be hostile for the uninitiated, regardless of gender, and this is often exacerbated by the contrast between the technical experience of an engineer comfortable in their territory, and the practical experience of the performer who may be in unfamiliar surroundings. Alan Williams (2012) describes the interaction between an engineer and a female singer who had complained about a headphone mix; the engineer did not take her seriously until he eventually went into the studio and listened through the headphones himself, at which point he realized that they were faulty: "the power inherent in headphone mixes contributed to an atmosphere of anxiety that never completely dissipated, even after correcting the problem" (2012: 123). A different aural landscape is experienced by the performer in the studio to that experienced by the engineer in the control room, and is bound to affect the recorded performance; this was a particular problem for this artist as she was not well-known and had not yet proven her skills beyond the studio. Williams goes on to observe: "The control over another musician was his to exercise, hers to challenge" (2012: 122). The potential pressures of this type of attitude are frequently underestimated; amongst musicians, a surly engineer who refuses to acknowledge the poor quality of sound "in the cans" can damage the reputation of a studio, and professional etiquette is unfortunately all too often neglected in studio training. The importance of an engineer who mirrors the gender of the artist is an important remedy against "male culture" in recording studios.

Self-Production and Laptop Production

Self-production for female artists is not a new concept; both Sandie Shaw and Dusty Springfield, British stars of the 1960s, produced their own music, and the Lover's Rock artist Carroll Thompson formed her own record and production company in the 1980s to release her music (see Steward and Garratt 1984; Palmer 2011: 123). In the USA, Joni Mitchell, Alicia Keys and Missy Elliott are all noted self-producers. In order to discover this fact, one often has to "read between the lines" of their biographies. This is an account by Sandie Shaw from an email interview with me that illustrates her involvement at every stage of the production process:

> The most important part was the A and R bit, which was done in a tiny demo room in Tin Pan Alley with room only for me, the writer, and a stand-up piano. He would run through songs or ideas for songs. I would choose which interested me, complete or make suggestions to improve them and to what they called "Sandiesise" [sic] them. It was important to me that the material was authentic for a contemporary young woman. When I had chosen three suitable songs, I took them and the songwriter, Chris Andrews, to see the arranger, Kenny Woodman. There we ran through suggestions for the arrangement and Kenny would write the dots then book the musicians for the session. I [always] used the same engineer, Bill. I worked with Bill and Kenny and Chris to get the sound right then went in the studio to a sound booth in amongst the musicians to add my voice, did a couple of takes, listened back to them, made adjustments and then recorded the master live. I never did more than three takes because I felt it lost the spontaneity. At the beginning it was only 6 track so very little room for maneuver so everything had to be got right at the same time on the same take. I chose two of the three songs to be an A and a B side and saved the other one for a possible album track.

> *When did you start to become interested in having control over your own sound, and in what ways did this manifest itself?*
>
> From the beginning.

In a similar way to Joni Mitchell, who reputedly "hid behind" Graham Nash for her first album, Sandie's production role was concealed. She continued:

> I could not read music and I did not know musical terms for what I wanted so I had to imitate the instrument to illustrate the parts/rhythm I wanted to the arranger. It was all a bit experimental with lots of laughs. My manager would not allow me to put my name as producer on the record label as she felt it would look amateurish, that girls did not do such things, and would imply that I could not afford a producer![9]

On being asked why she was allowed to have so much control over her work she replied: "The answer was because I was paying for it! This was the first independently produced work of its kind". In Chapter 6 I will discuss other forms of concealment within the music industry, but it is interesting to note here how acceptable it was not to acknowledge the agency of high-profile women artists in the 1960s in the creation of their own sonic identities.

The spread of laptop music technology has been particularly beneficial to female artist self-producers, as Paula Wolfe has noted (2012, 2019). The main impact has been on self-determination outside men's control and the influence of the "male ear", the equivalent musical gender filter to the concealed "male eye" in film making identified by Laura Mulvey (1975: 27).[10] The success of the US artist Grimes has been attributed to the ease of access provided by the music program Garageband (although she soon progressed to Ableton Live because of its potential for greater complexity). The journalist Art Tavana (2015) describes Garageband as a "gateway DAW" (Digital Audio Workstation), and both Wolfe and Tavana agree that it provides an initial audio programming stepping-stone for artists who want to define their "sound" before perhaps progressing further into a formal studio production setting. The democratizing effect of Garageband for those who can afford a computer and regular upgrades is undeniable, but it remains true that elevating one's music above the "noise" of internet production in order to make

---

9   Email interview with the author.
10 The "male ear" was a term used by Beverley Diamond in a paper presented at the Feminist Theory and Aesthetics Conference in Toronto in 1990, "Aesthetics and Canadian Women's Music", which is cited by Pegley and Caputo (1994).

money, still involves gatekeepers and a music industry system that is prejudiced against female artists who don't want to completely relinquish control of their music to male mediators. In the words of Emma Hooper, "gatekeepers are those who, very often, mediate not just between artists and audiences, but between artists and *opportunity*" (2020: 137; original emphasis). Home recording and doing-it-oneself can sound empowering and even almost cosy, but it has its own complicated discourses and aesthetics (Tomaz de Carvalho 2012). However, like Grimes, there are other women who have relished the control it gives them over their sound, as these two excerpts from press interviews attest. Maya Jane Coles, an entrepreneurial and proactive electronic musician, started her own label to retain control over her musical aesthetic and its distribution:

> I never thought, "I want to start a record label". I purely set it up as a platform to release my own stuff, because I didn't want to sign it to anyone else and be part of someone else's brand. I just thought, "I've built something for myself and I've got here myself, so I want to keep it that way and not give up my rights". It's a hell of a lot more work, but it's totally worth it. (Cook 2013)

Coles has had the experience of being largely marginalized by the media in spite of her success, as her former tutor "Impromaker", who identifies herself as a sound engineering tutor at The Roundhouse, remarks in this comment under Kitty Empire's article cited earlier in this chapter:

> Look up Maya Jane Coles and you will see a young female producer, DJ and artist at 20yrs she has already received an award from NESTA for creativity, Performed DJ sets at major UK festivals and at established London venues, had a track released through an independent that sold out. One question to leave on is why an already successful young producer who is known to many in the industry gets little coverage and support, would a young male producer with this type of early success have more support? My thought is probably yes. (Empire 2008)

The industry pressures towards gendering the final stages of production were resisted by the electronica artist producer, Ronika:

> Having trained as a sound engineer and produced or co-produced most of Selectadisc, it was vital to keep complete creative control. I've turned down big opportunities because my experience of people in the industry is very much, 'We'll get you in the studio with some big male producers". I wasn't seeing any female producers when I started doing this. One of the most important things about

the record was to make sure there were a load of tracks that had a female production credit on them. (Cragg 2014)

Men's Work in the Studio

Even in the 21st century we apparently still have to challenge the myth that "Women just aren't interested in this area of work". Continuing Massey's earlier interview responses:

> *PA*: Why do you think there are so few female record producers, especially in the genre of rock?
>
> *Massey*: The interesting thing is that the studio manager of almost every major recording facility is a woman. She's the person in charge – the person who is actually running things and very often the person doing the hiring and firing, so you would think that studios are perfectly willing to hire female staff. But since there are so few women music engineers and producers out there, my guess is that there are simply not that many women who are interested in doing this for a living. (Askar 2005)

Massey searches for a reason, after trying to identify a role in the profession where power is held by a woman.[11] Several of the women that I interviewed disputed this assumption with great force, for instance the mastering engineer Mandy Parnell's moment of realization, cited in Chapter 1. The producer/engineer Adrienne Aitken also rebuts the idea that it is men who naturally want to operate the controls and women who take a "softer" people-focused role: "The guy I was working with was a complete technophobe and I took to it like a duck to water".[12] Wolfe, too, notes that finding technology challenging is not exclusively a woman's prerogative, citing a communication from Darius Kedros in which he defines himself as a "natural technophobe" (Wolfe 2019: 81).

11 This point is further informed by US associate professor at Berklee, Susan Rogers, in an interview for BBC Online in 2012: "The bottom line is, women aren't interested", she says. "Right now, I currently teach engineering and production; and I also teach psychoacoustics and music cognition. In the psychology topics, the students are half women and half men. But in production and engineering, maybe one out of every 10 students is a young woman" (Savage 2012). Although the BBC article later qualifies these comments, and in her interview with the author Rogers made a much more nuanced case, remarks such as those made above are rarely interrogated by mainstream media who ignore the fact that the historical lack of role models is a major consideration in the gendering of studio practice.
12 Interview with author.

Explanations for the dearth of women recording engineers mirror those of the engineering trade in general.[13] For women, part of the reluctance to become involved with music technology, says Hinkle-Turner (citing Turkle 1988)[14] "can be traced to their awareness that many of the cultural constructions surrounding technology are directly at odds with other cultural constructions surrounding their femininity" (2006: 247–48). In Chapter 8 of this book, we shall see that Pauline Oliveiros's classes appear to have gradually been drained of their female participants. Situations like this happen, despite Cordelia Fine's recent research into the invisibility of gender construction in the home and the workplace which includes a discussion about women's employment in corporate engineering and technology jobs. As a response to remarks such as those noted above, she concludes that: "As the arguments that women lack the necessary intrinsic talent to succeed in male-dominated occupations become less and less convincing, the argument that women are just less interested has grown and flourished" (2010: 52).

Studio Etiquette

In their series of interviews with 20th century women in the British music industry, Steward and Garratt included some women who worked with audio technology. Some surprisingly negative remarks came from a female studio manager, not a male producer or engineer, echoing the experience of Laura B cited in Chapter 4:

> "You just can't see a group of girls going home with a soldering iron", noted Barbara. "And that's another question we ask – if they know how to use one. You want to know if they've got that sort of equipment and if they've linked this to that, and, invariably, the boys have. They get an earlier interest and they follow it through".
> (Steward and Garratt 1984: 76)

It might seem odd that a studio manager was not prepared to train an engineer to use a soldering iron. This is not difficult: in fact, it is a very basic skill that the author has witnessed to be the first thing to be taught to both male and female studio interns in university studio facilities. It is not unusual for

---

13 For a summary of women's employment in engineering, see Women's Engineering Society (n.d.). Only 6% of the general engineering workforce in the UK is female, and only 52% of co-ed state schools in the UK entered girls for physics "A" level, for instance.

14 Sherry Turkle's chapter "Computational Reticence: Why Women Fear the Intimate Machine" (1988).

women to stereotype women, and this also will be discussed in the conclusion, because internalized misogyny appears to be a common thread in studio practice, and was mentioned by several of my interviewees, one of whom wryly admitted that she had never employed a female assistant. This tension around gender can happen at any point in the production chain; Andrea Odintz reports Judy Clapp (engineer for the Meat Puppets and Red Hot Chili Peppers) as saying in an interview for *Musician* magazine:

> I've encountered a lot more competition and sexism from women ... I was once offered a job to work with a female artist, but she didn't want another woman around. She wanted to be the star of the show. You'd think that women would be more supportive [of one another], but it doesn't always work that way. (1997: 214)

One of the live sound engineers that I interviewed brought up a similar issue, requesting anonymity. We had the following conversation:

> Because of the nature of the business, and because of the fact that there are not many of us, it's very, very competitive; I think I've had more help from a male engineer, than a female engineer. Yes, it's something that's not spoken about, but it should be, and in a way I'm happier to work with male engineers than with women engineers.
>
> *Is that because you don't think they're any good?*
>
> No, it's not that, it's because I think they're going to be a nightmare. And maybe it's a defence mechanism. I find it very difficult to relate, or maybe sometimes I might say the wrong thing; I find it more difficult. And especially women who claim that there are *other* women who really hate women, they really, really support women but actually I don't find this to be true.
>
> *I think probably men do it to men as well.*
>
> Oh yeah, I see it with men, all the time.
>
> *I think it's partly the industry, you know. And maybe it's because you expect women not to be...*
>
> Very aggressive. That's the word I was looking for, very aggressive.

Returning once more to Askar's interview with Massey, the producer's ideas are expanded further:

HM: The other thing I find interesting is that there are a fair percentage of women who are mastering engineers. That seems to be one area where there seems to be equality and the one area where gender doesn't matter. Maybe that's because mastering engineers don't usually work directly with the artist; also, they often have more "normal" working hours than producers or recording engineers.[15] Women are also very well represented in management areas: a lot of artist managers and producer managers are women.

PA: There are more female record producers in jazz and classical music compared to rock. Do you think those genres are more welcoming for female record producers?

HM: Jazz and classical artists tend to be older and more mature. I think that's the reason why. If you are dealing with a room full of rock musicians who are younger ... I am sorry to say they often do not see women as equals, especially in music circles. There is still a lot of sexism in young males, something which may not be as prevalent among 40 or 50-year-old men. (Askar 2005)

It is interesting that Massey appears oblivious to his *own* attitudes and assumptions. He does not make any observation that the sexism in young males could be challenged by the introduction of more female trainees, or otherwise qualified (by experience) engineers to the studios. As he is an established producer, one would assume that he is capable of positive discrimination in his choice of apprentice engineers. The attribution of sexist attitudes only to *young* males also needs to be challenged; as reported in Chapter 4, one of the engineers that I interviewed wrote to me a few months after our conversation (and after her first ever session with older male musicians) to report harassment, despite reporting no prejudice in her workplace when I first interviewed her.

Reasons for Employing a (Female) Producer

Traditional producers could become increasingly unnecessary as laptop technology democratizes the process, although at the time of writing this seems unlikely. The producer's "brand" is still part of the marketing of pop and rock music; Steve Albini's "non-production" is just as important to his clients as Timbaland's determined sonic signature, and at the 2014 Art of Record Production Conference, during a panel on the skills needed to mix music for mobile phone speakers, one of the delegates reported that he was building a large analogue studio because he anticipated a surge in "real studio" work from

---

15 In my interview with mastering engineer Mandy Parnell in which she described working with Björk in Iceland, Parnell reported working 36-hour days.

teenage bands raised on their parents' Led Zeppelin albums who wanted not only an authentic sound but also a traditional studio experience.[16] Alongside the reestablishment of old-school studio set-ups this indicates the possibility that traditional working practices will re-establish themselves, even as a niche activity, with an increased demand for old-school producers as mediators even for feminist artists and bands. The author Mavis Bayton notes of her own all-female punk band The Mistakes that completing a project was much more likely when there was a project manager, because a collective approach to every aspect of music creation could prove to be a hindrance:

> The producer can be the fulcrum of record company pressure and influence over artistic output because he or she has more power than any band member, able to achieve commercial success, or, alternatively, wreck the sound ... self production can be problematic as individual band members may disagree, and often bands find it easier when an outsider produces them, especially as, the more democratic the atmosphere, the more disagreements there are likely to be. (1998: 162–63)

An upsurge in the involvement of women in bands ought to result in an increased need for female engineers and producers apropos Bayton's comments above. Some thinking-through both by these potential clients and by the providers of the services that they use might mean that female engineers become assets to the studios where they work. Younger women artists who are not self-producers may feel more confident working with a woman their age and have high expectations of their creative skills, as observed by Lauren Deakin Davies in Chapter 3.

The reasons for deliberately employing a woman producer can sometimes be completely justified; one producer that I interviewed (anonymized) reported a producer-songwriter who had not prepared his song adequately for a young, inexperienced girl group aged between 16 and 18. Employed to arrange the song, the producer discovered that the song was impossible for the group to sing:

> ... he had put it in a key that suits himself, he can't sing, but he shone in it ... I said "that song's for *you*, and you're not even a singer". Back in the day, a producer would sit down with a keyboard player and find out which key the song should be in for each type of singer. I said: "Where's all that gone? You've just got your track set in stone now, or if you're going to change it it'll be a big deal. Even if you

---

16 Studio sessions have now also become part of the Groupon "experience day" phenomenon as a lucrative way of monetizing down-time.

> change it with the bass line or whatever's carrying the song, will it even be that instrument any more?" ... "What if it was Barbra Streisand or Beyoncé, or somebody that's sold millions, and you just gave them the track and said 'Here's the song', with your voice on it? You wouldn't get a look in". The song has to be in a key that's suited, or at least near to them, otherwise they just won't even entertain it.

Because of her experience in the "world" of contemporary girl groups, this producer knew that the track would not be possible for the group to perform live:

> I said, "It's at least one tone, or a tone and a half too low; they can sing it in their studio, but when they go and do a showcase, I can guarantee that apart from the little bits that I've given to them, they're going to struggle live in a showcase". You can't let them mime in a showcase; for a label, they've got to sing, and then when they go and do TV, they can mime.

It can be simple business pragmatism that leads to a sustainable career in the recording industry for a woman professional, according to Mandy Parnell:

> That girl thing, you know. It's more accepted now but back then it was "Well, what are you doing *here*? It's a boy's thing". There was a bit of that but it wasn't major. And 'cos I was, you know, bleached blonde spiky hair and shitloads of make-up and scary as shit to these guys, I was a very, very fierce looking woman you know. I think they were more intimidated by me than I was by them. It's like any business though, it's just business. You have to be tough in business; it's just that same motto.

Ultimately, given the limited opportunities for women in the technical field and the assumptions about their inability to engage with technology, Sally Potter's comments, written in 1997, are still relevant:

> "Femininity" demands the appearance of lack of skill and emphasizes nurturance and appreciation of the skills of men ... success for women often means gaining the precarious position of token achiever in a male-dominated profession. This position is circumscribed in such a way that as more women achieve in a given area they are forced to compete with each other for the same space rather than the space itself expanding. (1997: 30)

Reproduction: Sound and Body

Women's physicality, the power of their bodies, is arguably most to the forefront during pregnancy, birth and motherhood, which threaten their creative, social and political engagement with the man-made world and appear to threaten men's sense of power in that world too. In his interviews with producers, Howard Massey cites childbearing as being a major issue with his female interviewees (though not the men, who he does not ask about fatherhood).[17] Motherhood was mentioned by only some of the women that the author spoke to. I deliberately did not ask them whether they had children or not, although information about this was volunteered in some cases, and Helen Atkinson was expecting a baby when the interview was undertaken, and said that she did not expect to continue working afterwards. However, in a later email conversation, she mentioned that she was working freelance from home, still using her laptop to create mixes for iTunes regardless of having a baby. Her colleague Isabel Gracefield Grundy was circumspect about the reality of potential motherhood:

> I think one really key thing is for female producers, I reckon that most producers break through and have their biggest success from the age of 30–40 and that as when, as a woman, if you haven't had kids already, you really need to be having children and I think that's really important; how you handle that is a huge dilemma for me and it sort of has been since I started. If you're a producer at your peak, you have to be working 80-hour weeks because that peak is short, and you have to make the most of it.

It seems that provided the woman studio professional has established a reputation for herself (as Helen Atkinson has), motherhood need not always be an obstacle, and nor need it interrupt the close relationship a woman producer

---

17 In Massey's first book, for instance, published in 2000 (*Behind the Glass: Top Record Producers Tell How They Craft the Hits*) out of 34 producers, one is a woman: Sylvia Massy. Sylvia occupies one whole page out of her seven-page interview talking about why there are so few women in the music business although Massey doesn't ask any of the male producers anything to do with their personal lives at all: it's all about kit. In the second book of interviews, published in 2009, Massey interviews more than 42 producers, three of whom are women. The question by now has moved to mid-interview, with the exception of the youngest female producer, Ann Mincieli; in her interview the question is asked at the very end, and she does not engage with it in great detail. This shifting of the question to later and later points during the interviews could indicate the beginning of awkwardness felt at asking the question – but also persistence.

has with machines. For some women, however, it does have practical ramifications, as Olga Fitzroy discovered when she realized that she could not share parental leave with her partner. She had to return to work quickly after the birth of her child, and has now become a campaigner against the "motherhood penalty" and gender pay gaps caused by entrenched social attitudes to parenthood (Fitzroy 2018).

The successful British songwriter and producer Kate Bush actively incorporated motherhood into her music, thus bridging the gap between the physical state of reproduction and the conceptual reproduction of "self" provided by recording technology. She is perhaps Britain's most famous female self-producer, pioneering the use of the Fairlight CMI synthesizer. Her relationship with technology is driven by curiosity: "'I loved the idea of a child being inside the computer: bringing you 'love and deeper understanding', she says. 'I do think that the technology we have now is absolutely incredible'" (Cameron 2011: 85). Bush's active incorporation of motherhood into her practice has involved using auto-tuned recordings of her son Bertie when he was aged 12 in the version of 'Deeper Understanding' on her album *Director's Cut*. Her romanticism when she remarks that, "computers make surprises", has something in common with Sherry Turkle's "Lusers" (2000: 191). One hacker Turkle spoke to said the computer "make[s] most people feel that they have a free will, perhaps even ... a soul" (2000: 181). But, as interviewer Keith Cameron points out, she is still ambivalent to other technologies and described mobile phone use as "enslavement": "While Kate the sonic pioneer embraces technology's liberating capabilities, Kate the individual fears its potential to denude the human spirit" (Cameron 2011: 85).

Bush, however, is a privileged woman and her confidence as a mother is not shared by every woman producer or engineer: motherhood is neither an option nor a choice for all women. In some cases, women choose not to have children because they don't want to risk disrupting their career. This was a choice made by the US producer Sylvia Massy, not only to Howard Massey in an interview in 2009, but also cited by Melinda Newman in a *Billboard* article in 2018:

> "The risk in losing the ability to have a family is too great. They'll find better things to do. I know it's an unpopular position, but I've always felt that", says Massy. "I think there will be [women] like me that have decided, 'I can do without a family because the young musicians I work with have been a substitute for family'". (Newman 2018)

Susan McClary notes that it "is supposed to be *Man* who gives birth to and tames the Machine" (2002: 138; original emphasis) but creativity can also be all-consuming for some women, replacing the satisfaction of physical reproduction just as easily as it does for men. Tara Rodgers relates sound manipulation to reproduction:

> Reproductive sounds are variously *produced* by bodies, technologies, environments, and their accompanying histories; *reproduced* in multiple reflections off reverberant surfaces or in recording media; *reproducible* within spaces of memory and storage that hold sounds for future playbacks; and *productive*, by generating multiple meanings in various contexts. (2010: 15; original emphasis)

In this, Rodgers is reclaiming the reproductive side of music creation for women, opening for them the potential to reach genius status in the same way as those men interviewed by Battersby.[18] Nevertheless, several of the women I spoke to had children, and did not mention any particular problem with motherhood interrupting their work. Indeed, in a more practical vein, Mandy Parnell has embraced the situation, and has taught her son to cut 7" acetates using a second-hand EMI desk and lathe (MusicTech 2018).

In this chapter I have explored the stereotyping of women as technophobes unable to engage with music technology. In general, the strictures imposed on what is and is not acceptable regarding women's engagement with both listening to music and music production have been controlled to such an extent that they have bordered on censorship and prejudice. It is remarkably sinister that decisions about how we hear what we hear in pop music are almost exclusively made by men, who control what young women and their male contemporaries listen to: women performers are overwhelmingly constructed by men. The myth of the Svengali or auteur producer has endured for much of the history of popular music. In the following chapter this concept, and its influence on female listeners, will be explored in greater detail. Yet Saran Headman's feisty comment from her email interview

---

18   This nurturing and parental relationship to technology and the product of its use is particularly evident in hacking; Turkle reports the computer nerd Anthony talking about his "brainchildren", saying that women don't need to have them, as they have the physical potential to give birth: "Men can't have babies, so they go have them on the machine. Women don't need the computer, they have them the other way. Why do you think people call ideas brainchildren? They are something you create that is entirely your own" (2000: 216). The assumption made by a male programmer that parenthood equates with motherhood is not unusual.

demonstrates the way that an attitude can be turned around to a woman engineer's advantage:

> I don't think my gender has ever gone against me. I think as most male producers or engineers expect me to be crap. Then I prove them wrong. The greatest power lies in the underestimated!

6 Gender Ventriloquism: Songwriting, Production and the Mediation of Women's Voices

By definition, recording is an artificial process with the potential to create misleading illusions. Fakery has been embedded in the recording process since its inception. In his book *Cowboys and Indies*, Gareth Murphy documents Thomas Edison's sleight-of-hand in the "tone tests" he undertook in 1913, during which audiences were invited to assess the difference between the quality of the playback of his recordings and a performance of the same piece by live singers, who had secretly been instructed to mimic the sounds of a record player with their voices (Murphy 2015: 26).[1] In fact, the aesthetic decisions surrounding listening to female voices have been mediated through male scientific bias for a century, according to *New Yorker* journalist Tina Tallon (2020). As music technology advances, new ways of creating illusions advance with it: for instance, Paul Théberge cites Baudrillard in his description of the ways that the invention of multi-tracking created a "simulacrum" in music, "the perfect copy for which there exists no original ... productive of the 'real' rather than merely reproductive" (1997: 169, 179). In pop music, where artificiality has become a signifier of its authenticity, according to Moore (2002), transplanting voices across audio and visual tracks through digital sampling has become common practice ever since the 1980s. In some respects, this has "rescued" the public profiles of women singers in pop music (especially those perceived to have "star" quality) from consignment to historical oblivion by male historians, unlike the female jazz vocalists described by Lara Pellegrinelli whose place in "vernacular culture" erased them from "'great man' histories" (2008: 42).

Recording technology has a deeply embedded relationship with gender stereotyping, and in this chapter, I will discuss the ways that control is exercised through studio production processes. A historical overview of how this

---

1   In 1972, Susan and John Harvith interviewed one of Edison's singers, Anna Case, about her mimicking of the machine (Harvith and Harvith 1987: 43–45).

happens, not only through different technological developments, but also through authorship, will highlight the nature of the concealed manipulation of women in the recording of popular music. In this and the following chapters, I am adding to the discourse on the ways that youth cultures are directed by hegemonic principles, as noted by Joanne Hollows:

> In feminist studies of youth culture, there is often a concern with the extent to which youth cultures reproduce gender inequalities and "damaging" modes of femininity, or, alternatively, whether youth cultures are sites in which new, more "progressive" modes of femininity are produced which challenge or resist existing gender relations. (2000: 8)

In my article for the 2018 *IASPM@Journal* special issue on "Gender Politics in the Music Industry" (Reddington 2018), I proposed the term "gender ventriloquism" to describe situations where men control the sound (and often the lyrical content) of songs that are supposedly empowering for women and girls, and this concept will be explored in the first part of this chapter. As we will see, in many genres of popular music, girls and women are still assumed to be singers (and sometimes themselves expect this to be their role), while it is men who are normally assumed to be instrumentalists or producers. Recording, vocal processing and production are overwhelmingly undertaken by men, although the sonic signature of female artists' vocal timbres and the youthful, spirited renditions of the songs create direct emotional links with their teenage audience. Male mediators have a great amount of control over not only what is being sung (the text) and the ways in which it is being sung (the aesthetics) but also what is being "heard" by young audiences. In a country music blog posting from November 2019, Hannah White describes listening to the radio on a car journey she was making with her daughter in which her daughter sang along to the lyrics of 'Into You' by Ariana Grande:

> She turned it up and sang along with her idol "a little less conversation, a little more touch my body". I remarked under my breath, more than a bit irritated "you do know that no woman would ever really say that". She told me I was old.

White continues:

> When my daughter is singing along to *Ariana Grande, Beyoncé* and the like, she justifiably believes the words she is hearing originate from the formidable women who are singing them. Like all of us, she uses music to frame her own emotional experiences and this lie told to my daughter will become a battle she will have with herself

when she is trying to create a respectful relationship. A little girl is learning about the world through the popular songs she consumes … Without challenge she is absorbing a blueprint on what an emotional and physical relationship is. (White 2019)[2]

In the latter part of the chapter, I will return to the producers and engineers that I have interviewed, and introduce the idea of reverse ventriloquism, where women record male artists rather than the other way around. We will see that the debate about whether or not this makes any difference to what we hear and the way we hear it is very much in its infancy, and is not always to the forefront in the technical and aesthetic decisions that are made in the studio—but occasionally, similar issues do occur, and intimacy and sexuality have become important in the recording of male vocals. However, to begin with, we will look at the concept of producer power, starting with the girl group phenomenon of the 1950s and 1960s and the ways in which male producers and songwriters put words into the mouths of young female artists and simultaneously co-opted their vocal signatures as conduits for their own ideas.

Relationships between "Auteur" Producers and Female Vocalists

The act of ventriloquism in male co-option of the personae of "powerful women" has rarely been explored, yet it is evident if we look back to the girl group music of the 1950s and 1960s through Charlotte Grieg's *Will You Still Love Me Tomorrow?* (1989). Despite her clear enthusiasm for the songs, throughout her book Grieg highlights the disposability and interchangeability of female vocalists such as Mary O'Leary of the group Reparata and the Delrons, who told her that: "Even if I had known upfront what the situation was, I would have still gone ahead and done it … You felt at the time if you got too smart, if you got too demanding, they'd find somebody else to do it … and that usually was the case" (1989: 76–77). Eddie Holland, who often wrote lyrics for women to sing, felt that he had a unique insight into women's ways of thinking, effectively spying on them under the guise of conversation: "I knew I was able to write in a way that appealed to women. I spend a lot of time listening to women talking about their views, their problems and so on. I find it interesting. Most men don't" (Grieg 1989: 135). Although this voyeuristic approach is common to most songwriters regardless of their gender, Grieg takes issue with Holland's "coldly manipulating" attitude and remarks:

2   https://www.bellesandgals.com/2019/11/01/if-i-were-a-boy-gender-inequality-in-the-music-industry/ (accessed 11 December 2019).

"Looking at it from a different perspective, it seems that the sexual politics of the day were such that in the music industry at least, only through women could men make public their private and shamefully human emotions" (ibid.). This is an important observation, not only because Holland was using women's voices to articulate imagined female emotions mediated through his gender. He, alongside many other producers and songwriters, was also using them to create song scenarios that were beneficial to men; using women as mouthpieces he intentionally facilitated social conditions that encouraged teenage women to behave in the way that they were "instructed to" by his songs. The thoughts and feelings of the actual women themselves whose conversations he was appropriating appeared to be of little consequence to him.

One of the most disturbing releases of this period was the single 'He Hit Me And It Felt Like A Kiss', released by The Crystals in 1962. This single, produced by Phil Spector, was written by Carole King (music) and Gerry Goffin (lyrics), after the pair had a conversation with their babysitter, the singer Little Eva, who reportedly discussed the way her possessive boyfriend beat her as being a manifestation of his love for her. Even at the time of release this caused a furore. There are other examples of shaky ethics in the pursuit of hit records; for instance, Mac McKintyre's choice of the song 'Tonight You Belong To Me' for his 11- and 14-year-old daughters to sing (Stras 2010: 39).[3] Grieg remarks that girl groups formed the precedent for the "sexy girl-woman" in pop (1989: 197) and later, they undoubtedly influenced the personae of artists such as Madonna, Rihanna, Lady Gaga and Beyoncé. Barbara Bradby has lauded the feisty sonic personae of these girl group singers (1990), but from a 21st century viewpoint, the recuperation of youthful, female auras by (often older) men takes on an unwholesome perspective. Despite the presence of women such as Carole King, Cynthia Weil and Ellie Greenwich in the songwriting teams (who did receive royalties as co-writers), it was rare for the bearers of the "empowering" message that was heard by their teen audiences to be properly remunerated for their work, or indeed credited at the time for their input.[4] As Laurie Stras has noted, "[Girl groups] ... were feminine archetypes

---

3   Shock violence and underage sex have long been part of the male songwriting oeuvre. A similar case occurred with Malcolm McLaren's 1980s band BowWowWow, which featured 14-year-old Anabella LeWin making sexual noises on the song 'Sexy Eiffel Tower'. She insisted in interviews that she was making the sounds of falling from the tower, which is probably what she was asked to do in the recording session.

4   I am grateful to Barbara Bradby for noting that many of these groups wrote or co-wrote their first releases. However, the male songwriters soon took over the role of writing their songs; even Ivy Jo Hunter, who co-wrote the Martha and the

for millions of adolescent baby-boomers on either side of the Atlantic: what girls were (or thought they should be), and what boys thought that girls were (or that they should be)" (2010: 8). These groups displayed "multiplicity"; according to Stras, "from their audiences there is a general willingness to go along with the proposition that the image presented – the one you are to accept – is, if not a lie, at least not the whole truth. It is an act between the viewer and the viewed" (2010: 19).

Jacqueline Warwick describes the auteur producer Phil Spector as a man who "deliberately obscured the identities of the singers he worked with, reasoning that invisible singers were interchangeable singers whose anonymity would never allow them to challenge his authority" (2004: 196). Darlene Love (who sang on many of Spector's productions) describes singing lead vocals on songs that were later attributed to other girl groups and that became hits, with no acknowledgement either financially or otherwise that it was her performance that was being used (in her autobiography, *My Name is Love*, 2013). Male producers have sometimes been unguarded in their contempt for the vocalists they work with. For example, Jon Stratton reports the (now disgraced) British songwriter and producer Jonathan King naming the "rather staid ladies in their thirties and forties" that he instructed to "sing like 15-year-old scrubbers" (which they found "hilarious") on the 1971 track 'Johnny Reggae' by The Piglets. Stratton notes the "derogatory" nature of the group's name, which was intended to reference the American girl groups, and notes that it not only insults the women themselves, but also the genre of music (Stratton 2014: 68).

According to Judith Butler, stereotypes are maintained in popular music via performances of "drag" versions of the feminine that contribute to the entrenchment of gender delineations in youth culture. Butler (1993) regards Aretha Franklin's 1967 recording of 'Natural Woman', for instance, to be that of a "drag queen" because the natural woman of the title is a male-constructed fantasy. The music was written by Carole King, lyrics written by Gerry Goffin, and title suggested by producer Jerry Wexler; Butler sees the artificiality of the way that the track was created as an inauthentic attempt to control perceptions of womanhood. This is before even considering that Aretha is a black woman and the creation of the natural woman of the title is a construct of a white writing and production team, thus providing an additional layer of artificiality, an example of "lenticular logic", a term originally applied by

---

Vandellas' 1964 hit 'Dancing in the Street' with Marvin Gaye and William "Mickey" Stevenson, was a man. In the case of the female songwriters in the Brill Building, even their history and influence have been downplayed, according to Ian Inglis (2003).

Tara McPherson (Stras 2010) to the multiple layers of race and gender complexity experienced by the black community in the Deep South of the USA, and applied by Stras to moral issues surrounding girl group music.[5] Further observations about femininity as drag were made by Mary-Ann Doane, who describes the roles of women in film as watched by female audiences as "the eviction of the female spectator from a discourse purportedly about her ... one which, in fact, narrativized her again and again" (1982: 77), with the discourse being a masquerade, "the decorative layer which conceals a non-identity" (1982: 81). As audiences, we are complicit in the acceptance of women artists as being powerful, even when their agency depends on a traditional female stereotype.

Disembodiment and its effect of lowering the value of women singers has been a continuous thread in the history of popular music and is also prevalent in histories of jazz music, which indicates the breadth of the problem (Pellegrinelli 2008). Women's skills as vocalists are frequently made invisible in discourses of popular music cultural history. In the 1970s and 1980s, as "second-wave" feminism started to break cover in the USA and Europe, the music industry still continued to perpetuate the idea that producers were all-powerful, and vocalists were either dispensable (McRobbie 2000; Stras 2010), or could be created out of any sort of raw material. Disregard for the professional contribution that vocalists made to pop and rock records was even expressed by Nile Rodgers during the 1970s, when he boasted that:

> we can make your secretary a star – all she's got to do is what we tell her to do. Point us to somebody in this building who is not a star and we will make them a star, no matter who it is, because we're going to make the record and our rhythm section is the star, we'll just put whoever in it. (Easlea 2004: 134)

The singing group Sister Sledge, who were taken under the wing of Rodgers' Chic Organization following their 1975 hit 'Mama Never Told Me', were not allowed to hear the songs written for them or even to see the lyrics until the recording session; sometimes they were fed the melody and lyric line by line (Easlea 2004: 136). Rodgers and Bernard Edwards' intention was supposedly to keep the singing "fresh", but as a working practice this approach appears

---

5 The plundering of the black music community in general for songs, style and personae was noted in detail by Charlie Gillett in his book *The Sound of the City* (1996), and provides a disturbing additional layer of entitlement by white men in the US music industry that set the tone for music industry practice throughout the 20th and now seemingly the 21st centuries.

to be borderline abusive. Later still, Lucy O'Brien documents an unnamed member of the electronic act 808 State disparaging women vocalists on house music as "just tinkly pianos and wailing slags" (2012: 237) in a similar critical vocabulary to that of Jonathan King, cited earlier. The return of vocalists to the bottom of the professional hierarchy was something that became particularly prevalent during the upsurge of dance music, despite the public perception of female singers as powerful people with agency, and this will be explored further in the following chapter. Where once the value of vocal timbres that "ring true" had been of vital importance to girl group music (Grieg 1989; Bradby 1990) there had now been a shift in the definition of authenticity, according to Warwick: "Ironically mastery of an instrument becomes a badge of musical truth, while bringing music out from within the body itself is dismissed as facile and 'inauthentic'" (2004: 193).

Simulation and Ventriloquism

Once a singer engages with a microphone, technological mediation begins to shift control along a chain of command that detaches their voice ever further from the sound source, becoming less and less "real". This "throwing of voices", described by Jason Toynbee, started with singing into microphones, which encouraged the creation of specific singing styles designed for, and affected by, their use (2000: 76–77; see also Katz 2010). The "throwing of voices" also opened up the potential for the transplantation of a woman's voice from the body that produced it, to a body and face that were considered to be more conventionally attractive than the original singer. This practice was first mooted early in the 20th century by the composer Leopold Stokowski, who proposed a version of Wagner's opera *Tannhäuser* in which the beautiful voice of a woman who was a "sore trial for the eye" would be mimed to by another woman who "may be accepted by the audience for a Venus" (Milner 2009: 67).

Prior to this in theatre, according to Richard Middleton, developments in 18th century practice had introduced disembodiment to performances, where "the projected voice, the voice thrown elsewhere" became commonplace (2006: 22). Middleton mapped this to contemporary popular music, where "the voice of the people is always plural, hybrid, compromised" (2006: 23). Similarly, in the world of film, by the time movies could "talk", ventriloquism was embedded in the production ethos, and professional singers were employed to "ghost" the voices of famous film actors whose singing voices were not regarded to be commensurate with their acting skills. Many different examples of historical transplantations of women's voices in both film and radio have been documented in the book *Mismatched Women: The Siren's Song through the Machine* (Fleeger 2014). Vocal overdubbing became a career in itself and was parodied in the 1952 film *Singin' in the Rain*.

The development of sampling further distanced the physical presence of the performer of the original vocals from the final recording, and has given rise to further feminist readings of the implications of recording for female voices. Susana Loza has described this as "sonic deconstruction" (2001: 350) by male producers, and the implications of this phenomenon are described in detail in Barbara Bradby's 1993 article, "Sampling Sexuality: Gender, Technology and the Body in Dance Music", which critiqued the construction of the dance track 'Ride on Time' by Black Box. They used the sampled vocals of Loleatta Holloway's 'Love Sensation' which was "performed" on video by a much younger model, Katrin Quinol, in exactly the same manner as that imagined by Stokowski. According to Bradby: "In effect, Loleatta Holloway had been doubly 'ripped off', since not only had her voice been stolen by others to make money, but her person had been usurped by Katrin Quinol's image" (1993: 170). Tim Lawrence (2015) reports Holloway's vocals as being sampled "more than 300 times" in his article on the real, personal consequences of this practice. Not only has her physical presence been lost as a normal part of the recording process, but she has further lost her identity when her disembodied voice was reproduced as processed sound and used by the producers as part of the musical arrangement.[6]

There is, however, a different perspective to this phenomenon. Mark Katz cites the example of Norman Cook's sampling of Camille Yarborough's song 'Take Yo' Praise' in his track 'Praise You' to discuss issues around the "bodiless voice" that "One could argue that through his sampling Cook digitally neuters". He describes his students' disappointment on meeting Yarborough who "did not see how she was exploited" (Katz 2010: 157). Showing a degree of respect for the originator of the sound that is not always demonstrated by producers, Cook had given Yarborough a co-composer credit plus a 60 per cent share of the royalties (Katz 2010: 158). Not only had Yarborough liked what Cook had done with her vocal on the track, but she was also adequately compensated financially for her voice being sampled, whereas Holloway had

---

6   This is in contrast to Théberge who attributes greater freedom to vocalists in the context of pop recording, since they have the "last laugh" in terms of self-expression on the finished track. See Goodwin's (1992) discussion of Théberge (1989). In 2020 Black Box claimed in an article in *The Guardian* newspaper that the sampled voice of Holloway was not used because the contract allowing its use was not returned in time. This adds an additional twist to the history of the song (Hann 2020).

not been.[7] However, the low status of some female singers is epitomized by this male journalist's description of the 1989 dance track by Lil Louis with "vocals" by singer Shawn Christopher, which combines Donna Haraway's 1991 cyborg thesis and Roland Barthes' 1977 description of the "grain of the voice" in a disturbing way:

> the grain of the voice in the orgasmic moans of Christopher, the vocalist on 'French Kiss'. Even her histrionic and theatrical cries of passion are just so much air shoved through a tube of meat within the world, and the magical synchronization of her moans and sighs with the ramping down and ramping up of the tempo of the drum machine embodies a kind of synthetic silicon/flesh interface which dissolves their boundaries. (Daniel 2011: 46)

Authorship and Perceptions of Power

In particular in hip hop and neo soul, authorship is blurred; samples that reference other eras and genres are assembled in combination to form a sonic bed for the top line to be sung over. This is a very different method to traditional Tin Pan Alley songwriting and potentially leaves the singer in a precarious financial position because the number of composers and copyright

---

7   Loss of control over one's voice has not been an exclusive malady for women, however. In 1940 a court case took place when singer Paul Whiteman realized that "the singer who records his voice loses control over it". Several high-profile artists including Bing Crosby had previously released records with the instruction "Not Licensed for Public Broadcast" for this reason (Chanan 1995: 110). By the 1950s, there was a debate about the copying of the "stylistic phrasing of the singer" that came to a head when the singer LaVern Baker wrote to congressman Charles Diggs Jr. in 1955 to complain about "thefting [sic] my music note for note" (Zak 2012: 53). This could be described as theft of the vocalist's aura; Zak describes precisely what the problem was at this time: "Cover records had traditionally been remakes of *songs*; copy records were remakes of *records*" (Zak 2012: 54; my emphasis). Separation of female vocal performances from the women's bodies that produced them was taken to an extreme by a yet more postmodern situation in 1991 described by Chanan, where the group The Beloved sampled Hildegard von Bingen's 'O Euchari' in their song 'The Sun Rising' resulting in a court case between Hyperion Records, who owned the copyright to Hildegard von Bingen's music, and Warner Brothers, The Beloved's label (Chanan 1995: 164). The Beloved case: *Hyperion Records Ltd v. Warner Music (UK) Ltd 1991*.

'The Sun Rising' also used an 8-second sample of 'O Euchari' sung by Emily Van Evera. The judge wanted it to go to full hearing but it was settled out of court. See Harrison (2014: 336–37); also discussed in Chanan (1995).

acknowledgements outnumbers the singer many times over.[8] Songwriting royalties can be distributed amongst many writers, and the concepts of authorship and, by implication, individual genius, are challenged – although this doesn't stop producers becoming wealthy, nor does it stop them developing an aura of individual success (see, for instance, Seabrook 2016).

In a prominent example of multiple authorship, Cher's distinctive hit 'Believe' was composed by a large group of men. According to Mark Taylor in an interview in *Sound on Sound* in 1999, this song had no less than six (male) writers.[9] Despite this, Kay Dickinson assigns compositional power to Cher, rather than the producers and songwriters, as the *user* of the vocoder effect, writing that "this attributes mastery to a woman, even if she was not part of that particular production process" (2001: 341). According to Dickinson, regardless of the concealment of the male writing and production team, Cher still acts out a story of empowerment. This is comparable to the attribution of power by Barbara Bradby to the girl groups as authors of their "sound", because we can hear the sonic signature of empowered women in this music. For them, however, this authorship was not reflected in composer royalty payments: the "sonic brand" belonged to Spector and other producers at the time.

One of the reasons Cher's agency and identity are rarely questioned is her considerable input into studio decisions. For instance, she suggested using a Neumann U67 microphone to record her vocals because she had been pleased with the results after a previous session with George Martin. Mark Taylor, the producer of the track:

> spent time alone in the studio painstakingly processing Cher's vocals in this way, and by the following morning, he was convinced he didn't have the nerve to play her what he'd done. "It was a bit radical," he laughs. "Basically, it was the destruction of her voice, so I was really nervous about playing it to her! In the end, I just thought it sounded so good, I had to at least let her hear it – so I hit Play. She was fantastic – she just said "it sounds great!", so the effect stayed. I was amazed by her reaction, and so excited, because I knew it was good. (Sillitoe 1999)

---

8   The website https://www.lostinmusic.org has been set up in order to try to disentangle copyright litigation and contribute to an ongoing conversation about authorship.
9   Brian Higgins, Matt Gray, Stuart McLennan and Tim Powell (for the first version, which had been "knocking around the Warner Brothers offices in demo form for months") plus Steve Torch and Paul Barry later on (Sillitoe 1999).

Taylor's remark that the vocal effects on 'Believe' resulted in the "destruction" of Cher's voice implies that he was aware of the potential of sonic manipulation to really disrupt a vocal performance. Dickinson feels that Cher's willingness to accept this sonic manipulation with enthusiasm, counteracts any implication that she has a lack of agency in her work:

> Although the Vocoder [sic][10] outwardly fits this bill (it is read as being done to, rather than done by, the artist's voice), the flagrant embrace of technological opacity we hear in its mechanized obviousness opens up further, perhaps more fascinating, questions circling some tenuous notions of single-handed musical genius. (2001: 337)

Despite my own misgivings, Cher's relationship with the producers and songwriters of 'Believe' appears to have been mutually satisfactory. The writers of the article noted that in addition to the "vocoder effect", the "telephoney" sound of Cher's voice gave an additional distinction to the track: "This idea came from the lady herself – she'd identified something similar on a Roachford record and asked Mark if he could reproduce it" (Sillitoe 1999). Mark Taylor continues:

> Roachford uses a restricted bandwidth, and filters the vocals heavily so that the top and bottom ends are wound off and the whole vocal is slightly distorted. It took a while to work out exactly what it was that Cher liked about this particular Roachford song, but in the end we realized it was the "telephoney" sound. I used the filter section on my Drawmer DS404 gate on the vocal before it went into the Talker to get that effect. (Sillitoe 1999)

Simon Frith noted that "The sound of the 'phone voice' in contemporary R'n'B is ... a marker of youthful communication and community; its use in the 1960s and 1970s was a sign of distance and separation" (Frith and Zagorski-Thomas 2012: 7). Ironically, Barbara Engh acknowledges that the telephone was the first technology that disembodied the human voice (1994: 121):

> Adorno claims that a woman's singing voice cannot be recorded well, because it demands the presence of her body. A man's voice is able to carry on in the absence of his body because his self is identical to his voice; his body disappears.[11]

---

10 The effect used was, in fact, Autotune.
11 Engh (1994), referencing Theodor Adorno (1928). Michael Chanan notes the acousmatic nature of recorded music, which means that it has already become

Ultimately Cher's entrepreneurial approach to her career has allowed her to demonstrate in public a savvy attitude to maintaining a broad demographic in her audience, through her engagement with myriad contemporary production styles in a similar fashion to that of Madonna, Beyoncé and many subsequent artists. Anthemic songs about female control are not always what they seem, however. In a scathing article about Beyoncé written in 2005 entitled "Beyoncé: She Didn't Write the Songs", a journalist sources the samples used for her backing tracks, exposing the musical content as a jigsaw of previously released material as part of the hip hop aesthetic.[12] Although this rather misogynistic article concentrated on the musical element of her songs, Beyoncé's 2011 hit 'Run the World (Girls)' was in fact written by a five-man production team if we include the producers who not only created the backing track, but also the top-line and lyrics. Beyoncé has a production credit, though no credit for the lyrics; her main input appears to be in the singing style, which differs from that in earlier recordings in its use of staccato, aggressive phrasing, and which of course is important since the voice used to deliver a song is often the emotional entry point for the listener. This is an example of the re-setting of boundaries in the songwriting and recording process when a star performer completes the song by adding his or her aura to the finished product and it comes to be regarded as an essential and marketable element of the final track. Her vocal performance has on at least one occasion been rewarded by a songwriting credit, and therefore additionally monetized, by the studio team. For instance, her performance of the song 'Irreplaceable' was deemed to be so valuable (according to the engineer Jon Marius Aareskjold who took part in the recording) that she was given a songwriting credit. This information was volunteered after the musicologist Joe Bennett presented a conference audience with the statement: "Vocalists add Value (do they add creativity?)" (Bennett 2014). Nonetheless, the triumphant press debunking of Beyoncé's girl-power as a songwriter, citing the number of male writers behind her hits,[13] reflects the fact that our image of women

---

"literally disembodied" (1995: 18). Although our attitude to embodiment in recorded music is presumed to have moved on since Adorno's claim, the feeling of an "airy nowhere, inhabited by voices and nothing else – Helloland" described by a reporter who visited the Boston Telephone Exchange in 1887 (Engh 1994: 122) is significant; the inhabitants of the "airy nowhere" are potentially airy nobodies until we assign meaning to them as performers with agency with musical, physical, conceptual and commercial embodiment.

12 https://www.foxnews.com/story/beyonce-takes-credit-for-writing-songs (accessed 16 December 2020).
13 Ibid.

and girls in pop and rock music is still often constructed by men, if not at the beginning of the songwriting process then through men's activities as gatekeepers and intermediaries, meaning that vital elements of the public profile of female artists, both visual and sonic, are not within their control.

The curious power relationship between a charismatic female artist and those who record her is further illustrated in the relationship between Madonna and her producers. In her case, there is a Möbius Strip situation of the selling of the idea of domination and control as part of a musical package, but capitulation in the studio to her studio engineer while she is creating the artifacts that express this domination. Stan Hawkins's article on Madonna's track 'Music' (2000) interrogates the vocal processing done by Mirwais Ahmadzaï in which "Madonna submits to a swirl of fancy vocal edits ... her over-processed vocal style guarantees a seductiveness that typifies her agency" (Whiteley, Bennett and Hawkins 2004: 184–85). This idea of "submission by choice" is ever-present in Madonna's back-story, but the point at which it became a choice and not a necessity is never clear in biographical information. Although agency is attributed to Madonna for the track itself, it is clear that she sub-attributes the technical experimentation to the producer of the session, Mirwais Ahmadzaï. Under the instruction of (presumably) executive producer Madonna, Mirwais provides a controlling sonic framework to encase Madonna's ideas, as she herself confirms: "As a songwriter, I'm really conservative ... I like to find somebody who's a little bit more avant garde in the production department".[14]

Hawkins believes that this deliberate sonic capitulation is part of Madonna's producer-ly persona: "In tracks such as *Music* we cannot fail to acknowledge the artist's location within virtual sonic space as an entity of embodiment" (Whiteley, Bennett and Hawkins 2004: 187). Although he writes convincingly of Madonna's "technical virtuosity" (189) and her detailed attention to every part of the production process, a different narrative emerges from the producers and engineers who work on her material. For instance, Guy Sigsworth clearly delineates the division of labour in their songwriting and production process, noting that a song has to be "finished enough to impress" before even being sent to an artist, who will often correspond regularly about changes they would like to make before they enter the studio; the old-school method of creating a piano and vocal rough sketch has now become obsolete. On the song 'What It Feels Like For A Girl', Sigsworth reflected:

14 http://web.archive.org/web/20130618234026/http://transcripts.cnn.com/2000/SHOWBIZ/Music/11/10/wb.madonna.album/index.html (accessed 5 June 2020).

> The Madonna song was done very quickly. I sent her a backing track, and she wrote a top line to it, we put it together and four days later we had a record. And what was kind of good for me was that we decided on day one that we liked all the noises I'd already used on the demo, and it was more a matter of repositioning them in the arrangement around M's top line. So the whole job, apart from recording the voice, was moving things around in Pro Tools.[15]

Sigsworth articulates what is, for him, a "nuts and bolts" approach to songwriting that conflicts with romantic academic readings of Madonna's songs. The lack of contradiction between the two narratives, that of Madonna and that of her co-producers, suggests that it is perhaps in no one's commercial and reputational interest to challenge the other's version of events: all stories are good stories when they lead to the shifting of product.

Later, we shall see that for some artists, clarity about authorship is a vital part of their perception of themselves as creative people who engage fluently with technology. Unlike Hawkins, Susan McClary reads empowerment into video versions of Madonna's songs rather than examining the actual production process undertaken, although through these readings she notes that "the music in music videos is largely responsible for the narrative continuity and the affective quality in the resultant work, even if it is the visual images we remember concretely" (2002: 161).

Helen Davies uses Kylie Minogue as an example of the tensions between passivity and agency in female artists' careers, noting her attempts to become a more credible artist in the perception of the public as her career progressed. Davies cites Phil Spector's control over the artists he worked with, and remarks that: "One factor in the granting of approval to Kylie was that she was perceived to have seized greater control over her music, in which light her earlier work was reassessed and gained a measure of credibility retrospectively" (2001: 299). But powerful women "risk forfeiting their femininity":

> If women are viewed as being manipulated by Svengali figures, then the performers are replaceable and dispensable, and therefore of no value. Women are traditionally assumed to be passive, and so are constantly suspected of being the victims of such manipulation. (2001: 299)

Mike Stock's attitude to Kylie was to infantilize her and commodify her vocal vulnerability. Bennett (2015) reports Stock enjoying the production challenges of what he regarded to be a lack of skill:

---

15 https://web.archive.org/web/20150924130251/http://www.soundonsound.com/sos/mar01/articles/guy.asp (accessed 26 November 2020).

One might argue further that her higher/weaker vocal range made a meaningful contribution to the melody, albeit a subtractive one, by imposing a constraint that was previously unknown to the songwriters. It is demonstrably true that the melody of the verse was changed as a result of the vocal constraints provided by Minogue.

According to Stock: "She couldn't sing well. She wasn't projecting well. She hates the fact that she sometimes sounds like a little tweeting bird but I loved that. It was engaging and I thought it was fragile and she was vulnerable".[16]

Davies noted another unfortunate accusation for female artists working with male producers; Natalie Imbruglia, who was criticized by the press for her producer choices—Radiohead producer Nigel Godrich, and Dave Stewart—was "perceived as attempting to gain status through working with 'credible' men" which "can thus simply increase suspicion that the woman is being manipulated or is using her sexuality to further her career" (2001: 302). However, in a similar way to Beyoncé, Imbruglia is one of those artists whose management insists on a songwriting credit (and thus a royalty) on songs by other writers that she covers. This is common practice, and joins the anticipated inclusion of studio engineers as "writers" of songs in the move to laterally monetize copyrights, presumably as a result of fear of shrinking income streams in the music industry as a whole.

The awkward relationship between men's control of studio technology and the impact of that on female vocalists and the message behind their songs is complicated further by the symbolic effect of rhythm. In an analysis of the expression of female empowerment in the R'n'B genre in 1991, Susan McClary pinpointed the way that technological intervention by male producers can revert the "empowered female" message of a track, by causing it to be dominated sonically by its male mediators:

> It is ... possible to appropriate the phallic energy of rock and to demonstrate ... that boys don't have any corner on that market. But that beat can always threaten to overwhelm: witness Janet Jackson's containment by producers Jimmy Jam and Terry Lewis in (ironically) her song 'Control'. (2002: 154)[17]

This "containment" retains the *illusion* of power in female hands; but through disembodiment enforced by a combination of vocal effects and male

16 http://joebennett.net/2015/02/27/saw-kylie-lucky/ - more-4305 (accessed 21 August 2015). Despite Mike Stock's comments, his colleague Matt Aitken reported to Pete Waterman "Actually ... this girl's got a really good voice" (Waterman 2000).
17 See also Jason Toynbee's discussion on Bradby's writing about the girl groups of the 1950s and 1960s (2000: 100).

mediation, it is men's idea of a powerful woman that we hear in pop. There is no awkward physicality to encounter, and McClary takes this point further: "The advent of the recording has been a Platonic dream come true, for with a disk [sic] one can have the pleasure of the sound without the troubling reminder of the bodies producing it" (2002: 136).

It is still normal for pop producers to undervalue the singers who animate their songs despite the positive readings of Warwick (2004) and Bradby (1990). Even in the 21st century, female vocalists sometimes feel they are puppets, manipulated by men who have no direct knowledge of youthful concerns, as demonstrated by Kelly Clarkson, who recently complained about her own lack of agency: "I just think it's funny that all these middle-aged guys told me, 'You don't know how a pop song needs to sound'. I'm a twenty-three-year-old-girl! But I was fighting those battles alone" (in Seabrook 2016: 137). Each generation of women has had to discover for themselves the lack of agency they have, and the enormous amount of concealed control men have over culture in general. Lauren Mayberry of the band Chvrches described her bitter disappointment at the realization that the singer and guitarist Avril Lavigne did not have agency in her songwriting, and provides a good example of how a false sense of empowerment can be engendered in young female audience members by the music industry machine:

> I was totally the target audience ... The marketing campaign was "She's just like you. She writes the songs". To a teenage girl writing songs in her bedroom, that's amazing. And then I woke up one day and realized it was all written by The Matrix [songwriting and production team]. Teenage me still loves that record ['Let Go'], but why did they sell it like that? I was pissed off that it was being sold as real. (Nicholson 2015)

Mayberry labels this as "deception", yet this type of working practice has been common in the music industry for more than 50 years, as we have seen.

The sense of male invasion of women artists' creative output and persona was most clearly articulated to the author during the process of researching this book, by an older female musician who had recently returned to performing and recording after a long break. She had started to work with a male producer who created beats for her tracks, which in his opinion became a significant contribution to the completed songs; the two started, and finished, a relationship during the recording process. She came to regard his beat making as an invasion of her material so she spent a long time untangling his work from her songs in order to return the authorship solely to herself. She felt very strongly that he had manipulated her; not only did he mark out his territory on her material, but he also diverted songwriting royalty income towards himself by doing so, and they were no longer her songs of personal liberation because of his sonic presence. By removing his sonic presence on her songs, she re-empowered herself and re-established autonomy over her material.

This illustrates that authorship disputes between men and women in the studio are about much more than division of royalties.[18] As producers have become increasingly acknowledged for programming and arranging songs written by women artists, the lucrative creative attribution or authorship of pop songs is becoming more and more complex. In future, composer acknowledgements may include the recording engineers themselves in the credits, as we will see later in this chapter. The process of collaborative songwriting in "song houses" continues the Fordist, production-line style of song manufacturing practised by Motown, and echoes the working methods of Phil Spector, with collaboration masking a lack of agency. The music industry itself appears to work as quickly to control new developments as artists do to escape them. Simon Frith has recently examined the ways in which this role functions, and cites Laing's 1969 description of recording as "one way in which 'pop music ties together art and industry in a Gordian knot'" (Laing 1969; Frith and Zagorski-Thomas 2012: 170). Women who wish to assert themselves as producers within this hectic ethos need to manage, or be managed, extremely smartly in order to survive in the long term: we still watch with the male gaze, and we listen with the male ear, even in the 21st century.

Artists who are aware of gender ventriloquism have various strategies to conquer it: Grimes mentioned in an interview the idea of reverse sampling, or as journalist Rachel Aroesti wrote, the "transform[ation] of dance music's parasitic tendencies". In the words of Grimes: "I'll hear some totally fucking crazy remix and I'm like 'What if it wasn't a remix? What if there were people actually making music like that and it wasn't a Mariah Carey vocal being sampled?'" (Aroesti 2015: 11). The complexity of this whole issue is perhaps expressed more simply by the Australian cabaret act Lady Sings It Better, who won a prize in the Sydney Fringe in 2016. An all-female act singing "offensive"

18 In another example, an historical spat on Twitter between Amy Winehouse and Mark Ronson, her producer, demonstrated a similar problem with co-authorship. Ronson originally stated on a Jools Holland show that: "Amy Winehouse would come to me with just a song and an acoustic guitar and then kind of you dream up the rhythm arrangement and track around it and you help arrange all sorts of things". Winehouse tweeted her objection to him taking so much credit for her success; eventually, Ronson had to capitulate and admit that his work with Winehouse had contributed greatly to his own success. http://www.bbc.co.uk/newsbeat/11376118 (accessed 2 August 2018).

songs such as Robin Thicke's 'Blurred Lines' or exposing the "*aggressive* sexuality" of Tom Jones' 'Delilah', their leader Maeve Marsden says:

> If I wanted to write an essay about misogynist lyrics, it would never get me to as wide an audience as a comedy cabaret show does. The more tools, approaches and strategies feminists have in their kit, the further the message goes. (Spring 2015: 17)[19]

Significantly, Hannah White reports, at the end of the blog posting cited earlier in this chapter, the following: "The song my daughter was singing, I later found out, is called 'Into You'. Co-written by *Grande* with, yes, four men: *Max Martin*, *Savan Kotecha*, *Alexander Kronlund* and *Ilya Salmanzadeh*". This leads me to the final part of this chapter, in which I start to explore what happens when traditional gender roles in the recording studio are interchanged.

Reverse Ventriloquism

Recent developments in the gendering of studio practice mean that equivalent acts of ventriloquism may occur where a male vocalist is recorded by a female producer/engineer. There are not yet enough established women engineers to be able to ascertain whether female to male ventriloquism is yet an issue, but I did raise this with some of the women that I interviewed.

The producer and songwriter Isobel Campbell probably comes closest to overt female/male ventriloquism of any of the producers that I interviewed. Formerly a member of the British band Belle and Sebastian, she chose to produce Mark Lanegan because of her response to his voice as a listener: "Mark's voice inspires me, to the point of obsession … The first time I saw him perform, I was shocked by how much pain there was in his voice; it was so moving" (Chick 2010). It is notable that Lanegan once refused to perform one of Campbell's songs, deeming it too suggestive:

> "He didn't realize what he was singing until halfway through, then he stopped and said, 'I can't sing this!'"
> "She says stuff in a certain way that I probably naturally wouldn't", says Lanegan.
> [Campbell:] "He said it would probably have been OK if I was singing it". (Chick 2010)

This interesting reversal of gender roles demonstrates a negotiation that has not placed power completely in Campbell's hands as a producer. Lanegan's

---

19 See also http://www.maevemarsden.com/productions/lady-sings-it-better/ (accessed 3 June 2020).

relative power within their working relationship allowed him to refuse to sing lyrics that he felt uncomfortable with, which reflects a very different working relationship to that of, for instance, Darlene Love and Phil Spector. In Chick's interview, Campbell is clear about her intention to speak through Lanegan's emotional vocal style as he voices her lyrics, stating that "My songs are drawn from my life, but his voice is perfect at narrating them, at expressing them". Wolfe, in her writing about media reporting and its relationship with Campbell's journey from singer-songwriter to producer, mentions the criticisms of Campbell's own voice by various reviewers; Campbell utilizes Lanegan's more emotional voice as an "authentic conduit to the Americana her songs seek to evoke" (Chick, cited by Wolfe 2016); Lanegan's voice is a mouthpiece, effectively making Campbell a ventriloquist, in this case co-opting her male artist's emotional range to animate her songs.

As the gender implications of male/female ventriloquism have become more apparent during the writing of this book, raised unbidden by some of the women I spoke to, I began to specifically ask about the way that my interview sample addressed expressions of sexuality in their recording sessions. Susan Rogers spoke candidly about the sexiness of some male voices that she had recorded, in the unusual social environment of a conversation at Halloween between a female-only group of students she was teaching:

> It was during a makeup class in Advanced Production at Berklee. Attendance was optional and as it turned out, only the female students attended that day. We drifted off the main topic and somehow found ourselves in, for me, brand new territory. We started talking about what we found sexy in male vocal performance. I have never been in a room with that many heterosexual female record makers and it was kind of intoxicating. I soaked up every minute. We took turns playing examples of things we liked and we spoke very openly about how the vocals made us feel. Because there were no men there we didn't have to worry about embarrassing anyone. I realized that this is what it must be like during many all-male sessions, which of course I have never seen.

London R'n'B producer JPL negotiates the sexual content in her male clients' singing and lyrics. On one occasion, the artist Zalon was exercising self-restraint in both his performance and his lyrical approach. It was she who suggested that: "We can push the boundary on that":

> I always say to men, if a woman likes a man, a man can get away with saying almost anything to her. It's when we don't like you it's like, "What did he say? That's a bit out of order, isn't it!". So we were

> able to bring that dynamic to the songwriting, and some of the maybe more risqué kind of lyrics: not as in cursing or anything like that, but "take me to bed" kind of lyrics.

The above conversation illustrates JPL giving Zalon permission to express his sexuality. This reversal of conventional gendered studio etiquette might potentially feel threatening to the artist. However, the male artists that JPL works with appear to enjoy the reversal of roles, and of course once they leave the studio for the outside world, they resume their normal gender roles.

In more mainstream audio engineering, Olga Fitzroy, the British engineer who has both pop music and TV and film soundtrack credits to her name, expresses a completely practical view on recording male vocalists:

> *Have you ever reversed the normal situation where a male engineer records a female artist, by recording a male vocalist? If so, what led to this decision being made, and do you think you heard his voice differently?*
>
> Quite often – it seems to me that most singers in bands are male, so I've often recorded male vocalists. I think the decision was made because I happened to be the person that had been booked to make the recording, perhaps I'd worked with that artist or someone connected with that artist before. If I'm trusted to record drums, guitar and strings, why not vocals? I don't think women in general hear things particularly differently to men. I've read articles saying that women have better hearing than men on average, but I don't think being a good engineer is about what frequencies are audible to you, it's more about aesthetic choices, and being competent.

Similarly, "Hannah", who has specialized in recording rock vocalists for many years, feels strongly that her decisions about sonic aesthetics are not affected by gender. In a similar way to Fitzroy, she aims for invisibility, or rather inaudibility, as a mediator, with the emphasis on the performance (and therefore the performer) concealing her role:

> *When you record male vocals, how aware are you of making the sound appealing to female listeners/audiences, and how does this affect the way you approach the sound?*
>
> I have never ever, ever thought about making male vocals sound more appealing to female listeners. I just go for what sounds good for whoever is listening and what suits the music. A good well-executed performance is the most important thing.

Lauren Deakin Davies, who predominantly works with singer-songwriters, feels that a less competitive recording environment gets better results. Identifying herself as gay, she remarks:

> Male sexiness isn't really something I'm looking out for. Something I find myself doing is helping men to sing falsetto better, or sing higher notes. Maybe they've sung a lot by themselves and so they go low, and they get to a high part and they really struggle and I feel like, "I can help you, teach you to hit those notes properly". If they were in a studio with a [male producer] and were trying to hit a high note and they couldn't, I feel like they'd be worried that the man was judging them and even taking the piss out of them for singing a high part. I'm really supportive.

In this chapter, I have described the concealed power exercised by male producers, who "produce" a version of femaleness that is embedded not only in the sounds that are created in the music that they produce, but also in the structures that surround the artists that they work with. These structures have to be negotiated by women artists, and indeed women producers who have to rationalize their activities within the business that has been run for decades by men for their own benefit. The insidiousness of the process of ventriloquism lies in its ability to remain concealed, and the reluctance of even enlightened women to admit the depth of control that men have over popular music. This reluctance is based not just on an unwillingness to acknowledge an unfair and oppressive situation that exists in plain sight, but also because to flag up the consequences of addressing this issue could result in the ending of the career of a woman producer working in a "man's profession". The ability of women producers to survive and thrive in this profession that displays such consolidated misogyny should not be underestimated. In the next chapter, I will discuss the strategies that women have developed in EDM (electronic dance music) to negotiate male mediation – referring to both music magazines and academic publications – to demonstrate the complex interface between producers in a genre that supposedly favours women producers, and the ways that they are written about.

7 Fighting Back Against Stereotyping: The Case of EDM

In the previous chapters, we have seen examples of the ways that dominant cultural values are and have been reinforced by gender roles in the recording of popular music. Paula Wolfe's extensive research into self-producing female singer-songwriters (2012, 2016, 2019) identifies a burgeoning world of activity by women in recording that is hemmed in by male gatekeepers in the music industry – an old guard of men who appear to be privately resistant to systemic change, even when they articulate an interest in public in the promotion of such women in the industry. Regardless of this, the sense of agency felt by women who not only write and play their own songs, but also create a sonic signature by recording and producing them, should not be underestimated. Although this has not been the main focus of my own research in this book, the movement towards autonomy in that area of the music industry is currently thriving, and the "world" of female electronic music production provides insights into the various ways that incursions into the music industry can be made and how they are received. Because this is a genre in which a visible presence is of lesser importance than it is in other genres, particularly mainstream commercial pop, looking at this area of music reveals different ways that music can be articulated by women practitioners who use music technology in their practice, the ways these are interpreted by commentators, and the nature of these apparent changes. In this chapter, I will examine this world and the insights it provides with regards to the production and reception of female generated music in general.

Although it is common in electronic dance music (EDM) for women to mediate their own music, rather than be mediators (as most of my interview subjects are), responses to a music genre such as this where women are establishing a power base will help to illustrate the impact of the alleged upsurge of powerful women in the music industry in general. This is a different gender story to that of R'n'B, a popular music genre that has run parallel to EDM, which "pits female singing against male rapping, reinscribing a longstanding (and unhelpfully binaristic) stereotyping of music as feminine, concerned with senses, and language as masculine, a rational structure" (Jarman-Ivens 2007: 18). In the genre of R'n'B, the female singer frequently shares her track with a male rapper who acts as a sort of male "minder", signifying her lack of independence and autonomy through her position within a track created sonically by a male producer and patrolled by a male voice standing alongside her. Susan McClary's observation about the "containment" of Janet Jackson, cited in Chapter 6, is taken one stage further.

Many of the issues concerning the way the contributions women make to the music industry are valued are illustrated particularly clearly in the interface between commentators and practitioners of EDM. We will see that, even here, a masculine definition of working practices takes precedence, but at least there appears to be an ongoing dialogue about what happens as the producers develop their skills and their practice towards becoming autonomous. I will present examples of the ways that dance music scenes are written about and how women are sometimes defined within that writing, before a discussion about the organizations that support women professionals (or not).

Historical Precedents in Dance Music

There has been the occasional release of female-produced tracks, most notably 1999's release *Female of the Species*, which featured 24 electronic music producers.[1] Yet the process of convincing the powers-that-be, and the public, that women are capable of making aesthetic musical choices and engaging with the technology in order to realize those choices, has been remarkably slow and has been disrupted in many different ways.

In the "Swinging Sixties", the first DJ at Los Angeles' Whisky-A-Go-Go club in 1964 was a woman, Joanie Labine.[2] She played records between bands from a booth suspended next to the stage. However, her role was later changed to that of go-go dancing, and she became a pioneer again, but this time in a physically sexualized, rather than a technological and musical, role.[3] Just being present in the club would have felt like a privilege at that time; changing her role to a performance of corporeal femininity amenable to the stereotypes attributed to her gender, and pushing aside her intellect, would have avoided any sort of challenge to her stereotyped identity as a nightclub hostess. According to Tami Gadir's (2016) research, sixty years later female DJs are still sometimes assumed to be the girlfriend of a male DJ, rather than a person

1   https://www.discogs.com/Various-Female-Of-The-Species/release/192038 (accessed 12 August 2018).
2   https://spychedelicsally.blogspot.com/2014/06/joanie-labine-first-female-dj-at.html (accessed 4 June 2020).
3   https://whiskyagogo.com/calendar/the-world-famous-whisky-a-go-go-part-1/ (accessed 24 November 2020).

with professional agency. Colleen Murphy's experience of being excluded from the venue she was due to play at, because of her gender, bears this out:

> One time I did get really angry, as I was playing with Josh Wink who was a really famous DJ at the time, in the '90s. I was playing at this club in New York, it was me, Josh Wink and Laurent Garnier and I was opening. So I got there early, there's already a queue outside, I show up with my record boxes and the bouncer won't let me in because he doesn't think Cosmo's a girl. Because I had Cosmo as my name so it could go either way, when really it's more of a male name. So I gave it to him big time, New York Style.

Sometimes, historical gaslighting can cover up awkward truths about attitudes towards women in the music industry, effectively ascribing power to them when they have had little, or none. In disco music, for instance, which was described by Nona Hendrix of the disco pop band Labelle in the BBC documentary *The Joy of Disco*, as a genre of music that "foregrounded women's sexuality", the marketing peripherals such as 12" single and album covers were often based on highly sexualized images of women. The documentary highlights the complex gender relations in the disco environment. One interviewee noted that the strong presence of women in discos at the outset legitimized the male-on-male dancing in the gay male clubs where the disco scene started up, because such dancing was illegal in the 1970s. By foregrounding women's sexuality, the music industry simultaneously monetized it and tied women's physicality to their musical skills; it could be strongly argued that it was women's *sex appeal* rather than their sexuality that was foregrounded.[4] Despite this, behind the scenes, LaBelle's manager Vicki Wickham was also the producer of their biggest-selling single, 'Lady Marmalade'.[5] Sylvia Robinson, later the founder of Sugarhill Records and whose single 'Pillow Talk' was co-produced with Michael Burton, is another example of the rare female producers of this era, and she also utilized her sexuality in order to become successful.

Towards the end of the 20th century, claims were made for a soft revolution in gender relations that was centred on electronic dance music and rave culture. In this field, the physical presence of the woman herself is minimized, and judgement of her sexuality, age, gender orientation and culture can be hidden behind a "mask" of sound, a tremendously useful tool, bypassing the pressure for a woman to maximize her youth and sexual persona at the expense of a deeper technological engagement with popular culture. The

---

4 http://www.bbc.co.uk/programmes/b01cqt72 (accessed 16 December 2020).
5 Wickham is listed as the producer of 35 singles on discogs.com from 1968 onwards.

career of US artist producer Laurie Anderson, who conceals her "self" in her music, is a useful illustration of the way an artist can conceal aspects of their physical persona within their music. McClary has documented Anderson's ability to embody herself in music within a mask of technology. Anderson, who spans the divide between experimental music, performance art and pop (her single 'O Superman' charted in the UK charts at number two in 1981), provides an interesting counterpoint to the discussion about Cher in the previous chapter. McClary writes of Anderson's music that:

> It is electronically saturated at the same time as it insists on the body – and not simply the neuter body that has been erased from consideration in music theory, but the problematic female body that traditionally has been the site of the spectacular. (1989–90: 104–128)

We could argue that Anderson's work demonstrates Hélène Cixous's theories about *éctriture feminine* (1976). Unlike the male producers who undertake "sonic deconstructions" of the female voice listed by Susana Loza in 2001, this deconstruction is undertaken by Anderson herself, and therefore signifies a different phenomenon. Rather than "embodying flexible sexualities, performative sexualities, sexualities that confront the cultural signs that, for better or worse, have inextricably defined the limits and spaces of our desires" (Loza 2001: 356), the vocal processing Anderson uses de-genders the message that she wants to deliver, disrupting the mask of femininity that would otherwise be the primary message heard by the listener. She interrupts an externalized impression of who she is by experimenting with self-generated vocal sounds, claiming an authenticity out of her bodily performance despite the inauthenticity of its mediation through technology. Anderson "deliberately plays with those anxieties. She insists on and problematizes her mediation" (McClary 2002: 137). Her sonic definition is self-generated and fights against those definitions imposed upon her by convention; in this she performs a radical representation of being a woman while also avoiding the assimilation of androgyny with maleness.

Anderson's disguise has an entirely different effect to the masking of Cher's vocals in 'Believe' or Loleatta Holloway's concealment behind Katrin Quinol's body that I discussed in the previous chapter. Her hidden-ness is a deliberate performative choice, and forms part of the conceptual approach she has to her work. Rejection of the decorative aspects of femininity allows a woman sound artist and performer to reinvent the ways that a woman can sound, as well as the way that she looks. Anderson's experimental approaches to self-production are therefore an important contribution to the discourse about women and production because she re-casts herself as a sonic being, demonstrating her creative agency and her skills simultaneously: artificiality is reclaimed as a female tool. Ironically, in defining herself against convention, her work also serves to acknowledge the power of convention.

Control over one's identity remains a constant struggle for women performers. Twenty-first-century artists who work within the artistic, and less traditional, side of popular music reject male definitions and incorporate their agency into their work. Björk is one example of the tech-savvy women in the music industry who have had little tolerance for their roles being defined by men. Björk's irritation with the constant assumption that she is technologically incompetent led to an online diatribe in the magazine *Pitchfork* in 2008 that was followed up in 2015 with a further articulation of her feelings about attribution of skills in her musical releases.[6] Sophie Heawood, a journalist for *The Guardian* and fan of Björk since childhood, supported her against the conjecture that "she must have got a man in", citing the article:

> "With the last album that Kanye did, he got all the best beatmakers on the planet", she said, while making it clear she was not knocking him for this. "A lot of the time he wasn't even there. Yet no one would question his authorship *for a second* ... I did 80% of the beats on *Vespertine* and it took me *three years* to work on that album – it was like doing a huge embroidery piece". (Heawood 2015)

Percussion was added in the last two weeks of production by Matmos, the electronic musicians who have been credited with producing the entire album ever since, despite repeatedly denying it (Heawood 2015: 5). The fact that during this seven-year period so little progress was made in mainstream attitudes to women and music technology, despite the emphasis on women's increasing power in the music industry from some quarters, increased interest in the international organization female:pressure[7] based in Berlin and which promotes women and non-gender-specific people in EDM and other genres of music that involve interaction with music technology. The site acts as a global network for female producer and DJ events, opportunities and so on, and includes information about organizations that have female-enabling policies, quotas, or women-only foci, and is a constant forum for discussion on all of these issues.

---

6 https://pitchfork.com/features/interview/9582-the-invisible-woman-a-conversation-with-bjork/ (accessed 16 December 2020).

7 http://www.femalepressure.net/fempress.html (accessed 16 December 2020).

Björk is an artist who follows through her observations on gender roles in the music industry with affirmative action. I include here an edited transcription of the conversation that I had with Mandy Parnell after speaking with her about Björk's comments to *Pitchfork*. The conversation illustrates the intense working schedule undertaken in the completion of the *Vespertine* album, and the practical effects of working relationships with an all-female team; in its authenticity, it illustrates just how normally a group of women working together on a high-profile music project interact towards its completion. Parnell has referred to Björk as being "innovative" as a musician and producer. After a falling-out with her original mastering engineer in New York (also a woman) and what musicians term an "ears rest" while on holiday, Björk returned with a new approach to what had seemed like a completed project. Mandy relates:

> When she came back she sat down and listened to the album without the iPad stuff or anything. She said "I don't think it's strong enough as an album". She made a very big decision; everything was packaged, ready to go. It was all [shrink-wrapped]. Sealed, signed, delivered in the boxes ready to be shipped. And she was discussing it with Derek at [record label] One Little Indian (he's been around since the punk days), a character very supportive of his artists. She decided to recall it all, go back into the studio and call on some of the guys who had done some of the programming for her and change it up.

Björk decided to contact her one-time keyboard player Leila Arab, an electronic music artist who discreetly mentors many other artists, according to Parnell. Leila recommended Mandy Parnell for the mastering part of the project while the work was being re-edited. Gradually, Mandy became increasingly involved:

> It started off with Derek going "Can you re-cut the vinyl, Björk's not happy with the vinyl", and I was like "OK", and then it was "Can you re-do the CD?" Actually she's re-doing some stuff on it, do you think we could fly you to Iceland for playback because her daughter's out there, her daughter's seven, eight, she doesn't want to leave her, she's preparing for the best of all concerts, she's having to rewrite the show for the festival and she was headlining, so there was a lot of work for her. "If you think we could fly you out for playback" ... OK, another phone call. "Do you think you could take out a mobile rig?". It's very unusual for mastering to do that 'cos normally you do it on your own. "We can try, I don't know whether it will work".

The mixes that Mandy was given were not in stereo, an unusual situation, but she sat and worked closely with Björk:

> She's editing on ProTools, very much a producer/engineer: there's nothing she can't do that anyone else in her team can do ... There's a lot of people that can sit on the couch and give orders, but there's not a lot of people that can sit in the chair and do it all, and she can. She's very much in control of that. It was a crazy, crazy few days.

The working situation became so intense that the male studio employees avoided the trio of women producers:

> Leila came down to the studio one day for playback and all the men in the studio, it's a studio complex out there, they hid because they were terrified of the three of us in this room ... I'd actually had to brief Leila and Björk separately ... they're both my clients, but they're both very strong and very opinionated. So I sat at the back while they discussed it all and did whatever, and just made notes ... Most of the females I've worked with are very much in control, and know what's going on. Even female artists that come in, there's not many that don't know what's going on and couldn't deal with it if they needed to at some level.

From the above account, we can see that three women engineers/producers had complete artistic control over Björk's album, working through their own conflicts over how it should sound in order to create the final product. There is no hint of a need for male involvement: in studio parlance, they "drove the studio" themselves. Decisions about the personnel needed for the project's completion were made by Björk and Leila Arab; Mandy Parnell was trusted to supply the skills that the duo lacked. The tension they experienced was normal, and was resolved in order to make the music "work". This is an example of hands-on production, a total engagement with music technology at every stage of the process by three skilled women practitioners.

Self-Determination, Embodiment and "Control"

Most successful female performers have to negotiate the relationship between their physical appearance and their sound. Semi-ironic performances of female sexuality like that of Madonna (and later, the Spice Girls) are complex to read from a feminist perspective. Any artist whose performance of the female gender is supposedly a deliberate parody stimulates a two-way response. Sheila Whiteley, writing about Madonna, cites an observation by Luce Irigaray to point out that:

> mimicking is not without its perils. The distinction between mimicking the patriarchal definition of woman in order to subvert it and merely fulfilling this definition is not clear. In her attempts to overdo this definition, woman may be drawn back into it. (Whiteley 2000: 142)

One of Madonna's main champions, Camille Paglia, asserts that:

> The old-guard establishment feminists who still loathe Madonna have a sexual ideology problem. I am radically pro-pornography and pro-prostitution. Hence I perceive Madonna's strutting sexual exhibitionism not as cheapness and triviality but as the full, florid expression of the whore's ancient rule over men. Incompetent amateurs have given prostitution a bad name.[8] (1992: 11)

Whiteley provides a more nuanced viewpoint, noting that Madonna is "hailed as a heroine of self-actualization", proving that "feminism is not only for the serious" (2000: 225). In contrast, bell hooks criticizes the attempts by women academics to co-opt Madonna as a feminist icon. She states that:

> The desire to "appear cool" or "down" has led to the production of a body of cultural studies work in the United States that appropriates and rewrites the scripts and meanings of popular culture in ways that attribute to diverse cultural practices' subversive, radical transgressive intent and power even when there is little evidence to suggest this is the case. This has been especially true of the academic work produced about popular icons (Madonna, for example). (1994: 4)[9]

It is difficult to disentangle Madonna's sonic power from the power of her appearance and reputation; even McClary focuses more on what Madonna looks like and her skills as a dancer rather than her music itself when writing about female power in music (2002: 148–66). Stan Hawkins examines Madonna's relationship with production much more closely, commenting on her "technical virtuosity":

8   This attempt by Paglia to recuperate prostitution as an empowerment of women could be seen as a response to writers such as the anonymous objector to Aphra Benn cited by Lock (1976) in Battersby (1989) who said that rather than being fit to be named as muses, women were "much fitter for prostitution" (see Battersby 1989: 39).
9   hooks' tone is one of disappointment after the publication of Madonna's book *Sex* in 1999, accusing her of making "right-wing antifeminist statements that, if uttered in another context, might have provoked public protest and outrage" (1994: 18).

> Time and time again, Madonna snaps up the trends in the market and rapidly reshapes them in a bid to entertain us.[10] The result of all this is that her productions emerge with a controlled primacy where technical virtuosity forms an irresistible part of desire and fantasy in our reception and enjoyment of pop. (Hawkins 2004: 189)

Madonna's successful template of executive production, where she synthesizes the latest trends and branding (both musical and visual), has inspired many later artists including the Spice Girls, Beyoncé and Lady Gaga who elicit similar heated discussion, and thus generate welcome media column-inches and increase sales in a similar way (see Lieb 2013).

Self-determination by woman artists can be swiftly incorporated by the music industry, as exemplified by the potentially abrasive challenge posed by female bands of the Riot Grrrl subculture in the 1990s, whose stance was later recuperated by the Spice Girls (Leonard 2007: 156–61). Helen Davies notes that after co-opting the slogan "Girl Power", by 1996 "the Spice Girls conform[ed] completely to the conventional image of female pop performers, albeit in a camp, supposedly semi-ironic way, with their presentation as manufactured, talentless sex objects" (2001: 308). Effectively, it became men's idea of Girl Power. Nicola Dibben's attribution of polysemy in reactions to the Spice Girls led her to muse that the group's attempts to build an audience of men through their traditional approach to sex appeal (presented with faux-irony), and an audience of women through "power" (my quote marks) risked backfiring: "Within this context such tactics can be used to cynical and exploitative ends, serving the interests of the dominant economic order while providing the consumer with the illusion of autonomy" (1999: 351). Her discussion focuses on the valorizing of "relevance" over resistance in pop music (1999: 352). She writes:

> Both Madonna and the Spice Girls are "producerly" texts: the audience is able to make meanings that connect with their social experience which, for young females, is primarily one of powerlessness and subordination, and to create a resistant meaning. (1999: 348)

Yet she is cautious about what she terms "appropriating the signs of patriarchal ideologies" as a marketing strategy. The practice of combining traditional feminine attributes and style not only satisfies the voyeurism of a heterosexual male audience, as Luce Irigaray warned, but also limits the creativity of the artists by forcing them into a role defined by hegemonic precedent, which Dibben describes as "representation of empowerment which simultaneously

---

10   Or make money.

retains patriarchal notions of 'female desirability' for the female audience". She warns that: "The modes of resistance offered by such tactics therefore contain within them their own downfall: their political power is compromised by working within the forms provided by the dominant ideology" (1999: 351). Opinions about the degree to which an artist's physical appearance should be part of their persona pass from the mainstream into the margins. Tara Rodgers notes that in the artist world of US electronica: "After working hard to gain public recognition for their technical proficiency, women face renewed pressure to cultivate their appearance" (2010: 16).

Mutual agreement between the suppliers of money and the sellers of the commodity in pop is infinitely more liberating for the individuals at the centre of the transaction than it is for the teenage audiences that they claim to speak to and for. Through disembodiment and manipulation by producers and engineers, it is the male idea of a powerful woman we hear and we are encouraged to engage with: what John Shepherd calls "a masculinized version of femininity" (1991: 169). Because there is no awkward physicality to encounter in recorded music, he continues:

> If women symbolize the source of life, the social interactions that are the source of our being as people, and if sexual relatedness provides a biological code for these same processes, then women tend to become equated with sex. In order to be "successful" in a male-dominated society, they must package themselves (or be packaged, as in advertising images) as objects amenable to the control of men. (1991: 156)

Women's Roles in Electronic Music Scenes

Electronic dance music is a distinct genre with a history that runs parallel to that of mainstream pop. It (arguably) allows women to control their own sound, and to demonstrate this by the direct operation of the machines that create their music. Back in 1992 Andrew Goodwin challenged the idea that developments in music technology were leading to democratization of the music industry, commenting that pop rapper Betty Boo (Alison Clarkson) was the only female producer he had seen "actually pictured operating a piece of new musical hardware", when she appeared in a *Smash Hits* feature. He continues:

> For now it needs to be said that, for whatever reason, the democratizing function of the new technologies of pop seems to stop short of opening up the new forms of composition and engineering to women – probably for socially complex reasons to do with the

> identification of technology with masculinity. In other words, it is the boys, still, who are playing with the toys. (1992: 92)

Keyboards are used universally as midi controllers, although they are gendered as the women's instrument; computer keyboards are similar to the typewriter and therefore "not a technology associated with muscles, manual skills and all-male environments" (Gavanas and Reitsamer 2013: 55). Despite this, there was little discernible progress in the development of keyboard-heavy electronic music forms in 1980s pop for women as creators of tracks, rather than as singers and topline artists. For a long time, the electronic music genre seems to have been stuck in the same gender rut as other forms of popular music, despite its potential to disrupt the narrative that has become normal in subcultural music production, in which "Subcultural capital would seem to be a currency which correlates with and legitimizes unequal social status" according to Thornton (1995: 104). This seems to have been due in part to the retrogressive infrastructure surrounding the music, just as in more mainstream pop music. For instance, in the world of 1990s rave music that Thornton explored, both young women who thought of themselves as "one of the boys" and the young men involved in the scene sneered at the "Sharon and Tracey" element of the crowd, looking upon them as passengers in a scene that (according to those "in the know") they had no deeper understanding of. The response to rave music by its core aficionados was felt to be of more worth as its more widespread (often female) consumers were filtered out according to their "coolness" or lack thereof.

These attitudes contradict the beliefs of Marcia Citron (1993), who valorized the listening of women audiences as part of a musical transaction. As Angela McRobbie noted of the early rave events:

> For raves to succeed they have to attract a large number of people. Rave organizers as a result tend to be older, male and already have had some experience in club promotion, often starting as DJs in smaller clubs and illegal radio stations. Girlfriends help on the till, behind the bar, or else do "PR" by going round pubs distributing flyers. The rave culture industry thereby reproduces the same sexual division of labour which exists not just in the pop music industry but also in most other types of work and employment. (1993: 420)

This division of labour along gender lines was acknowledged by Whiteley; while admitting that there had been "significant inroads by women into the music industry" in the 1990s, she noted that there were still traditionally gendered roles especially in the areas of engineering and DJing. Whiteley describes a topless model who has become "DJ Rap", appearing on the cover of *Ministry* magazine in July 1998, and quotes Brian Logan's remark that "for all clubbing's subculture (which stresses equality on the dance floor) its attitude is more Stone Age than New Age" (2000: 4). She also criticizes an advertisement in *Mixmag* for an all-female DJ tour that focused purely on the looks of the women, noting that: "the club scene is now over ten years old and was never intended to be about good looks. The flyers, the adverts and, indeed, television's treatment of club culture, however, continued to suggest otherwise" (2000: 5).

Several years later, Gavanas and Reitsamer noted the annoyance expressed by experienced DJs when faced with the sexualization of their profession, which should, they feel, be based purely on music rather than physical appearance:

> when femininity is highlighted in controversial ways it becomes heavily debated among female and male DJs alike. According to a Berlin-based DJ, one of the worst aspects of club culture is that "tits are worth more than ten years of experience and skill" and that DJs who capitalize on sexualized marketing are a "kick in the face for us who do it with quality for years". (2013: 64)

Dance music, whilst being an accepted route into production for DJs, creates a fertile source of debate about gender and production. Jeremy Gilbert and Ewan Pearson acknowledge and integrate some feminist viewpoints in their 1999 discourse on dance music. However, the distinction between *feminine* and the *female* that is articulated clearly by Christine Battersby (1989) is problematic in their work; physical engagement is felt by dancers in audiences for many other types of music apart from dance music and is not exclusively a "feminine" phenomenon, as they assert. Gilbert and Pearson state that techno music is androgynous, and referring to Maria Pini's research from 1997, they claim that dance music "opens up a new space for the exploration of new forms of identity and pleasure" for women (1999: 97). Yet women are not represented well in the sonic articulation of dance music. The absence of female vocals, or the chopped-up female voice if it is there at all, does *not* affirm gender equality in any way. In focusing on electronic groove, the machine is prioritized, and the story becomes the human body's reaction to the track, as described by Gilbert and Pearson's comment about house music, which disparages (mostly women's) vocal presence in the music by using the idea of "de-emphasis":

> in the mix and arrangement of vocal house tracks, as in disco, the rhythm is not subsumed, or de-emphasized by the presence of vocal

or song, and the song structure is often "opened out", extended beyond four minutes of verse, bridge, chorus. (1999: 74)

A female listener could interpret this dissecting of the woman's sonic presence as exclusion and exclusivity, maybe even representative of misogyny rather than androgyny. If the main area of popular music that women have been allowed to inhabit is that of vocalist, as we saw in the previous chapter, surely removing even this presence is a move backwards rather than forwards.

Since 1999, when Gilbert and Pearson's book was published, there has been a furious debate and disappointment in dance music circles about gender issues. An example of this appears in *The Quietus* in 2011, where Angus Finlayson wrote:

> It was dismaying to find that an implicit disdain for women could sit comfortably alongside a love for underground dance music – because, although perhaps it's not immediately obvious, the politics at the core of dance music culture lean the other way: towards an ethos of equality and inclusion which seems increasingly obscure or forgotten about.[11]

Finlayson notes that at the time the article was written, DJ Mag's top 100 did not feature a single female DJ. He regrets the promotion of dance music as "soft porn with a sheen of arty respectability", yet even he stops short of noting that the problem is that the music is made by men.[12]

The embedded misogyny in dance music culture has been examined more recently in Tami Gadir's research on DJ culture in Edinburgh and Oslo, which reveals that male (and some female) DJs feel that "the voice undermines the 'underground' authenticity of the music that DJs choose to perform". Her interviewees are scornful about "girly" tracks, tracks defined by "prominent or catchy melodic riffs (particularly those in high registers); vocal lines (particularly those involving female voices); and soft or 'fluffy' timbres – as some participants referred to them", which are at odds with what one of her DJs refers to as "good electronic music" (2016: 122). Although she observes that there have been "certain scenes where the act of dancing has been a conscious act of activism against homophobia, sexism, classism, racism etc.", the research that she undertook "[prompted me] to underline the plethora of dancing spaces in

---

11 https://thequietus.com/articles/07384-dance-music-misogyny (accessed 13 January 2021).
12 An indication of the heated discussion around this issue can be found, for example, at http://herbeats.com/2011/11/a-few-personal-thoughts-on-a-disturbing-trend-towards-misogyny/ (accessed 3 February 2016).

which gender equality is not achieved" (Gadir 2015). Until internalized misogyny ceases to be an issue in popular culture in general, gender divisions will remain in place regardless of the appearance of social change. Even Loza, who challenges the way that electronic music producers, amongst others, "passionately fabricate the human-machine hybrid known as the cyborg, the fembot and the post-human" (2001: 349) and who discusses the way that the standard gender binary is disrupted by "sonic drag" and "polymorphous performativity" as vocalists shift across the gender spectrum (2001: 355), stops short of criticizing the fact that all of this is acted-out over a male sonic bed. Current pop music production is supported by videos that emphasize hyper-embodiment in sound as well as visual images, according to Hawkins (2013) and Hansen (2011), involving the aural processing of vocals being enhanced by compression to increase the volume levels of sighing, breathing and other intimate body sounds. I was told by a female dance music vocalist recently that ASMR (autonomous sensory meridian response) recording techniques using binaural microphones have found their way into dance music production, were being used to enhance the sensuality of her voice by her producer, and that this is common practice. The pornographication of what we hear in pop music is apparently quite deliberate.

The fact that music and dancing inform gender behaviour, rather than the other way around, is borne out by Tia DeNora's research. She attributes "social calm" to some music forms, citing "music's role as a device of collective ordering, how music may be employed, albeit at times unwittingly, as a means of organizing potentially disparate individuals such that their actions may appear to be intersubjective, mutually oriented, co-ordinated, trained and aligned" (2000: 109). Describing musical entrainment, she writes of dance: "As a series of bodily gestures ... dance and more mundane and subconscious forms of choreography are media for the autodidactic accumulation of self and gender awareness" (2000: 78). This might suggest that the act of dancing collectively affirms and/or conceals gender divisions, rather than breaking them down in any environment other than the venue at which the dance event is being held. Again, the implications of this music being created by almost exclusively male producers for audiences in the many different dance genres should not be underestimated. Dibben's discussion of polysemy in an article about Madonna and the Spice Girls, cited earlier, further informs the situation of women in dance culture which: "allows listeners to situate themselves amid competing ideological forces and in so doing plays out in material form very real tensions of female identity" (1999: 352). Mainstream dance floors are still gendered according to traditional male/female roles, and women DJs still negotiate their way through a scene whose structure is gendered as male, as we saw earlier through Colleen Murphy's experience.

Twenty-first-century academic writers still caution against the temptation to herald a new epiphany for female users of music technology. Tara Rodgers criticizes the excuses made by those who document the history of electronic music making:

> Some of the most important contributions to the study of electronic music and sound have positioned women as "outside the scope of study" (citing Kahn 1999: 13–14), defined DJ cultures as "distinctly masculine" (citing Reynolds 1998: 274–75) or like Fikentscher, use observational statistics [fewer than one in ten DJs is female] to explain the dearth of female engagement in the scene (2000: 124 n. 3). (2010: 11)

Rodgers is criticizing the patrilineality of histories of women sound artists; another example of this is the film *Modulations: Cinema for the Ear* (1998) which profiles 80 men in electronic music, and no women (2010: 14). There is still work to be done in order to make women's work in electronic music visible.

Ultimately, the question that is never fully addressed by many authors on dance music and EDM is how it can be seen as liberating for people of different genders and sexual orientation to dance to music that is made by an overwhelming majority of male producers. Cultural commentators could be accused of trying to read significant social change into subcultures that show signs of only superficial acknowledgement of societal progress in terms of gender, treating feminism merely as a fashion rather than as a politically empowering movement. As Thornton observed, subcultural capital was still very much a male concern towards the end of the 20th century. In her writing on female rock journalism, Joanne Hollows reiterates Thornton's remarks, underlining the complete embedded-ness of male values in all aspects of the music industry: "like girls who invest in 'subcultural capital', feminist critics are not immune to the feelings of cultural distinction which comes from being 'culturally one of the boys'" (Hollows 2000: 174–75). Being "in the know" about male-dominated scenes still elevates women writers above their contemporaries (indeed, the recent phenomenon of Poptimism, in which the value of girly music is reassessed, may be a reaction against this tendency). From the opposite perspective, Holly Kruse, referring to critics who "explore different subject positions", cites Suzanne Moore's concept of "gender tourism" which, according to Moore, is used "primarily as a means by which male theorists are able to take trips into the world of femininity"

(Kruse 2002: 148). It is too easy to explore the idea of feminism and femininity without actually committing to a deeper engagement with societal change. The celebration of breakthoughs for women participants in a subculture without noting the underlying male structures, both business- and production-wise, does not give a true account of the control that men still have over access to the more empowering and active parts of subcultural engagement. It does not acknowledge their positions of historical and contemporary privilege.

As Jacques Attali noted, "Possessing the means of recording ... allows one to impose one's own noise and to silence others" (1999: 87) and this applies to archiving as much as it does to the creation of music. Hegemonic practice and thought-processes are woven through every element of the musical product in pop and rock, both in its creation and its consumption: in lyrics, melody, timbre, rhythm, dynamics, orchestration (and not least through video and photographic representations of the artists). Media debates about sexualization, misogyny and young people have ensured that there is a continuous cycle of focus on these factors which entraps each generation as they "come of pop age", in a celebration of their own moment that is *felt* as a subversive response to previous generations. Yet, until more women are active curators of histories targeted at mainstream consumption, change will continue to be very slow. The *Electro* exhibition at the Philharmonie de Paris dedicated to electronic music in 2019, for instance, had a very poor representation of women artists (female:pressure had a presence, but almost in a ghettoized way) and of non-white practitioners.[13] Given the strong pan-European presence of women in electronic music, this was very surprising.

The technological processes described in this chapter can be co-opted and further weaponized against women in the name of art. Awkward women who disrupt the entrenched values of the world of popular music may simply be replaced by machine-generated versions of themselves, according to Loza. She noted in 2001 the ways that an increase in female empowerment in studio production is being challenged by the increasing presence of "the salacious fembot [which] allows heterosexual males to contemporaneously manage the threats posed by rampant technology and unbridled female sexuality" (2001: 351). Loza predicted that biddable robot women who perform feminine sexuality for their male creators and consumers would pose a real threat to feminist society. In a similar vein, several years later, Sean Eads expresses concern at David Toop's celebration of digital voice processing, which Eads

---

13 https://philharmoniedeparis.fr/en/electro-exhibition (accessed 18 September 2019).

feels will lead to an increasing acceptance of "cyborg" music and its reduction of singing to strings of vocaloids (Toop 2005; Eads 2015). Vocaloids are units of processed sound that can be used to construct virtual (female) pop stars such as Hatsune Miku, an avatar that demonstrates ventriloquism taken to an extreme just as Loza predicted; Hatsune Miku's gigs are even reviewed as live events (Cliff 2020). Pop music production reflects changes not just in gender delineations and perceptions, but also in what is possible to create through technology, and the novelty of non-existent female pop stars co-exists alongside real women who are redefining what it means to be a woman in 21st century pop music.

Getting into the Scene: Negotiating Ways through Male Territory in Electronic Music

Some women learn electronic music production skills at youth projects, some from dedicated audio courses, and some from informal mentoring, which has its own set of problems. Jennifer Brown's 1996 Master's thesis gives an interesting insight into undergraduate music technology learning in Australia:

> I came to realize that a major part of the learning of audio-engineering and electronic musical instruments took place, not from attending classes, but from working the studio equipment with peers in self-styled co-operative learning situations ... The few successful women seemed to be those who became "one of the boys", cruising their scene and observing the nuances of male culture. (1996: viii–ix)

As we saw earlier, becoming "one of the boys", partly in order to assimilate but also partly because of lack of role models, is a common approach of women to their roles in the music industry in general. Rebekah Farrugia, writing on female producers of EDM, identifies a major issue that excludes women from electronic music scenes in Philadelphia, where her research was undertaken. Access to networks that are set up to protect the territory and subcultural capital of the genre is still controlled by men: "the opportunities to learn to produce is [sic] ... more limited for women who have less access to the informal, male-centred social networks through which tricks of the trade are often passed along" (Farrugia 2010: 89). She quotes Chicago's Kate Simco: "You have to prove yourself coolness wise. Hanging out, I've had to prove myself way harder than guys do. Some guys just don't know how to hang out with me. It took me a long time for me to prove myself" (2010: 90). It is a very short step from peer-to-peer sharing, to networking amongst an exclusive elite within a subculture, and in this respect subcultural studio activity would appear to replicate the mainstream music industry in its attitudes to women and their audio technology skills.

There are an increasing number of women artists, both well-known and outside the mainstream, who program, engineer and produce their own music; there are also women artists who should be able to, but who find their control over their own musical product nibbled away at by invariably male studio personnel in a gatekeeping practice which can have dire financial consequences for them. It cannot be denied that the lack of visibility and awareness of women's skills is sometimes down to lack of confidence in the women themselves which prevents them from claiming a "professional" role, as a comment on the music journalist Kitty Empire's blog posting observed:

> I have been fortunate to interview the likes of MIA, Beyonce and Mary J Blige and they all point out that women simply don't get the credit. Mary J Blige said that she didn't realize for years that she was supposed to be getting co-producer and songwriter credits, while both Alicia Keys and MIA said their ideas had been systematically dismissed for years. It took time for their male cohorts to begin to view them even semi-seriously as songwriters and music-makers.[14]

Outside the mainstream, the independent and DIY nature of recording echoes this point about labelling, or naming, of practitioners in the production process; as a response to the author's Facebook posting about this research, folk artist Kath Tait, who has co-produced or solo-produced/engineered seven albums of her own material since 1982, sent me the following observation that even after producing her second album: "once again, the word 'producer' never crossed my mind at the time".[15] As women musicians become more successful they have more say in their own creative process both in rock and pop, and occasionally themselves become producers of other female artists (Mayhew 2014: 149–62), or as we have seen in the case of Björk, Leila Arab and Mandy Parnell, create teams of trusted colleagues.

Changes in the Recording Industry at the Frontline

I will now discuss the music industry's attempt to rectify the dearth of visible female producers and engineers in the British music industry. In March 2013, a discussion about the "current crop of high-profile women in music" which

---

14 Comment on blog by hattiecollins, 7 April 2008 10.52 in response to Kitty Empire, https://www.theguardian.com/music/musicblog/2008/apr/05/inthissunday-sobserver (accessed 16 December 2020).
15 Personal email, 27 November 2010.

"seems to reflect a healthy and diverse industry", by a group of female music industry professionals, noted that:

> Emeli Sandé's album *Our Version of Events* is the biggest-selling record of the year so far. Meanwhile, Adele has continued to dominate both sides of the Atlantic, the pinnacle of her year being the six awards she scooped at the Grammys back in February. Closer to home, women songwriters received seven nominations in four of the judged Ivor Novello Award categories. They won three of those, and also picked up the Ivor's Inspiration Award and Songwriter of the Year. (*M Magazine*, 8 March 2013)

However, in terms of membership of the Performing Rights Society, a membership organization that administers songwriter royalties,

> [it] has a ratio of 13 percent female to 87 percent male, a figure that remains pretty constant among both new joiners and existing members. Sarah Rodgers, Chairman of the British Academy of Songwriters Composers and Authors (BASCA), says that her society's membership is 20 percent female to 80 percent male. Meanwhile, the Music Producers' Guild (MPG) is even more divided, with women making up less than four percent of its members.[16]

These figures suggest that while women appeared to be gaining more power and recognition in the music industry, the relative success of a few high-profile women (such as Adele) did not reflect a genuine change in equality of opportunity in the industry itself. In 2016, five female practitioners won MPG awards out of a total of sixteen in a move possibly stimulated by the article; the previous year it had been only one out of fifteen. After the rebalancing of awards according to gender in 2016, the MPG seems to have pulled back slightly in subsequent years; on their website they make a point of noting their efforts to reward female practitioners, perhaps unsurprisingly stating that the breakthrough engineer award category was "totally dominated by women".[17] An apparent hurried response to a drastic gender imbalance in a powerful and hitherto respected organization shows exactly how threatened the mainstream industry organizations can be by exposure of their practices. For instance, the singer Charlotte Church used the 2013 BBC6 Music John Peel lecture to criticize the male hold over the British music industry, and in 2016 Laura Marling started a website, *Reversal of the Muse*, to highlight the

---

16   M, PRS For Music Online Magazine, issue M48, http://www.m-magazine.co.uk/features/women-in-music (accessed 14 July 2013).
17   https://mpg.org.uk/news/2019-awards-winners/ (accessed 31 January 2020).

achievements of women musicians who had control over their own careers.[18] In the USA, a similar sense of dismay is articulated, with attempts to rationalize the gender imbalance behind the scenes, as attested by an article in *Billboard* in 2018 about the Grammys (Newman 2018). The artist Grimes, long a producer of her own music, regularly tweets about autonomy in the studio, and Missy Elliott responded angrily to a Twitter query of "Where are all the female producers?" in 2018. Still, however, the gender balance is greatly skewed in favour of men; for instance, a study by the Annenberg Inclusion Initiative, published in 2018, noted that by 2018 in the USA, only 12.3 per cent of songwriters and 2 per cent of producers were female, in a sample of 700 songs. The ratios were, of course, even worse for women who were not from white backgrounds (Smith, Choueti and Pieper 2018).

It is possible that permanent change could come about when the groundswell of community initiatives and small organizations that provide safe spaces for women to learn about music technology meets movement from above, such as the changes initiated by the PRS, MPG and so on; this will be discussed in more depth in the concluding chapter. However, without the mainstream music industry media on board, and serious commitment from men at the top of the music organizations, progress may still be painstakingly slow. Paula Wolfe notes that in 2007, for instance, 80 per cent of the member companies in AIM (the Association of Independent Music) were led by men (Alison Wenham, cited in Wolfe 2019: 28) and that "What may appear as a free for all at the bottom end … remains firmly guarded at the top" (2019: 139). A major problem continues to be the necessity to prove oneself to be "as good as a man" within the industry. A leading professional audio organization in Britain, according to several of the women that I interviewed, despite its recent attempts to rectify its practice, has a history of discord and bullying which culminated in the following tweet (since deleted): "[Female producer] joins a panel of intelligent and articulate women to discuss women in music". The tweet speaks for itself, and led to one prospective female panel member leaving the organization. She told me about the hidden misogyny that she experienced:

> I was a co-opted member of the director's board for about a year, and I went to their meetings, and everything I said was just trashed, and in the end I thought "Why am I turning up here just to listen to all of these old guys argue and shout me down?" and I just thought, "No I'm not doing this anymore" … No-one's come out and said, "Women can't produce", or "What would women know

---

18 https://www.reversalofthemuse.com (accessed 3 June 2020).

about technology", or "What would girls know about production", or whatever, but it's almost everything that they don't say, or everything they try to say and get so wrong that blows the whole thing open as to exactly what it is.

The difficulties of entering a "male" profession as either a token woman or a "special" woman who is "just as good as a man" inevitably have to be negotiated by female members rather than through joint decisions, illustrated by a woman producer's description of her attempt to improve the situation:

> I put it forward to the [organization] once that for one of our panels … I [would pose] the same question the BBC asked in their article, "Why aren't there more women in the business?": "Why aren't there more women producers, why are there even so few engineers in the broader scale?". And they said, "That's a brilliant idea, let's do that".

The response to the proposal when it was later put to the membership illustrates the complexity of the situation. Women who have reached what they feel is a precarious position in an organization overwhelmingly populated by men, and who have had to fight hard to achieve respect, can be afraid of the potential consequences of change (and possibly competition for that space, cf. Potter 1997), no matter how positive that change might prove to be:

> One of the women members, I don't remember who it was (there's not that many), came on board but she's more established, and she responded to that and said "I absolutely think that shouldn't be a discussion point", and she totally went off on one about the fact that there shouldn't be a mention of whether you're female or male. She really ranted about it and scared off the boys, who said "Oh we better not upset anybody, so we better not discuss it", and I responded, "It's not whether or not we have to justify that we're women, this is a cold hard fact, there aren't many of us. Can that not be discussed as a point? It's a fact. We're not trying to justify anything. Discuss, you know!" (anonymous)

In another situation, Mandy Parnell clearly expressed the way she feels about the pressures on women professionals to have a collective approach to supporting each other:

> I have met female engineers and I mentor a couple of them. There's a girl in America where the Women's Audio Mission were really on her case to join and she really felt uncomfortable about it. I bumped into her at the opening party of a famous studio. She was asking me what did I think about these groups and I was like, I've never got

> involved with them 'cos I just haven't; it's just not my thing. I work, you know. I go out to the AES, I go to a couple of networking things, but I don't really have time to be honest with you; there's so much I want to do in there [studio]. It's not for me to get involved with that. And I said to her "If you don't feel comfortable with it you shouldn't do it". They were really putting pressure on her.

As in so many areas of work previously dominated by men, where women are pioneers, they have responsibility not just for doing a good professional job, but also for representing their entire gender in a frequently hostile environment. Adrienne Aitken's words describe the apparently impossible conundrum facing all women in a male-defined workplace:

> What they're saying is that if you even mention gender then you're defining that there should be a difference, and that it needs to be quantified that you're a woman but you're actually as good as a bloke, and if you're as good as a bloke, a bloke doesn't have to quantify that he's a bloke, he's just an engineer, so you shouldn't have to quantify that you're a woman, you're just an engineer!

Finally, it is notable that many men also do not like the way they are stereotyped. In conversation with Susan Rogers at the 2014 ARP conference in Oslo, she talked about her approach to male artists in the studio: "For me as a woman pulling a performance from a musician I unapologetically use a different technique, and I'm sure there are a lot of men out there who like that". Male producers will say "Come on, be a guy!" but Roger's interactions with male artists are deliberately gentler. And ever practical, JPL learned her studio etiquette after an audience with Nile Rodgers.

> He said, "A lot of the time what people don't understand is it's great to work with female producers, but a lot of men think they can't be themselves". I took heed of that when I heard that in 2005, 2006. I made an adjustment to make sure that guys can always be themselves around me so if they wanted to pass wind in front of me, they could, if they wanted to swear, they could, you know it's about creating that atmosphere for them to be able to create and be honest ... That's your job, you know. When it goes wrong they're going to blame you, when it goes right they're going to pat themselves on the back, but that's your job, that's what you signed up to do. So when I got that I realized it's not about me: It's about getting everybody else what they need.

8 Education, Inspiration and Potential for Change

This chapter considers the role of music education in empowering women to use their technical skills in the studio. Through a combination of my own primary research in higher education (HE) institutions and published literature on music education and music technology education in secondary schools and HE since the mid-1990s, I will discuss areas of positive change and areas of entrenched practice from the perspective of gender.

My reasons for identifying music technology education as a strategy for challenging and changing the male-identified culture of professional studio practice are largely to do with popular culture's tendency to be short-term in its engagement with social progress. During the course of the chapter, we will see that it is not just music industry culture that defines the gender polarities within popular music; government policy also has a role to play (Born and Devine 2015). Western youth culture alternately resists and embraces mainstream and more subversive activities, often using music to articulate tensions that include attitudes to young women and girls. Joanne Hollows expresses an ambivalence (discussed at various points of this book) that is found at the heart of much writing about women and pop music (notably Dibben 1999; Davies 2001; Leonard 2007; Lieb 2013):

> In feminist studies of youth culture, there is often a concern with the extent to which youth cultures reproduce gender inequalities and "damaging" modes of femininity, or, alternatively, whether youth cultures are sites in which new, more "progressive" modes of femininity are produced which challenge or resist existing gender relations. (Hollows 2000: 8)

The intersection of progressive music technology education with self-determined cultural activity by young people should provide some sort of environment where progress could be facilitated. Cultural change in terms of gender roles in the music industry is dependent not just on the activities of the producers and consumers (Fiske 1997), but ultimately needs to become a mainstream priority, especially given the resistance to change by male industry mediators described by Wolfe (2019: 51). Perhaps through a formal music technology education that includes gender parity, we can embed a more enlightened set of values, and normalize a more progressive approach to the use of music technology in the professional world of music production. This is significant given that, as noted in the discussion that follows, the gendered nature of the music industry and the continued gendering of musical roles can be traced back to severe and pervasive issues within educational experiences and barriers experienced by girls. These experiences firmly support assumptions entrenched in historical perceptions of appropriate musical activities for girls and women that underline their femaleness, femininity and compliance. Attributes such as quietness (playing stringed instruments rather than brass instruments, for instance), stillness (seated facing a piano rather than the mobility facilitated by being a guitarist, or the physical dynamics employed by a drummer), embodiment and sexuality (being a singer, so the corporeal "female" becomes part of the sound), and most importantly, a lack of technical skill (Born and Devine 2016) are all assumed to be part of the portfolio of the female musician. Effectively, boys and men are assumed to make the best music producers and engineers, because they have the right sort of personality, and the right sort of brain.

Education and Learning: My Interview Sample

Within the educational system, potential issues of concern with music technology teaching are varied. Firstly, there are questions about what music technology is and what it is for, and indeed the same questions apply to music itself, starting with the fundamental question of whether music is a science (akin to mathematics) or an art (akin to painting). Georgina Born and Kyle Devine set out these differences in 2015, delineating the different foci of traditional music degrees and the new music technology degrees that started to proliferate in the late 1990s when the concept of the creative industries was developed alongside a rapid expansion of university places. This knowledge-based economy was to co-exist with the service economy in the post-industrial era (2015: 142). Secondly, an issue that concerns those in the music industry itself is whether music-making is a learnable skill, or a measurement of inherent genius. Thirdly, do men and women listen and hear things differently? Lastly, who decided that music technology was a "boy's thing"?

We will see in this chapter that the dominant discussions in the industry about women and music technology are not only mirrored by educational policy, but are also further entrenched by it, despite the impressions of progress given by media publicity in the last decade regarding the increase in women engineers. This final point is important because, as Hopkins and Berkers have noted, music technology has become a vital component in the aesthetic development of music (2020: 46). This means that the exclusion of women from learning music technology will also exclude them from the evolution of music itself, and the opportunity to articulate their gender authentically in the future development of music.

Studio engineering and production combine a set of skills that are not normally associated with each other in school education in Britain: technical skills and the development of an aesthetic imagination. Formal music education itself can be very useful to music producers, especially if instrumental scores are being used, and a basic knowledge of time signatures and rhythm is essential even for elementary levels of studio engineering and production. Helen Atkinson has identified her music theory knowledge as being a competency that helped her greatly in her work as an engineer at RAK Studios. Sound engineering also reaches a professional level when knowledge of physics and electronics are part of the skill set, together with an ability to work with increasingly complex software. Good communication skills are vital too, combined with an artistic sensibility and a sensitivity to musical genres and trends.

The women that I interviewed have different combinations of these skills, learned in a variety of environments; we have seen that some moved into production and engineering from songwriting, some from science backgrounds, and some from musical backgrounds. Contrary to Wolfe's research published in 2019, many of them did not have university-level education (although eleven of my interviewees did had university qualifications, one had dropped out, fifteen had not been to university, and eight did not mention this in their interview). Some, like JPL (psychology) and Dot Allen (zoology), had degrees in apparently unrelated subjects. Many had filled in gaps in their knowledge by taking short courses at different points in their careers to update their knowledge (for instance, a course to train women in sound engineering at the Arts Council-funded Ovatones in London was mentioned by Dot Allen). More unusually, Adrienne Aitken had originally planned to enrol on a course affiliated with Canterbury University; when she realized that she would not graduate until she was 21 years old, she decided instead to work in a publishing company, Carling Music, where she learned about the music industry through direct experience. She expressed gratitude to her parents for supporting her decision, which "shaped my ability to be able to express myself". From a more technical perspective, it appears that the ability to envision oneself behind a mixing desk in a studio, in control of a session, from an early age was a major motivating factor. Despite the fact that there has been a lack of precedent and few female role models in the industry, my research has shown that a set of relevant skills and an *imagined* future role have allowed women to feel confident in moving into an area of employment as a pioneer, thus becoming a role model herself for others who follow behind.

Schools and Universities

After presenting a paper on women and music technology publications at the ARP conference in 2010 in Leeds, I was approached by a lecturer from a private university who told me that his female music production students refused to engage with the technology involved in the creation of their musical backing tracks. He described them sitting applying make-up while their male colleagues constructed the tracks they were waiting to sing on. I suggested that he should employ a female instructor, and was interested to discover a few years later that one of the women I was interviewing had been taken on in that role at the university in question. I did not find out whether behaviour had changed in the class after this, although I later encountered the director of the programme in question at a social event and he denied that there had ever been a problem. This gaslighting was quite extraordinary, and demonstrates in this case a desire to cover up what had been a serious problem to do with diversity in teaching and learning.

In a later interview, Terrie Harris told me that she had noticed many more female engineers at the festivals where she worked in live sound, and said that this may well have been to do with proactive approaches to equality in higher education in the last 30 years.

The British government has been devaluing the arts in general, including music, in the curriculum for some years. For instance, in 2010 an English Baccalaureate was applied to school performance tables by the then coalition government at Key stage 4 that measured English, mathematics, science, a language and history or geography, but no arts subjects at all. The introduction of the EBacc (as it was dubbed) as an alternative to traditional 'A' levels was promoted further in 2015.[1] Despite this, and despite the closing down of youth provision (which often included informal music technology courses) by local councils due to austerity politics introduced by the Conservative government in 2010,[2] university-level music production and technology courses have thrived, as has the provision of private short courses. Helen Elizabeth Davies reports there being 1,500 higher education music courses across the

---

1   https://commonslibrary.parliament.uk/research-briefings/sn06045/ (accessed 26 November 2020).
2   See https://www.theguardian.com/uk/2010/jun/22/budget-2010-vat-austerity-plan (accessed 16 December 2020).

UK in 2016,[3] an increase from around 80 in 1996 (Davies 2020; Laing 1999). Unfortunately, as Wolfe (2019) has noted, music graduates face a shrinking market of professional recording studios and, of course, competition from DIY producers who have not been through the university system and who have been building their skills and networks outside those institutions.

In theory, both universities and short course providers should create gender-neutral spaces where gender orientation, age and background do not act as barriers to access and learning, but this does not always happen in practice. When I first entered higher education as a lecturer teaching studio-based subjects in 1997, although young women and young men had supposedly undertaken equal music technology training in the studios at the university, there were still some final-year female undergraduate students hanging about in the corridor each morning who told me they were "waiting for my producer". I became concerned by their lack of motivation, agency and (apparently) skills and, with a grant from the government's Total Equality Fund in May 2002, I ran two separate programming workshops with the same content, for male and female students respectively, so I could observe and compare their skills and confidence. These sessions lasted an hour each and were attended voluntarily by students who signed up for them in advance. Although this was simple and basic research, the findings indicated that there was apparently no difference in the students' ability to learn, whatever their gender; within an hour, each group transcribed and re-programmed a simple drum pattern using Logic. However, I noted an interesting and significant outcome from the male student group which I had not anticipated. A female student had missed the other workshop and asked to participate in the male group. After ensuring that the male students didn't mind, I allowed her to join us. Within a very short period of time, one of the male students had borrowed her bag to lean on, and another had asked her if he could borrow a pen, which she provided for him. These requests put her immediately in a subordinate position to the male students in the group, and I have gone on to observe "borrowing the pen from female students" tactics on many occasions since then, which would be amusing if it were not so irritating.

A subsequent part of the research project involved a female student questioning a group of female students about their experience of learning in the university studios. Through these focus groups, it became clear that male students had been provided with greater access to advanced music technology in the sixth form at secondary school than female students. Male students therefore arrived at the university with more developed skills, and this in turn led

3   https://www.ukmusic.org/skills-academy/music-academic-partnership/ (accessed 26 January 2020) and Laing (1999).

to them "talking ahead" during the technical demonstration sessions. Those who were less experienced (i.e., the young women) got left behind. Davies also notes this in her research with students at LIPA (Liverpool Institute for Performing Arts, UK): "by the time musicians reach higher education, their gender roles and practices are well established" (Davies 2020: 30). As an attempt to remedy the problem, I started running catch-up sessions outside the formal timetable (which also encouraged some male students who had felt "left behind" to attend), and one of my male colleagues introduced a drop-in element to a formal module where anyone could access expert advice during their recording sessions. The latter offering was used predominantly by female students, and informally my colleague fed back to me that the technical aspects of their work had greatly improved. My research was, however, received far less warmly by other male colleagues.

In a competitive environment laced with anxiety, such as that experienced by students of whichever gender in their first year at university, it is tempting to excuse the desire of those with knowledge to demonstrate this whenever they could. One-upmanship can be demonstrated by something as apparently simple as knowing how to use the specific terminology – effectively the language – of music technology. Unfortunately, the lingo associated with studio practice is often the first stumbling block to access. Mavis Bayton noted the ways that apparently coded technical language in studio environments was felt to be alienating to some of the women musicians that she interviewed (1998: 6, 95). Expertise must be signalled, as Thomas Porcello noted:

> the process of learning to be a sound engineer must be thought of in great part as a process in learning to speak like one; an important part of becoming a professionalized "expert" is gaining the ability (and the sanction) to speak authoritatively as an expert. (2004: 735)

Signalling expertise through knowledge of technical terminology is therefore part of an engineer's or producer's professional toolkit, asserting their right to work proactively in a studio setting whether in learning or earning situations. This expertise creates an exclusive community.

Exclusivity of language contributes to a range of covert ways that music education can stereotype and exclude female students. Another is the critical ear, noted by Lucy Green, who observed young male pupils "listening out" as their female contemporaries played instruments that they perceived to be male-gendered (1997: 55; Bogdanovic 2015). Green discovered that this critical listening caused territorial divisions, not only practically in what the male students expected to see, but also conceptually in the way that they *heard the music being played*. This extra layer of difficulty for women musicians in achieving a sense of belonging has also been noted by Kathleen McKeage in her research into the world of jazz education in the US, where she notes that "women must not only master their instrument, but must negotiate a place within a traditionally male-dominated community" (2004: 354; see also Rustin and Tucker 2008). This means that the learning task of women music students is twofold, unlike that of their male contemporaries.

McKeage cites research by J. S. Eccles (1987) that adds to the explanation of the dearth of women in "male professions" and their unwillingness to imagine themselves in traditional male roles. Although this research was published more than 40 years ago, it is still applicable. According to McKeage:

> (a) they may not be able to connect success in certain fields to any kind of career, (b) girls may have a more realistic appraisal of their abilities than boys and may better understand the cost in time and effort, and (c) girls may understand that success in a male-dominated field does not guarantee acceptance within that field. (2004: 345)

A major deterrent for women, therefore, is the realization that discrimination will have to be overcome in the workplace even after acquiring the skills they need to become professional. The implications of this effectively mean that girls are judged by higher standards than boys when they move into "male" territory:

> This delineation will throw off their gendered subjectivity, expose their femininity in the delineations of the music, problematize it. For boys, contrastingly, the masculine delineation will correspond with, and help to affirm, their sense of gendered identity as they find it reflected in the music. (Green 1997: 218)

This is something that I have observed in my own research into studio practice in education, and is echoed at a professional level by the apparent surprise at "articulate women" producers expressed by the tweet from the professional audio organization discussed in the previous chapter.

Gender gatekeeping in educational settings as a practice was also highlighted by Victoria Armstrong's extensive 2011 study into music technology education in secondary schools, which shows that despite some improvements (notably when music technology teaching in schools involves female as well as male teachers), there are still some values and judgements that will take many years to overturn. Armstrong has observed that there appears to be a general lack of agency in schools' engagement with IT, let alone music technology, and that there is an embedded technological determinist approach:

"Technologies are ... assumed to have a natural trajectory, and their development and use cannot be challenged or struggled over" (2011: 22). There is a correlation between her research and that of Valerie Walkerdine (2004), whose research into girls and mathematics provides an insight into the way that maths teachers' response to pupils is tailored to the gender of the recipient.

Research by Alison Ward – now a live sound engineer (interviewed in this book), but previously an undergraduate Commercial Music student at the University of Westminster – revealed that young women were not expected to be interested in music technology options by staff at secondary education level (Ward 2001). Alison's research, which was undertaken in 2001 in schools in northwest London,[4] bears out Armstrong's findings, which are still pertinent. Given that London is seen to be the hub of Britain's creative industries, this frankly old-fashioned approach to gender roles is disturbing.

In 2013, I conducted some (unpublished) follow-up primary research in mixed and single-sex (girls) schools in the northeast quadrant of Greater London. The take-up was poor, although some interesting responses to the questions were gathered from teachers at five of the schools that were approached. When asked the question "Why do you think there are so few female producers and engineers?" the following responses were received:

- Most girls that I have taught are only interested in performance or teaching as a potential career.
- Not enough role models or project-based workshops aimed at just female students. Lack of money to deliver workshops.
- Perception of the industry as male dominated may put others off. We get many more female students doing "straight" music A-level, so perhaps they are not so keen to be using the computers and completing those sorts of tech-based tasks.
- Males are more dominated [sic], it's traditional.
- Possibly self-perpetuating – seen as a male-dominated profession?
- Not sure.

What was notable was the resigned nature of most of the responses, as though there was no desire or need to challenge the status quo. This became even more apparent in some of the responses to the next question, which was, "What do you think could change this state of affairs?"

---

4   The thesis began with 19 photographs of proprietorial looking men behind large mixing desks, all from Sound on Sound.

- I have tried, but most girls only do music at AS Level and drop it at the end of Year 12.
- Funds, projects promoting better pathways and opportunities.
- Better female producers.
- More inclusion of Music Technology in music lessons at school. Wider availability of Music Technology at A Level?
- [No response].

Boys' Clubs and Token Women

Research like this underlines the extent of the systemic shift that will need to occur in order for change to become permanent, rather than a novelty that will fade when the attention of the public, and the music industry, becomes distracted by the next fad. Although the research detailed above relates to music education and does not relate to debates within the music industry itself, if there are fewer female graduates than male graduates with music technology and production skills, then this will feed into the state of the industry. This is why we should be questioning imposed gender delineations both at school and in further and higher education. We should use the energy burst of this interest in girls and women taking up STEM subjects to propel this desire for skills acquisition, fairness, opportunity and entrepreneurship in order to rectify the gender discrepancy. However, things are not so easy at the interface. Implied criticism of colleagues' attitudes and teaching methods can be difficult to overcome; equally, implied criticism of male students' attitudes and implications of any anti-male bias in teaching can also be problematic. Echoing the resigned tone of the teachers who took part in my research into London schools, Davies confirms that at the moment, "when preparing students for a career in the music industry, popular music higher education currently contributes more to the maintenance than to the disruption of the music industry 'boys' club', due to gender inequalities earlier in the musical pipeline" (2020: 29). As we shall see, female students can at times play a role in their own subordination, forced into these roles by overarching, entrenched patriarchal controls.

Norma Coates (1997: 60) discussed the "displaced abjection" which was identified by Stallybrass and White (1986) as a factor within the "common sense" placing of women in rock, which warrants a discussion on the way that young women police their *own* deviation from gendered roles. Nicola Dibben cites Angela McRobbie's observation that "it is their own culture which itself is the most effective agent of social control for girls" (Dibben 1999: 350). This indicates that there can also be problems sited within female students themselves; one of these is internalized sexism, where a girl or woman will not only criticize others for "stepping out of line" but may also prevent herself from undertaking challenging activities for the same reason. Steve Bearman, Neill Korobov and Avril Thorne describe the way this happens:

> internalized sexism is not merely sexism perpetrated by women upon women. Sexism involves two distinct groups, one of which is systematically denied power by the other. In contrast, internalized sexism involves the internal dynamics within an oppressed group. It helps to maintain sexism as a whole via a system of social expectations and pressures enacted between women. (2009: 14)

One of the results of this internalization of low expectation is "learned helplessness" where mistakes are felt to reflect lack of ability rather than lack of experience (Elliott and Dweck 1988). These feelings of powerlessness may be expressed as "assertions of incompetence" which may in turn reinforce the "sense of powerlessness and powerless behavior" (Bearman, Korobov and Thorne 2009: 10), where the student feels that they are going to fail to learn before they even begin. Hopkins and Berkers report "self-excluding" activities by females in music technology teaching environments (2020: 55). This is also common to some mathematics teaching,[5] and is borne out by the story of one student taught by an FE educator interviewed for this book. We were talking about girls-only music technology courses:

> I think it's really interesting that those girls are doing music tech; it's obviously just females there, so there's no intimidation from guys. They've never felt uncomfortable. There was one girl in particular I can think of in my pop class, I think she was the only girl actually; that was probably why she didn't feel confident about even putting a microphone on a stand. She's a singer, and she'd been asking these guys to help. I said look, you need to learn how to do these things yourself because there might be one day when they're not there to help you. But she would just naturally let them go ahead and do it for her because she was feeling a wee bit intimidated by them; so I think it is important that they have a female tutor as well.

On the other hand, a conversation with a male music technology teacher/mentor who works in after-school workshops for Islington Music Education Hub illuminates a different perspective. On being asked why he thought it was better to teach girls and boys together, he replied: "I just think that it's a real reflection of the real world, 'cos at some point they're going to have

---

5   As cited by Dame Celia Hoyles, Athena Swan Lecture at University of East London, 24 March 2015.

to mix with others; it's just a better way to do it".[6] Davies, too, reported the awareness of her young female interviewees that they were ultimately going to have to be able to work in mixed environments in the "real world" (2020: 39). However, my own research and lecturing experience in music production has often shown that reflecting the real world does not always help, especially at entry level. This is also borne out by research as diverse as Sarah Baker and Bruce Cohen in their work with girls and DJing (2007), and Eric Teichman in his research on young women and jazz improvisation (2018).

However, a determined approach from an early age means that some young producers can capitalize on opportunities for learning that they are offered, whatever their gender. Higher education can also provide good opportunities for female music technology students to progress, thrive and network. Laura Leitch had the opportunity to record the music of the band the Pearlfishers while she was an undergraduate at the University of the West of Scotland because her tutor, David Scott, was a member of the band and he trusted her skills enough to record with her. Her confidence was boosted by the experience: "afterwards ... David told me he thought that some of the tracks were recorded better than they could have been in a professional studio".[7]

Conversely, university courses in production and/or sound engineering do not always provide the skills needed in contemporary recording. In a discussion with Paula Wolfe, Katia Isakoff describes the "old guard" of male music producers working in British universities, teaching what are now, "outdated working practices" (in Wolfe 2019: 74–75). This is an extension of the control exercised by the "boys' club" in the music industry in general observed by Leonard (2016) and Davies (2020), or the "old boys' club" (Hooper 2020: 140). There is a similar level of drop-out rates in music production and technology courses to that of STEM subjects in general, where there is a "leaky pipeline" of girls' disengagement, between education and employment (Davies 2020: 2).

To return to my interview data, although Janet Beat's experience of outright sexism occurred in the 1970s, she was correct in her observation that the "anti-woman" attitude is sometimes driven underground. Stereotyping

6   From author's interview, 2014.
7   Laura had been one of a dwindling number of students on a mixed afterschool course at Stirling Tollbooth, but she was determined to stay the course:

> I learnt a fair amount there, although they used Cubase rather than Pro Tools; I now use Pro Tools. The course at the Tollbooth was once a week for about six weeks and we learned the techniques and then recorded a local band on the penultimate week; and then on the final week we helped to mix it. There ended up only being two of us in the class.

is a complex phenomenon, and many women in science and technology are reluctant to report such experiences, where to "create a fuss" would cause problems with co-workers and their career advancement. In my experience of researching the musical professions of women, women may initially deny having had any problems and then follow up with an email or phone call to describe what have sometimes been harrowing experiences.

Not only do women in this area have to contend with the challenging of stereotypes; they now have to address the problem of an academic backlash by researchers such as Scott Harrison (2015: 40, cited in Armstrong 2011: 2) who argued that "gender research in music education has been increasingly dominated by feminist theory" resulting in girls' musical experiences and needs being privileged over their male counterparts.[8] This is an example of a phenomenon where awareness of stereotyping results in an increased subconscious or even conscious use of it, according to research by Michelle Duguid and Melissa Thomas-Hunt (2015: 343–44). I have had direct experience of this backlash in my own teaching, expressed not only by a male colleague but also male students, in almost identical terms to Harrison's, and it is an example of what Nesrine Malik describes as the "myth of the political correctness crisis" (2019: 57–94).

Previous moves to encourage more women to take up music technology professions through education have faced limitations. Elizabeth Hinkle-Turner noted that by the end of the 1960s there were electro-acoustic music facilities in many US music colleges, many started by women. Although she discusses more than 100 women in her book, she talks of "a decline in interest and technical activity among young women" that she has discovered during the course of her research: "several instructors have expressed frustration with their attempts at recruiting women students". She continues:

> Pauline Oliveiros has even sent announcements to several listservs encouraging the enrolment of women in the Mills College electronic music program, which, although originally a women-only curriculum, now often primarily has male students on its class rolls! (2006: 247)

Confidence

Music Technology teaching at school had motivated Helen Atkinson in her ambition to be a sound engineer, and she and Chantal Epp were the only women I interviewed who had learned how to program and/or record music

---

8   Harrison, Scott (unpublished paper), cited by Victoria Armstrong at UEL's Femusetech event, 2015.

at school. It is significant that Helen had to specifically ask her teachers to take the Music Technology "A" level. For some women, other skills and opportunities at school or in higher education provided groundwork for a feeling that the world was open to them in terms of their ambitions. There seems to be a number of factors that develop confidence in young women learning and applying their knowledge of music technology. The experiences of the women included within this study suggest that the earlier that this process of learning begins, the greater the confidence they have in their skills. Gemma Whitfield, a graduate of the University of East London and now a DJ and producer of house and techno, attended an all-girls Catholic secondary school where she felt the female staff "really wanted to instil the idea that we could do anything the boys could do".[9] She told me that her two most useful GCSEs were Design Technology and Music:

> For my DT GCSE I chose to specialize in product design. Over the course of two years, I learnt how to solder, operate band saws, sanding machines and a jigsaw cutter, using CAD/CAM laser machines to print out my own designs onto acrylic and make my own buzz wire games. And I learnt about the principles of electronic circuits and wiring. It was all very practical and hands on, and I really enjoyed it – I've actually been able to use the skills that I picked up in those DT classes to create my own guitar pedals.

Even after becoming a graduate, these skills are still proving to be essential:

> I.T. classes were really useful – especially the programming/HTML coding side. Learning the basics of programming has been really useful in my everyday work with digital audio workstations, and also in the creation of my own software synths in Pure Data and Max for Live. I think that being introduced to working with computers & understanding software from a young age has made me really confident in my understanding of these applications.

Isobel Campbell stressed the importance of hands-on professional experience *after* her university course at Strathcyde University:

> You can read books and attend lectures on sound recording but for me nothing compared to the actual real physical, practical time

---

9   There is an interesting parallel here with Lucy O'Brien's experience of being taught by nuns, as described in my 2012 book, *The Lost Women of Rock Music*. The nuns were enabling of Lucy's punk band and encouraged the group as women to express their strength through music making.

> spent in the studio. Audio equipment becomes less and less intimidating the more time spent around it. Well, that's what it was like for me. Being hands on and spending real time in the studio I feel I absorbed things by osmosis. From 1996 till 2010 I spent most days of the year in studios. The studio is one of my favourite places. For me it's similar to how a painter might feel about a blank canvas. There are so many sonic possibilities and the possibilities are endless. I get really excited thinking about it.

The course itself had been "cold, hard and unappealing ... It seemed impossible to understand what the teacher was talking about. So, I used to have to rely on other students that I was friendly with to show me the ropes".

Sadly, gender attitudes in formal education still appear to be closely linked to a belief in technological determinism (see Armstrong 2011), and that concept itself has to be challenged in order to instigate change. Machines create a conceptual muddle, according to Sherry Turkle, who uses Marx's distinction between tools and machines to describe the "Janus-like" nature of the computer, now at the heart of most recording studios: "Tools are extensions of their users; machines impose their own rhythm, their rules, on the people who work with them, to the point where it is no longer clear who or what is being used" (2000: 159). If we take this into account, responsibility for the personal misuse of technology can be excused as a side issue thrown up by the control of the machine over what men do, rather than the decisions made by men who operate the technology in the music industry. There is an ongoing reluctance to blame men for the situations in which they exclude women from their worlds and make them feel uncomfortable. Even scholars such as Hooper have commented that "there are no overt 'bad guys' on which to lay the blame, instead, there are systems and patterns, which are much more subtle, unconscious and difficult to trace" (2020: 145). Women studio professionals sometimes subscribe to this approach: a recent interview by Amy Raphael with the prizewinning engineer Catherine Marks, which reiterates many of the subjects covered by the women that I have interviewed, attempts to rationalize seedy behaviour by a male colleague that would be deemed unacceptable in a more formal workplace situation (Raphael 2019: 259).

Until it becomes part of male (and female) musicians' professional etiquette not to be taken aback by, say, encountering a female engineer in a recording studio, and until the invisible bridge between IT and more conservative music teaching has been broached in schools, it is difficult to see where the potential for change in music technology education exists. As educators, it is important to teach both male and female students that they should expect a high degree of competence from studio professionals, whatever their gender:

this is an employability skill. It is also important to regularly audit one's own tendency to stereotype, whatever one's gender, and to accept that the change may appear to be rapid and painful for some in the workplace.

Other Learning Environments

A local youth initiative can be the catalyst for a career as a female engineer; both Helen Atkinson and Saran Headman learned confidence and skills from such organizations. Saran explains:

> I went to volunteer at the local studio provided by the council Youth Team in St. Albans. I had always had a love for knobs and dials since seeing my Mom's equipment, and not being allowed to touch it. So when I saw the desk, some sort of Allen and Heath 24/8, I was in love and determined to learn how to use it. I invited friends of mine who were rappers to record with me, either singing on their tracks or assisting Rob Naylor the engineer.

The increased interest by women in recording processes is stimulating an increased demand for learning and training opportunities for them. In London for instance, at the time of writing, the DIY Space for London runs live sound engineering courses, and there are many non-university audio recording courses that encourage women applicants, such as the Point Blank Music School (an international organization), where Bamz, a beat-maker for the successful hip hop artist Nadia Rose, learned her craft (Bamz n.d.). In Huddersfield, the "Go Compose!" project encourages school-age girls to compose electronic music,[10] in Hull there is The Warren (a mixed environment with a "safe space" for girls to visit if they need to) and in Manchester, Brighter Sound (Davies 2020). In a similar way to Girls Rock Camps such as Kate Nash's Girls After School Music Club, which was started in 2011[11] and Girls Rock Regina in Canada (see Marsh 2018), community-based access courses that support girls' aspirations are an important supplement to, and sometimes replacement for, music education in schools. They are intended as feminist interventions: that is to say, they actively promote confidence and challenge the status quo of assumed male competence and autonomy. In her article on the Girls Rock Camp Alliance, Charity Marsh directly refers to the #MeToo and #TimesUp campaigns, demanding accountability for

---

10 https://gocompose.soundandmusic.org/university-of-huddersfield/ (accessed 24 November 2020).

11 See https://www.antimusic.com/news/11/feb/07Kate_Nashs_Rock_N_Roll_for_Girls_After_School_Music_Club.shtml (accessed 19 September 2019).

"the attitudes, corruption, gender violence, and the ongoing subjugation of women and girls that maintain and celebrate the status quo, limiting the ways in which girls and women are allowed to participate" (2018: 89). Within this research, a participant noted that her knowledge of the entire process of writing, playing and recording empowered her, helping her to "productively navigate some of the sexism she experiences" (2018: 94). Sarah Baker and Bruce Cohen's research into girls and DJing details the ways in which the international Playing for Life initiative engaged with girls as hands-on participants in a variety of male-dominated musical activities. Significantly, the clear impact of girl-only learning groups was startling (Baker and Cohen 2007). However, it should also be noted that interventions can successfully be made by male facilitators sympathetic to the situation.

The founder of east London's CD Rom and electronic music producer showcase night, Tony Nwachukwu, noted a diversity of participants at his events from the start in 2002, but noticed a difference in confidence between men and women participants:

> I was always interested in why there was this gender imbalance. Men are not afraid to share. Asking those questions to females who come to CDR it's more like a "big ask": it's a really big thing to share something you're not sure about. There's an imbalance in sharing something that's not quite ready. There was a layer of insecurity that was happening and that was something that really bothered me. My goal is for it to be for everyone, and I wanted to correct this gender balance. And something that I didn't want to do is create "CDR for Women". There are ways that you can present an open diverse environment without having to really spell it out. That was my thinking. So we did things like when we had guests, whether they were artists showing their work or doing a DJ set, the line up would be all women and we wouldn't talk about it: we would just see it.

Tony's next solution will be to put together a "crew" of female producer-educators, using what he describes as female-led pedagogy to demonstrably create a safe environment for women to learn. Tony stresses the openness of this project, called WMXN, to everyone, with its difference being that learning happens, as he says, "through a female lens". New learning materials will be created, with much of the approach being developed through experience he has had working with black women and women from other ethnicities. This material will bypass the technical-first approach of most manuals, and also aims to make the studio environment less intimidating. Tony feels it is really important that mixed music technology learning spaces exist as well as women-only environments. He believes that it is really important that men become involved, *"because men have to understand"*[12] (my italics). He is one of several men whose approaches to gender and diversity have been much appreciated by those who have come into contact with them, as we have seen from the experiences of, for instance, Cathy Cuvelier and Lauren Deakin Davies.

Despite competition and a shrinking jobs market, there can also be opportunities in larger studios for more traditional internships, as experienced by Isabel Gracefield Grundy, Samantha Bennett and Felix Mackintosh, for instance. Although these opportunities are more often open to young men, if gender is hidden at the point of employing studio interns a much more random selection is made. Anonymized CVs rebalanced the genders at RAK Studios one year, according to Helen Atkinson:

> I don't think it's uneven at the start, because last year's apprenticeship programme had pretty much 50/50 girls and boys, I don't know what we had this year because they come depersonalized and the few CVs that we shortlisted all happened to be boys.

RAK is a large commercial studio with a formal internship programme, so it is possible to conduct "blind" reviews of CVs in a similar way to the auditions conducted for places in major orchestras, which not only increased the number of women in the orchestras but also discouraged nepotism.[13] In relation to same-gender mentoring, one of the producers interviewed by the author realized during the course of her interview that she had never made a conscious decision to mentor a female intern in her studio. Conversely, the engineer Olga Fitzroy has mentored female engineers, and has positive feelings about opportunities for women in studio positions:

> I recently had a student from the Tonmeister course come and shadow me for a day, and have kept in touch with her as she went about finding a work placement for her year in industry. Hopefully I gave her some useful advice, but she seemed bright and motivated and sensible, so was on the right track anyway. I've worked with Fiona Cruickshank at AIR a lot, from when she first started on her placement year from university, and have tried to follow the example of all the engineers and assistants at AIR, by trying to pass on knowledge whenever possible, and as we seem to have gravitated

---

12 See https://cdr-projects.com (accessed 27 September 2019).
13 See in the UK, https://www.theguardian.com/women-in-leadership/2013/oct/14/blind-auditions-orchestras-gender-bias and in the USA, http://gap.hks.harvard.edu/orchestrating-impartiality-impact-"blind"-auditions-female-musicians (both accessed 2 August 2018) and Goldin and Rouse (2000).

towards the same group of clients (or they towards us), we have worked together quite a lot over the years.

Olga feels that the lack of opportunity has little to do with the gender of the applicants for a dwindling number of studio jobs:

> I think the girls that have got as far as getting a job in a studio face exactly the same difficulties faced by any young people in this industry – there are definitely opportunities, but as there are fewer commercial studios than there have been in the past, the traditional route of tea-boy/girl, assistant engineer, engineer, is open to only a small number of people … If anything, girls might be at a slight advantage, as they are often more memorable to clients than the boys.[14]

To conclude this chapter, I return to the 2015 findings of Born and Devine, research that included my own institution in London. This research is particularly revealing in terms of the continuing male student bias in Music Technology courses in higher education. As Born and Devine note, at the time of the expansion of university capacity in the late 1990s, there was a political concern about the mitigation of youth unemployment, in particular that of young white working-class males (2015: 143). Music Technology degrees were set up in part "to attract and absorb what HE policy debate deems to be this problematic demographic" (144) resulting, at the time, in a 90 per cent male intake on these courses. In addition to this, like Blickenstaff (2005), and Hopkins and Berkers (2020), the researchers had identified a "leaky pipeline" between early adolescent interest and engagement with STEM subjects at school and their eventual decisions about higher education (147).

It is therefore important to note that opportunities for women to enter the music industry as studio engineers through education are funnelled down a narrow channel that is restricted not only by social factors such as sexism and "tradition", but also by government policy. Fundamental changes in thought at each level of the music industry – from government policy to everyday engagement between individuals – will be necessary in order to disrupt the entrenched ethos. However, if it is possible to change policy so drastically in order to absorb excess young white males, the potential is also there to make changes that benefit women, and, of course, people from a range of cultural backgrounds.

14 Trina Shoemaker, who worked as a secretary at Capitol Records and a maid at Ultra Sonic in New Orleans (Wolfe 2019: 64) and Isabel Gracefield Grundy, who made connections by making tea in a complex where she was working on dance music (see Chapter 2), are rare exceptions to the type of tea-boy/girl route into studio careers.

9 Conclusion

In this book I have explored the lived experiences of women producers, mainly in the pop music world, and their professional practice. They described their initial engagements with sound, music and recordings in Chapter 1, after which Chapter 2 followed their progress as they developed their understanding of the way that recorded music is made, either through visiting recording studios, seeing live music being mixed at a gig, or becoming involved in audio through radio. I documented examples of their first steps into recording studio environments, with an exploration of the many different ways that they secured their work and crucially, developed their self-definition as producers and/or engineers. In Chapter 3, survival strategies and moves towards specialization – in which one becomes the "go-to" person for particular types of work – illustrated the importance of ingenuity and resilience, combined with ongoing skill and personal network development; all of which are necessary to sustain a viable career in audio production. Chapter 4 addressed their engagement with clients and other professionals, and perhaps marked the turning point of the book: no matter how skilled or experienced a female professional is, she still has to negotiate the interface between her own practice and that of an industry working environment which is set up to favour men, issues that are explored in greater detail in Chapter 5. In that chapter I described the role of (largely covert) societal and professional gatekeeping in creating and maintaining stereotypical roles for women in the studio. Challenges by feminist writers to this historical maintenance of the status quo were applied to a variety of different real-life working situations to demonstrate the sophistry of these widely held assumptions.

In Chapter 6, I described the transplanting of female voices by male producers, a process that changes sonic and visual aesthetics which, alongside the voicing of female experience by male songwriters as an established practice, has controlled the ways in which women are perceived through the lens of popular music. This practice has reinforced the belief that women should enter the profession of pop music production to redress the resulting gender stereotyping, but as a concealed working practice it has not always been to the forefront in studies of women producers. I also began a speculative conversation about what happens when the situation is reversed, and women record men's voices. In Chapter 7, I described the ways in which electronic music production can liberate women from a dominant male-gaze focus on their physical appearance, and critically considered the established "ungendered" nature of EDM (suggested by academics and music industry professionals alike). In doing so, I demonstrated that this dominant discourse of gender-free music production hides persistent traditional gender delineations, evident in the downgrading or exclusion of (female) voices in the music genre. Towards the end of the chapter, I discussed the ways that some large music industry organizations make temporary or even superficial changes in response to adverse publicity about power relations within them. In Chapter 8, I focused upon music technology education in secondary schools and less formal settings. This chapter was positioned in the book to set up a concluding discussion relating to the changes necessary for addressing the imbalance of female producers and engineers in the professional worlds of sound engineering and production in popular music. The complexities and entrenched problems relating to the educational trajectory of female pupils in the UK represent a key barrier to be addressed. Within this concluding chapter, I will round up further issues that might affect the landscape of the industry for female professionals, and summarize the situation at the time of writing.

Creating and Sustaining a Place in the Profession

Throughout my research in this area (which has taken place informally over almost twenty years, and formally over more than ten), there has been a constant sense of evolution in the music industry. This has been tied closely to changes in technology, taste, distribution methods, playback devices, and stresses in the global economy that affect the disposable income of music fans. These changes have impacted not only on the roles of music recording professionals, but also on availability of work. In addition, the definition of what music production actually *is* has become increasingly fragmented since the early days of pop music recording. In her book on production, *Recording Unhinged*, Sylvia Massy divides current producer roles into three different categories:

> The musician/producer usually creates all the music and often writes the songs, bringing in vocal talent to front the project. The engineer/producer will craft the sound of an existing project, often using equipment and technique to create the magic in the studio. The fan/producer may never actually touch the console, but will help choose the songs and guide the project by bringing the right people together. (2016: 187–88)

Perhaps it is telling that a dedicated music producer should leave out the role of the self-producer that potentially creates such a challenge within the profession, and perhaps this omission is not unintentional.

It is still vital for anyone making a living in the creative industries, let alone a music professional who fits one of Massy's definitions, to remain up to date not only in terms of the aesthetics of musical taste, but also in terms of the incorporation of innovative technology into their practice. Continuing relevance is vital for pioneering female producers, to prevent them from becoming, effectively, "old girls". When I asked Mandy Parnell, for instance, how she updates her skills, she told me:

> I go to AES every year, the Audio Engineering Society convention. They have two a year, one in Europe and one in America. One year it'll be New York, the next year San Francisco ... they have lectures, very full on lectures. I just went out in October specifically for three lectures. I read, and just chat to people and then come back and do lots of research and explore it.

This type of professional networking can be costly but is of great value, not just as a source of current information but also in terms of profile. Being seen to be a studio professional in an environment of like-minded people not only engenders respect within the industry, but also has an effect on one's self-respect. In a less formal process, but with a similar result of giving a sense of embeddedness within a music scene, JPL described an ongoing conversation between herself and the young artists she was working with, "bombard[ing]" them with new material to listen to, whilst in response they send her the newest beats coming up from the street. This keeps her ideas fresh and ensures that she is able to communicate in an informed way with new artists about their ideas when it comes to producing their sessions.

This symbiotic relationship directs us to one of the signs that women have achieved parity with men in studio engineering and audio production communities: the expectation and acknowledgement by their *male* clients that they are competent because of their established reputation and expertise. This is something that was noted not just by JPL, but also by Felix Mackintosh, Ms Melody, Olga Fitzroy and "Hannah". Avril Mackintosh has been working behind the scenes for many years with male vocalists, and she was one of three engineers shortlisted in 2017 for a Music Producer's Guild award as Recording Engineer of the Year for the album *Solas*, by The Answer, after one of the original nominees, Neil Comber, withdrew, unusually acknowledging that he did not have the skills that the award pertained to:

> "Whilst I am incredibly grateful for the MPG nomination, the engineering work I have undertaken has only been in relation to producing and mixing these records", Comber says. "For this reason, I feel there are people far more deserving to be shortlisted who work predominantly as Recording Engineers".[1]

This is a generous and self-effacing public statement to make, and indeed recently the MPG appears to have taken on board its responsibility to recognize talented women audio workers. In Comber's statement, he highlights the distinct role that recording engineers play as facilitators of decisions that musicians and producers make by bridging the gaps between the ideas, the musicianship, and the capture of that combination onto hard disk.

With regards to the MPG there is a continued recognition of the achievements of female producers and engineers; in 2018 Catherine Marks was awarded Producer of the Year,[2] and Imogen Heap was given the Award for Inspiration. Heap has since become involved in a very wide portfolio of activities, from composing songs for films such as *The Chronicles of Narnia*, to the co-invention of the Mi.Mu glove that uses hand gestures to create music[3] and, more recently, the use of Blockchain technology in music contracts. Heap, in fact, could be cited as yet another definition of a producer, that of the producer/entrepreneur who includes technological innovation as part of their practice. Because of the high industry profiles and spread of practice displayed by the women who have so far been given MPG awards, any rolling back of the recognition of female achievement would be difficult to justify. The organization still has diversity work to do, however. In order to support the small steps they have made, they must be continually celebrated and built upon. If we cannot see women achieve, we are not able to be inspired by them.

Visibility is another key issue to the development of more diversity in the music industry, in particular the elevation and celebration of emerging and successful women engineers and producers by male colleagues. In the introduction to this book, I mentioned the isolated nature of women's engineering and production practice in the mainstream record industry. Support from other women colleagues can be vital, but as Mandy Parnell has acknowledged, women-only organizations and professional panels simply don't suit every woman. There are issues such as availability of time for meetings, reputational branding as an "awkward feminist", and also a reluctance to engender the

1 https://www.mpg.org.uk/news/avril-mackintosh/ (accessed 1 June 2020).
2 For examples of her work see http://www.catherinejmarks.com/work/4561792981 (accessed 12 August 2018).
3 See http://www.imogenheap.co.uk/thegloves/ (accessed 12 August 2018).

feeling that the producer or engineer *needs* the support of other women, and is therefore by implication too weak to survive on her own in the industry. In common with other musical and scientific activities that are gendered as male, a combination of visible role models, access and good fortune will enable more women to become involved in sound engineering and production.[4]

Professional Spaces and Women Producers

The ubiquity of laptops and associated music software has increased access to creativity but not necessarily to income streams or recognition in the mainstream music industry. In fact, as we have seen, once women show an ability to produce music at home, it becomes a lesser activity than music produced by men at home.[5] Jennifer Brown's concept of the "electronic cottage" industry has had an interesting effect on territorial traditions, as the small businesses created in the home expand. Some women are moving out of the bedroom and into studios as spaces of production, whereas some men have moved *into* the bedroom and created studios at home. Paul Théberge commented on this process shortly after it began to expand, noting that: "the privacy of domestic space becomes the ideal site of musical expression and inspiration rather than the more public realms of night club and stage" (1997: 218). A certain romance began to attach itself to home-made music, with its implication of resistance to corporate labels and professional studio trickery, two of the major drivers of popular music.

As an inverse example of the out-of-the-bedroom-into-the-studio route (in an interesting reversal of what has come to be regarded as a normal progression for women producers from home set-ups to larger studios), Laura B has moved in the opposite direction. A career that started with an intern

---

4   The cases of self-determination in the independent music scene in the UK in music technology practice reported by Mavis Bayton in the 1990s, with female artists such as Andrea Stallard of Mambo Taxi and Skin of Skunk Anansie taking sound engineering courses, or setting up a home studio respectively, in order to achieve a degree of studio expertise before entering the commercial studio to record (1998: 162), possibly came too late in their careers to allow the artists concerned to thrive at the centre of the mainstream British music industry and become role models for a younger generation of prospective producers, although Stallard still plays live music in the band Ye Nuns, and Skin has recently collaborated on a techno album under the pseudonym Juvenal.

5   Although laptop production is hailed as a breakthrough for home producers, before this Portastudios were readily available (enabling multi-track recording onto cassettes), and before that, it was possible to record onto disc using machines in railway stations and other public places and, indeed, sometimes in the home itself. See Brock-Nannestad (2012).

role for the Clash's live performances developed into working as an assistant engineer on Roger Waters' album *The Pros and Cons of Hitch Hiking*, working with the Pet Shop Boys, and through that on to industrial music and EDM, all in prestigious professional studios. She now works as a solo producer on EDM, enjoying the autonomy of her role and the control she has over her own music, back at home again. She has gravitated towards creating her own music, and mastering music for other acts. Mastering, which prepares a finished track with specific sonic qualities for (e.g.) radio play, or for being played in large spaces at EDM events, is still a specialist skill, although she told me that a lot of people still do not understand the value of it.

The "invasion" of the home space as studio space by men potentially provokes the same problems as Keightley's audiophile battleground mentioned in Chapter 5, with tension caused by noise and equipment shattering the peace of those who live there. Doreen Massey's comment about "the conceptualization of space" underlines the importance of creative space belonging to the producer, and that sense of belonging increasing her confidence, in this case in the development of the user's technical skills (Massey 1994). The confidence-building exercise of starting on a small home-based scale was mentioned by two of my interviewees, Terrie Harris and Chantal Epp, and this tallies with Wolfe's research (2012). Epp runs her entire business from her laptop, using it to program beats, download tracks (in accordance with a PRS licence) for mash-ups, and then marketing the resulting tracks via Twitter. Harris started recording in the kitchen of her home until recording drums became a problem for her neighbours.

Unfortunately, as self-production has flourished, even as a stepping stone into a more professional studio set-up for finishing recordings, there is a corresponding decreasing need for technical studio workers, as noted earlier in this chapter; the profession is already full to capacity. Spare labour capacity is going to become a problem for everyone in an increasingly technologized world, and careers in art and music – already challenged by the democratizing process of social media distribution – are likely to become even more fought-over. Unlike other situations where women have "been allowed" into male musical territory, such as when there have been skills shortages (see, for instance, Mary-Ann Clawson's work on bass guitarists, 1999), there is no perceptible skills shortage in audio engineering and production. While celebrating the new trend in valorization of electronic music genres due to "upward pressure" from music technology degrees (2015: 161), Born and Devine have noted the "potential overproduction of students in the MT degree sector. Simply put, where will all these graduates go?'" (2015: 167). To mitigate this, if enough women artists decide that they want to work exclusively with women studio engineers and producers, then those studio managers who refuse to employ female engineers (as described by Laura B in Chapter 4) may find that they have made a poor business decision, and larger commercial studios may decide that it makes good business sense to have women engineers on their roster. This would mean, however, a more enlightened approach to gender and music technology training than we have at present, whether this training takes place in studios themselves (notably, RAK's approach to CV applications for internship vacancies), in community settings, or in formal higher education. Indeed, Lauren Deakin Davies and Isabel Gracefield Grundy are both developing reputations as experts in facilitating the recordings of female artists who feel that it is important that their ideas are mediated by like-minded recordists. Both received support in their early careers that bypassed their gender, as we have seen from their interviews.

There will still be a need for professional recording practitioners, not least because of the upsurge in the use and accessibility of home recording technology which, it has already been observed, does not always result in the leap of skills from amateur to professional status. Home recording technology has become so popular that it could be compared to the ubiquitous piano in the Victorian parlour, but taking these home recordings to the level of radio-broadcast production standards, for instance, requires time to hone audio skills that may not be within the reach of every home practitioner.

Why Should We Encourage Women to be Sound Engineers and Producers?

If we substitute the word "controller" for producer when we think about the ways pop music is created, the perspective changes considerably. It is notable that even Prince, with his encouragement and respect for women musicians and engineers, recorded his vocals in isolation (Murphy 2015), which might suggest that he was unwilling to expose the processes involved in capturing his voice (his potentially most vulnerable and emotional musical tool), to the scrutiny of the studio staff that he trusted with the more technological, machine-based side of his recordings, despite his "alpha male" persona (Beaumont-Thomas 2016).[6]

To return to Doreen Massey, given that the way that we imagine space "is one of the axes along which we conceptualize and experience the world" (1994: 251), the sonic space inhabited by vocalists in popular music is, as we

---

6   https://www.theguardian.com/music/2017/nov/09/princes-sound-engineer-susan-rogers-he-needed-to-be-the-alpha-male-to-get-things-done (accessed 16 December 2020).

have seen in Chapters 6 and 7, a site of competition, potential conflict, and most importantly, *control* in popular music genres. Sonic capitulation, submission to control by a producer, and gender stereotyping are part of the music production process for both male and female artists, but these have a particular resonance for women because of their position in society in general. Gendered social controls are reflected and utilized in the songwriting and recording processes, not only in the crafting of the sound of the recorded product (the industrial process), but also, by implication, in the product itself (the social-historical process). The producer, of course, affects the product; therefore, the gender of the producer affects the gender of the product. This throws a light upon why it is so important to re-evaluate the stereotyping of roles in the music industry. As Schmutz and Faupel observe in their research into popular music canons:

> Even where women have achieved consecration in popular music, the ways in which their inclusion is legitimated draws on existing frameworks about gender that emphasize female dependency in contrast with male agency. In subtle ways, this gendered discourse limits the amount and types of critical legitimacy female artists can accrue. Even when consecrated, female musicians are not fully legitimated. (2010: 704)

This is underlined by the perception of the influence of girl group music on the canon established by the Beatles, Red Hot Chili Peppers and Aerosmith; the historical evaluation of this relationship displays a "behind-every-great-man" mentality, according to Laurie Stras (2010: 7). Unlike the behind-every-great-woman aspects of the male Svengalis, the gender rules of the music industry and society in general unbalance any potential equity in this phenomenon.

The concepts of control and ventriloquism that are described in Chapter 6 were carefully considered by some of the women that I interviewed: this is evident in the ways that they defined themselves. Ms Melody is a "translator" of her grime rappers' music, and Terrie Harris sees herself as a "caretaker" of live sound, definitions that are gender non-specific and that allow their users to determine themselves without external stereotyping. Conversely, JPL has been described by others in her executive production role as a "conjuror", and Isobel Campbell by Mark Lanegan as a "benevolent dictator", both definitions that imply power over what happens in the studio when they are driving a session. However, it was Chantal Epp who articulated her self-effacing position most clearly:

> I don't really like talking about the work that I do … You know, "This is my work, I've done it, it's so good". I just don't like that whole

self-promotion kind of thing, so I've worked my way around it by saying, "We have done this", talking about it in the third person. I've left my business anonymous. People know who I am, and they know it's my business if they know me, but in terms of Twitter and things like that I haven't got my picture on my website or the Twitter page. In a way it makes the business look bigger, and then also I don't have to talk about the work that I'm doing because I don't like that personally.

Other Gendered Setbacks "Behind the Scenes"

Even when they want to be acknowledged, lack of credit for their technical and production skills is still a major problem for women working behind the scenes in the music industry. Björk was able to fight back against this because of her fame, and artists such as Madonna and Beyoncé are credited as co-producers for the same reason (Mayhew 2004). But the problem of being uncredited as a producer on Florence Welch's music that was faced by Isa Summers, cited in the introduction, is not uncommon. Cathy Cuvelier described a similar situation in the reggae community:

> When I decided to build my own studio was when I realized I had to ask too much from people and wasn't gaining anything. I worked in a lot of studios and I wasn't credited on the production of so much stuff. It wasn't about the money, it was about the work I did and the recognition of what I did, and I was wiped out like I never existed, and I suffered a lot with that.

A significant label did not credit her for her work, but she took direct action: "I went straight to the studio and took all the files. But they did press a series of 7 inches; they only pressed a thousand, which wasn't a lot to be distributed."

In such a competitive industry, a female producer who has formerly been assumed to be lower skilled than a male one, and who actually delivers better productions, can be regarded as a threat. Indeed, Wolfe notes that this may even happen in mentoring situations between a male mentor and a female mentee (2019: 78). JPL now employs a lawyer to protect her contribution as a recording engineer after her success in recording started to make the producers on some of the tracks she worked on feel threatened:

> It's happened a few times ... I get brought in to do one track and end up getting most of the album, so then the male producer starts talking about my mix, or my this and my that ... sometimes I just realise it's people's egos. It's not easy for men to admit that in a particular part of the process that a woman might be better at it than them.

Having a supportive family and team really helps her to survive. As she said, "I have to count to ten a lot of the time". She steps back from the situation and tries to become objective, relishing her role as a black woman in a white man's world:

> Once my lawyer said to me "Jac, you have it hard because you're a black woman who does music that usually white middle-aged 50-year-old males would do, so when people hear your records they're like 'Great!' [and] when they meet you it's like 'Huh?'".
> But I kind of understand that and I know what I'm working with ... for some reasons people will love me and for the same reasons some people – loathe me is too strong, but you know it's that kind of thing – who does she think she is?

This balance of being allowed a certain amount of power but being challenged when overstepping the mark was also familiar to Ms Melody, whose experience of being racially profiled was described in Chapter 4. She is completely conscious of her position in relationship to her clients:

> ... despite the fact I was surrounded by thousands of pounds worth of equipment the fact that I did not pose any physical threat to them held the key. They relaxed in my company, let go of their inhibitions and egos and undertook a protective role over me. They also bragged about having a female engineer as though I was this prized procession. At times it felt a little patronising but there was another part that I found very sweet and endearing.

Ms Melody speculated about how much easier her career might have been had she been a white male, in particular the amount of time it took her to establish her reputation as a skilled producer. The music industry in general often seems to congratulate itself on its diversity, but when we actually hear from black professionals within the industry (often when they are in a position where they have nothing to lose) the story they tell is rather different. The Black Lives Matter protests of 2020 led Keith Harris (Steve Wonder's International manager) to write an open letter about his own experiences in the British and US music industry. At the time of writing, Keith is in his late sixties, and in the letter he documented some of the attitudes he experienced both himself during his lifetime and as an observer within the music industry. He commented:

> I would like to remind you all that this awareness of racism in the industry should not last for one day, or one week, or one year. This should last forever. I would like to see other young black people in

the industry rise to the positions of authority and seniority that their talent merits. (Harris 2020)

It is permanent, attitudinal change that young people in particular would like to see established, with solidarity between groups supporting change in racial, gender, body and disability awareness and acceptance. So, in relation to the gender imbalance evidenced throughout the pages of this book, we need to see women engineers and producers from diverse backgrounds being recognized by mainstream industry bodies such as the MPG as part of normal practice. Such everyday normalizing of a more diverse workforce is more powerful than extraordinary events which respond to passing media interest in the lack of diversity within the music (and many other) industries. This approach, however, requires consistent reflection, action and research into the issues and possible resolutions of a long-standing and pervasive issue, detailed throughout this book.

Some Positive Developments

Meanwhile, in STEM subjects in general, women continue to speak out against gender prejudice. In 2018, Dr Michaela Kendall made a Freedom of Information Request which revealed that 90 per cent of engineering grants were awarded to male-led teams (Weale and Barr 2018),[7] and as an example of institutional policy change in 2015, Glasgow College introduced a girls-only engineering course to try to redress the issue of gender imbalance (Stewart 2015).[8] In tech, an element of cool has helped women to assert their right to be involved in technology in a hands-on capacity; for instance in Berlin, the diminutive "ette" (see Dale Spender, *Man Made Language*, 1990) has been recuperated by the Berlin Geekettes, an organization formed to consolidate women's rights to be geeks.[9] In music itself, there are campaigns to address the gender balance in festival programming after research by the BBC in 2018 exposed a very poor ratio of male to female acts (Reality Check Team 2018).[10] The Canadian film *Play Your Gender*, released in 2017, has been screened internationally and exposes the lack of women producers in Canada, demonstrating

7 https://www.theguardian.com/education/2018/aug/10/female-scientists-urge-research-grants-reform-tackle-gender-bias (accessed 12 August 2018).
8 http://www.eveningtimes.co.uk/news/13644875.Engineering_a_girls_only_course_at_Glasgow_College/ (accessed 12 August 2018).
9 http://www.geekettes.io (accessed 24 September 2019).
10 https://www.bbc.co.uk/news/entertainment-arts-44655719 (accessed 12 August 2018).

that this is an issue that is experienced in other countries that appear to have an enlightened approach to gendered professions.[11]

Initiatives such as Keychange (the Performing Rights Society Foundation (PRSF)-led and EU-supported initiative to work towards a 50:50 gender balance in the music industry by 2022)[12] and research by members of the international organization female:pressure will also contribute to the possibility of change, by raising awareness and consolidating communities of campaigners. Perhaps one of the strongest indicators of positive change is the commercialization of the idea of women as producers and DJs, by companies such as Smirnoff, through their Equalizing Music initiative (Hanna and Taylor 2017).[13] Yet the fate of women in production could fall into the trap of being a momentary interest, a gimmick that passes before male autonomy is reasserted. Unfortunately, as Born and Devine have noted, "the gendered mediation of contemporary (music-)technological design shows an astonishing capacity to endure" (2016: 5). The plethora of new initiatives at the time of writing can seem encouraging, but until they have become established and can be evaluated with hindsight, it is very difficult to celebrate their achievements.

The contribution made by this book to the history of women in studio professions is far from comprehensive. Once I started to speak about my research, more information came to light: women studio engineers in Liverpool; Stockhausen's women tape editors; a woman engineer in Newcastle who cuts music direct-to-disc. There are women who have been working in this profession for years without being singled out for attention, for example Felicity Hassell, who assisted her husband John in his dub-plate cutting studio in Barnes, London. Although she is mentioned in an online article as making cups of tea, in the BBC documentary referred to in the same article she is shown loading tapes onto the 2" tape machine; it is likely that she was actually an assistant engineer, or would have been given that title if she had been a man.[14] Beryl Ritchie was a cutting engineer based in Scotland who cut Mike Oldfield's *Tubular Bells* and who is seldom lauded for her pioneering skills.[15] Mandy Parnell discovered sound women in Germany whom she had never

11 https://www.youtube.com/watch?v=dH-Kjt8g9ow (accessed 24 September 2019).
12 https://keychange.eu (accessed 16 December 2020).
13 https://www.multivu.com/players/English/8054251-smirnoff-equalizing-music-womens-day/ (accessed 2 February 2020).
14 https://soundofthehound.com/2011/06/25/the-strange-origin-of-the-uk-reggae-big-bass-sound-john-hassell-recordings-barnes/ (accessed 13 August 2018).
15 https://www.theguardian.com/music/2013/jul/08/beryl-ritchie-obituary (accessed 24 September 2019).

come across, and another while in America: "'I just went out to Skywalker Ranch and there's an elderly female engineer out there that everyone knows in America and I'd never heard of her 'cos she's just not been in the circle I was in".[16] It is only relatively recently that the important cultural contributions of Delia Derbyshire at the BBC Radiophonic Workshop, and work of the experimental electronic musician Daphne Oram, have begun to be appreciated. Within music genres associated with black communities in Britain and the United States, there is a whole range of issues associated with gender and what is termed music of black origin. For instance, in the British grime scene it is apparently easier for white women to penetrate the tightly knit genre than for black women, with "misogynoir" a pernicious issue. Digital artist Abigail Adeoti – director of *Gash* (2018), a documentary that follows the experiences of women in the black British music industry – laments in an interview with *The Guardian* that black women lack cultural space "even in the spaces that are created from their own culture". She continues: "The colourism and intercommunal racism within urban media is a serious issue that nobody dares speak on" (Adegoke 2018). This makes Ms Melody's success all the more unusual. Yet Sylvia Robinson, founder of Sugar Hill Records, was one of the first acknowledged pioneers of hip hop production and her success inspired other US producers such as Missy Elliott. A silo effect appears to close opportunities down as soon as pop music changes direction, which is why the continual raising of visibility by industry bodies such as the Music Producer's Guild is so vital. Support by music journalists is also essential. Building on the documentation of black British music history being undertaken by Mykaell Riley at the University of Westminster's Black Music Research Unit (which includes a history of women sound system operators[17]), the journalist Emma Finamore (2017) documented women in the current sound system scene in *i-D* magazine.[18] The documentation and reporting of women's practice across the wide spectrum of activities within the music industry help to establish and normalize their presence within it.

There is, of course, a more depressing story to be told, that of women whose careers have failed in this area. Without specifically intending to, I have for the large part presented a positive view of women's professional studio activities, filtered through survivor bias. Balancing the knowledge that to be a gender pioneer is of great value, with a responsibility for realistic communication

16 https://www.skysound.com/people/leslie-ann-jones/ (accessed 19 September 2019).
17 http://basscultureduk.com/about/ (accessed 16 December 2020).
18 https://i-d.vice.com/en_uk/article/8x8y5v/how-women-are-shaping-a-new-uk-sound-system-scene (accessed 10 June 2020).

about the specific difficulties embedded in this process, is very difficult. Any individual's story of their professional life might highlight different issues, according to their intended audience. In fact, I was pleasantly surprised by the positivity that was expressed in the interviews, while acknowledging to myself that this is an automatic reflex to the networking opportunity that I have provided by highlighting their voices: by writing about the women in this book, I am consolidating their own histories within record production. In this process, I have occasionally anonymized and edited the interviews after reflection about the issues raised, while needing to stress aspects of the working environment that might not be documented elsewhere.

Music production is a fast-developing area of creative empowerment and business opportunity in the creative industry, and continuing documentation and archiving are important in order to both acknowledge and consolidate women's presence in studio practice. The gaps in the archives of women's practice in the music industry are being addressed as increasing awareness of our often hidden practice comes to the forefront. In academia for instance, Reitsamer (2019) and Dever (2017) both challenge and acknowledge the mediation involved in the documentation of women's musical practice in Europe and in modes of feminist research in general respectively (see also Baker 2019). Despite the biases I myself hold as a writer of women's histories (white, educated, female), until the use of women producers is normal practice in all genres of music and not just music created by and for women, we will remain in the position of Genet (1971) and Lorde (2018), who found themselves not only operating in a straight, white man's world, but also trying to overturn man made language (Spender 1990). This language used in a field of creative endeavour controlled by men cannot help but produce gendered music. It is not the music alone that makes meaning, but the people who create it and the people who listen to it. Embedded not just in the technical processes, but also running through the entire business model and aesthetics of the music industry, is the same patriarchal structure that underlies industrialized Western societies; inevitably, change will feel slow, but there are signs that it will happen.

Bibliography

Adegoke, Yomi (2018). "Why Black Women are Still a Minority in the Grime Scene". *The Guardian*, 9 February. https://www.theguardian.com/music/2018/feb/09/black-women-still-minority-grime-scene (accessed 19 January 2020).

Adichie, Chimamande Ngozi (2014). "I Decided to Call Myself a Happy Feminist". *The Guardian*, 17 October. https://www.theguardian.com/books/2014/oct/17/chimamanda-ngozi-adichie-extract-we-should-all-be-feminists (accessed 2 June 2020).

Adorno, Theodor (1928). "The Curves of the Needle", trans. Thomas Y. Levin. *October 55*, 1990: 49–55. https://www.jstor.org/stable/778935?seq=1 (accessed 14 January 2021).

Armstrong, Victoria (2011). *Technology and the Gendering of Music Education*. Farnham and Burlington, VT: Ashgate.

Aroesti, Rachel (2015). "Kiss with a Fist". *The Guardian Guide*, 31 October–6 November: 11.

Askar, Paris (2005). "Howard Massey: Record Producer and Music Industry Author", 22 March. https://web.archive.org/web/20061022053148/http://blog.lownoiserecords.com/howardmassey.html (accessed 24 June 2020).

Attali, Jacques (1999). *Noise: The Political Economy of Music*. Minneapolis and London: University of Minneapolis Press.

Baker, Sarah, ed. (2019). *Preserving Popular Music Heritage: Do-it-Yourself, Do-it-Together*. London: Routledge.

Baker, Sarah, and Bruce Cohen (2007). "From Snuggling and Snogging to Sampling and Scratching: Girls' Nonparticipation in Community-Based Music Activities". *Youth & Society* 39.3: 316–39. https://doi.org/10.1177/0044118X06296696

Bamz (n.d.). "An Introduction to Bamz: Producer and Nadia Rose Collaborator". https://plus.pointblankmusicschool.com/introduction-to-bamz/ (accessed 3 June 2020).

Barthes, Roland (1977). *Image-Music-Text*. New York: Hill and Wang.

Battersby, Christine (1989). *Gender and Genius: Towards a Feminist Aesthetics*. London: Women's Press Limited.

Bayton, Mavis (1998). *Frock Rock: Women Performing Popular Music*. Oxford and New York: Oxford University Press.

Bearman, Steve, Neill Korobov, and Avril Thorne (2009). "The Fabric of Internalized Sexism". *Journal of Integrated Social Sciences* 1.1: 10–47.

Beaumont-Thomas, Ben (2016). "Prince's Sound Engineer, Susan Rogers: 'He needed to be the alpha male to get things done'". *The Guardian*, 9 November. https://www.theguardian.com/music/2017/nov/09/princes-sound-engineer-susan-rogers-he-needed-to-be-the-alpha-male-to-get-things-done (accessed 16 December 2020).

Bennett, Joe (2014). *The Death of the Songwriter: Attribution of Creative Ownership in Popular Music Production*. The 9th Art of Record Production Conference: Record

Production in the Internet Age. University of Oslo, Norway, 4 December, http://researchspace.bathspa.ac.uk/5039/1/DeathsongwriterOslo%20-%20final.pdf (accessed 9 February 2016).

Bennett, Joe (2015). "Creative Processes in Stock, Aitken and Waterman's 'I Should Be So Lucky'". http://joebennett.net/2015/02/27/saw-kylie-lucky/#more-4305 (accessed 21 August 2015).

Berg, Maxine (1984). "Responses to Machinery in 18th Century England". *Bulletin of the Society of the Study of Labour History* 49 (Autumn).

Black Music Research Unit (n.d.). http://basscultureduk.com/about/ (accessed 10 June 2020).

Blickenstaff, Jacob Clark (2005). "Women and Science Careers: Leaky Pipeline or Gender Filter?" *Gender and Education* 17.4: 369–86. https://doi.org/10.1080/09540250500145072

Bogdanovic, D. (2015). *Gender and Equality in Music Higher Education. A Report Commissioned and Funded by the National Association for Music in Higher Education.* Currently unavailable.

Born, Georgina, and Kyle Devine (2015). "Music Technology, Gender, and Class: Digitization, Education and Social Change in Britain". *Twentieth-Century Music* 12.2: 135–72. https://doi.org/10.1017/S1478572215000018

Born, Georgina, and Kyle Devine, eds. (2016). "Gender, Creativity and Education in Digital Music and Sound Art". *Contemporary Music Review* 35.1: 1–20. https://doi.org/10.1080/07494467.2016.1177255

Bourdieu, Pierre (2001). *Masculine Domination.* Cambridge: Polity.

Bradby, Barbara (1990). "Do-Talk and Don't-Talk: The Division of the Subject in Girl-Group Music". In *On Record: Rock, Pop and the Written Word*, edited by Simon Frith and Andrew Goodwin, 341–68. London: Routledge.

Bradby, Barbara (1993). "Sampling Sexuality: Gender, Technology and the Body in Dance Music". *Popular Music* 12.2: 155–76. https://doi.org/10.1017/S0261143000005535

Brock-Nannestad, George (2012). "The Lacquer Disc for Immediate Playback: Professional Recording and Home Recording from the 1920s to the 1950s". In *The Art of Record Production: An Introductory Reader for a New Academic Field*, edited by Simon Frith and Simon Zagorski-Thomas, 13–27. Farnham: Ashgate.

Brown, Jennifer M. (1996). "De-gendering the Electronic Soundscape: Women, Power and Technology in Contemporary Music". Master's thesis, Southern Cross University.

Butler, Judith (1985). "Performative Arts and Gender Constitution: An Essay in Phenomenology and Feminist Theory". *Theatre Journal* 40.4: 519–31. https://doi.org/10.2307/3207893

Butler, Judith (1993). "Imitation and Gender Insubordination". In *The Lesbian and Gay Studies Reader*, edited by Henry Abelove, Michèle Aina Barale, and David Halperin, 307–20. New York: Routledge.

Butler, Judith (1990). *Gender Trouble and the Subversion of Identity.* New York: Routledge.

Buxbaum, Edwin C. (1949). "On Playing Music LOUD". *Saturday Review of Literature*, 25 June: 51.

Cameron, Keith (2011). "Kate Bush Interview". *Mojo* 211 (June): 85.

Chanan, Michael (1995). *Repeated Takes: A Short History of Recording and Its Effects on Music*. London and New York: Verso.

Chick, Stevie (2010). "'I write the songs; he's the eye-candy': Isobel Campbell and Mark Lanegan". *The Guardian*, 28 October. https://www.theguardian.com/music/2010/oct/28/isobel-campbell-mark-lanegan-interview (accessed 16 December 2020).

Citron, Marcia J. (1993). *Gender and the Musical Canon*. Cambridge: Cambridge University Press.

Cixous, Hélène (1976). "The Laugh of the Medusa", trans. Keith Cohen and Paula Cohen. *Signs: Journal of Women in Culture and Society* 1.4: 875–94.

Clawson, Mary Ann (1999). "When Women Play the Bass: Instrument Specialization and Gender Interpretation in Alternative Rock Music". *Gender & Society* 13.2: 193–210. https://doi.org/10.1177/089124399013002003

Cliff, Aimee (2020). "Hatsune Miku review: Hologram Star Fired up Crowdsourced Power Pop". *The Guardian*, 20 January. https://www.theguardian.com/music/2020/jan/12/hatsune-miku-review-london-o2-academy-brixton-london (accessed 3 June 2020).

Coates, Norma (1997). "(R)Evolution Now? Rock and the Political Potential of Gender". In *Sexing the Groove: Popular Music and Gender*, edited by Sheila Whiteley, 50–64. New York: Routledge.

Cohen, Sara (1991). *Rock Culture in Liverpool: Popular Music in the Making*. Oxford: Clarendon Press.

Cook, John (2013). "Just the Beginning". Interview with Maya Jane Coles, in *Trap* 013 (February/March): 34–38. Camouflage Media Ltd.

Costley, Carol, Geoffrey C. Elliott, and Paul Gibbs (2010). *Doing Work based Research: Approaches to Enquiry for Insider-Researchers*. London: Sage.

Cragg, Michael (2014). "One to Watch: Ronika". *The Observer New Review*, 25 April. https://www.theguardian.com/music/2014/may/23/ronika-one-to-watch-nottingham-disco-believe-it (accessed 14 January 2021).

Daniel, Drew (2011). "All Sound is Queer". *The Wire* 333 (November): 46.

Davies, Helen (2001). "All Rock and Roll is Homosocial: The Representation of Women in the British Rock Music Press". *Popular Music* 20.3: 295–313. https://doi.org/10.1017/S0261143001001519

Davies, Helen Elizabeth (2020). "Preparing for the 'Real World'? Exploring Gender Issues in the Music Industry and the Role of Vocational Popular Music Education in the UK". In *Towards Gender Equality in the Music Industry: Education, Practice and Strategies for Change*, edited by Catherine Strong and Sarah Raine, 29–44. London and New York: Bloomsbury.

DeNora, Tia (2000). *Music in Everyday Life*. Cambridge: Cambridge University Press. https://doi.org/10.1017/CBO9780511489433

Dever, Maryanne (2017). "Archives and New Modes of Feminist Research". *Australian Feminist Studies* 32(91–92): 1–4. https://doi.org/10.1080/08164649.2017.1357017

Diamond, Beverley (1990). "Aesthetics and Canadian Women's Music". Unpublished paper, Feminist Theory and Aesthetics Conference, Toronto, Ontario, October.

Dibben, Nicola (1999). "Representations of Femininity in Popular Music". *Popular Music* 18.3: 331–55. https://doi.org/10.1017/S0261143000008904

Dickinson, Kay (2001). "'Believe'? Digitalised Female Identity and Camp". *Popular Music* 20.3: 333–47. https://doi.org/10.1017/S0261143001001532

Doane, Mary Ann (1982). "Film and the Masquerade: Theorising the Female Spectator". *Screen* 23(3/4): 74–87. https://doi.org/10.1093/screen/23.3-4.74

Duguid, Michelle M., and Melissa C. Thomas-Hunt (2015). "Condoning Stereotyping? How Awareness of Stereotyping Prevalence Impacts Expression of Stereotypes". *Journal of Applied Psychology* 100.2: 343–59. https://doi.org/10.1037/a0037908

Eads, Sean Jackson (2015). "Voice of the Machine". *Senior Capstone Projects* 424. https://digitalwindow.vassar.edu/cgi/viewcontent.cgi?article=1423&context=senior_capstone https://digitalwindow.vassar.edu/senior_capstone/424 accessed 31/12/2020

Easlea, Darryl (2004). *Everybody Dance: Chic and the Politics of Disco.* London: Helter Skelter.

Eccles, J. S. (1987). "Gender Roles and Women's Achievement-related Decisions". *Psychology of Women Quarterly* 11.2: 135–72. https://doi.org/10.1111/j.1471-6402.1987.tb00781.x

Elliott, Elaine S., and Carol S. Dweck (1988). "Goals: An Approach to Motivation and Achievement". *Journal of Personality and Social Psychology* 54.1: 5–12. https://doi.org/10.1037/0022-3514.54.1.5

Empire, Kitty (2008). "Where are the Female Geeks?" *The Guardian Blogposts.* https://www.theguardian.com/music/musicblog/2008/apr/05/inthissundaysobserver (accessed 30 December 2020).

Engh, Barbara (1994). "Adorno and the Sirens: Tele:phonographic Bodies". In *Embodied Voices: Representing Female Vocality in Western Culture*, edited by Leslie C. Dunn and Nancy A. Jones, 120–35. Cambridge: Cambridge University Press.

Evans, Claire (2018). *Broad Band: The Untold Story of the Women who Made the Internet.* London: Portfolio.

Farrugia, Rebekah (2010). "'Let's Have at It!' Conversations with EDM Producers Kate Simko and DJ Denise". *Dancecult: Journal of Electronic Dance Music Culture* 1.2: 87–93. https://doi.org/10.12801/1947-5403.2010.01.02.06

Fikentscher, Kai (2000). *"You Better Work!" Underground Dance Music in New York City.* Hanover, NH: University Press of New England.

Finamore, Emma (2017). "How Women are Shaping a New UK Sound System Scene". https://i-d.vice.com/en_uk/article/8x8y5v/how-women-are-shaping-a-new-uk-sound-system-scene (accessed 10 June 2020).

Fine, Cordelia (2010). *Delusions of Gender: The Real Science behind Sex Differences.* London: Icon Books.

Finlayson, Angus (2011). "Lesbian Propaganda and Other Myths: Misogyny in Dance Music". *The Quietus*, 14 November. https://thequietus.com/articles/07384-dance-music-misogyny (accessed 24 November 2020).

Finnegan, Ruth (2007). *The Hidden Musicians: Music-making in an English Town.* Middletown, CT: Wesleyan University Press.

Fiske, John (1997). *Reading the Popular.* London: Routledge.

Fitzroy, Olga (2018). "Award-winning engineer Olga Fitzroy on why the biz should embrace shared parental leave to help close the gender pay gap". *MusicWeek*, 17 January. https://www.musicweek.com/opinion/read/award-winning-engineer-olga-fitzroy-on-why-the-biz-should-embrace-shared-parental-leave-to-help-close-the-gender-pay-gap/071144 (accessed 12 September 2019).

Fleeger, Jennifer (2014). *Mismatched Women: The Siren's Song through the Machine*. Oxford: Oxford University Press. https://doi.org/10.1093/acprof:oso/9780199936892.001.0001

Frith, Simon (1983). *Sound Effects: Youth, Leisure and the Politics of Rock'n'Roll*. London: Constable.

Frith, Simon (1988). *Music for Pleasure*. London: Polity.

Frith, Simon (2012). "The Place of the Producer in the Discourse of Rock". In *The Art of Record Production: An Introductory Reader for a New Academic Field*, edited by Simon Frith and Simon Zagorski-Thomas, 207–221. Farnham and Burlington, VT: Ashgate.

Frith, Simon, and Angela McRobbie (1978). "Rock and Sexuality". *Screen Education* 29: 3–19.

Frith, Simon, and Simon Zagorski-Thomas, eds. (2012). *The Art of Record Production: An Introductory Reader for a New Academic Field*. Farnham and Burlington, VT: Ashgate.

Gadir, Tami (2015). "Underground, Overrated: Gender Normativity in Dance Music and DJ Cultures". Paper presentation, KISMIF conference, Porto.

Gadir, Tami (2016). "Resistance or Reiteration? Rethinking Gender in DJ Cultures". *Contemporary Music Review* 35.1: 115–29. https://doi.org/10.1080/07494467.2016.1176767

Gaines, Donna (1992). *Teenage Wasteland: Suburbia's Dead End Kids*. New York: HarperPerennia.

Gaston-Bird, Leslie (2019). *Women in Audio*. New York: Routledge. https://doi.org/10.4324/9780429455940

Gavanas, Anna, and Rosa Reitsamer (2013). "DJ Technologies, Social Networks and Gendered Trajectories in European DJ Cultures". In *DJ Culture in the Mix: Power, Technology and Social Change in Electronic Dance Music*, edited by Bernardo Alexander Attias, Anna Gavanas, and Hillegonda C. Rietveld, 51–77. London: Bloomsbury.

Genet, Jean (1971). Introduction to *Soledad Brother: The Prison Letters of George Jackson*. Harmondsworth: Penguin.

Gilbert, Jeremy, and Ewan Pearson (1999). *Discographies: Dance Music, Culture and the Politics of Sound*. London and New York: Routledge.

Gillett, Charlie (1996). *The Sound of the City: The Rise of Rock'n'Roll*. London: Da Capo.

Goldin, Claudia, and Cecilia Rouse (2000). "Orchestrating Impartiality: The Impact of 'Blind' Auditions on Female Musicians". *American Economic Review* 90.4: 715–41. https://doi.org/10.1257/aer.90.4.715

Goodwin, Andrew (1992). "Rationalization and Democratization in the New Technologies of Popular Music". In *Popular Music and Communication*, edited by James Lull, 75–100. London: Sage.

Green, Lucy (1997). *Music, Gender, Education*. Cambridge: Cambridge University Press.

Grieg, Charlotte (1989). *Will You Still Love Me Tomorrow? Girl Groups from the 50s on...* London: Virago.

Hann, Michael (2020). "Black Box: How We Made Ride on Time". *The Guardian*, 16 June. https://www.theguardian.com/music/2020/jun/16/how-we-made-black-box-ride-on-time (accessed 16 December 2020).

Hanna, Eileen, and Carla Clunis Taylor (2017). "Smirnoff Launches the 'Equalizing Music' Initiative in an Effort to Double the Number of Women Headliners by 2020". https://www.multivu.com/players/English/8054251-smirnoff-equalizing-music-womens-day/ (accessed 2 February 2020).

Hansen, Kai Arne (2011). "Hardly That Kind of Girl?: On Female Representations in Mainstream Pop Videos". MA thesis, University of Oslo.
https://www.duo.uio.no/handle/10852/26969

Haraway, Donna (1991). *Simians, Cyborgs and Women: The Reinvention of Nature*. London: Free Association Books.

Harris, Keith (2020). "'Make sure this is not another false dawn': Keith Harris' Open Letter to the Music Industry". *MusicWeek*, 1 June. https://www.musicweek.com/management/read/make-sure-this-is-not-another-false-dawn-keith-harris-open-letter-to-the-music-industry/079952 (accessed 25 June 2020).

Harrison, Ann (2014). *Music: The Business. The Essential Guide to the Law and the Deals*. London: Random House.

Harrison, Scott (2015). "Boys on the Outer: Themes in Male Engagement with Music". *Journal of Boyhood Studies* 4.1: 39–53.

Harvith, John, and Susan Edwards Harvith (1987). *Edison, Musicians, and the Phonograph: A Century in Retrospect*. Connecticut: Greenwood Press.

Hawkins, Stan (2004). "On Performativity and Production in Madonna's 'Music'". In *Music, Space and Place: Popular Music and Cultural Identity*, edited by Sheila Whiteley, Andy Bennett, and Stan Hawkins, 180–90. Farnham and Burlington, VT: Ashgate.

Hawkins, Stan (2013). "Aesthetics and Hyperembodiment in Pop Video: Rihanna's 'Umbrella'". In *Oxford Handbook of New Audiovisual Aesthetics*, edited by Claudia Gorbmann, Carol Vernalis, and John Richardson, 466–82. Oxford: Oxford University Press. https://doi.org/10.1093/oxfordhb/9780199733866.013.002

Hawkins, Stan, ed. (2019). *The Bloomsbury Handbook of Popular Music Video Analysis*. London: Bloomsbury.

Heawood, Sophie (2015). "If Bjork can't stop a man from stealing the limelight, what hope is there for the rest of us?" *The Guardian Weekend*, 31 January: 5.

Hinkle-Turner, Elizabeth (2006). *Women Composers and Music Technology in the United States: Crossing the Line*. Aldershot and Burlington, VT: Ashgate.

Hollows, Joanne (2000). *Feminism, Femininity and Popular Culture*. Manchester and New York: Manchester University Press.

hooks, bell (1994). *Outlaw Culture: Resisting Representations*. London and New York: Routledge.

Hooper, Emma (2020). "The Gatekeeper Gap: Searching for Solutions to the UK's Ongoing Imbalance in Music Creation". In *Towards Gender Equality in the Music Industry: Education, Practice and Strategies for Change*, edited by Catherine Strong and Sarah Raine, 131–44. London and New York: Bloomsbury.

Hopkins, Emma, and Pauwke Berkers (2020). "Engineering a Place for Women: Gendered Experiences of the Music Technology Classroom". In *Towards Gender Equality in the Music Industry: Education, Practice and Strategies for Change*, edited by Catherine Strong and Sarah Raine, 45–58. London and New York: Bloomsbury.

Inglis, Ian (2003). "'Some Kind of Wonderful': The Creative Legacy of the Brill Building". *American Music* 21.2 (Summer): 214–35. https://doi.org/10.2307/3250565

Jarman-Ivens, Freya, ed. (2007). *Oh Boy! Masculinities and Popular Music*. London and New York: Routledge.

Jung, Carl Gustav (1945). "The Relations between the Ego and the Unconscious", trans R. F. C. Hull. In *Collected Works*, vol. VII. Eds. H. Read, M. Fordham and G. Adler (1953). London: Routledge.

Kahn, Douglas (1999). *Noise, Water, Meat: A History of Sound in the Arts*. Cambridge, MA and London: MIT. https://doi.org/10.7551/mitpress/5030.001.0001

Kaplan, E. Ann (1990). *Rocking Around the Clock: Music, Television, Postmodernism and Consumer Culture*. London and New York: Routledge.

Kariv, Daphna (2013). *Female Entrepreneurship and the New Venture Creation: An International Overview*. New York: Routledge. https://doi.org/10.4324/9780203140987

Katz, Mark (2010). *Capturing Sound: How Technology has Changed Music*. Berkeley and London: University of California Press. https://doi.org/10.1525/9780520947351

Keightley, Keir (1996). "'Turn it Down!' She Shrieked: Gender, Domestic Space, and High Fidelity, 1948–59". *Popular Music* 15.2: 149–77. http://www.jstor.org/stable/931216 (accessed 8 July 2014). https://doi.org/10.1017/S0261143000008096

Kruse, Holly (2002). "Abandoning the Absolute: Transcendence and Gender in Popular Music Discourse". In *Pop Music and the Press*, edited by Steve Jones, 134–55. Philadelphia: Temple University Press.

Laing, Dave (1969). *The Sound of Our Time*. London: Sheed and Ward.

Laing, Dave (1999). "The Economic Importance of Music in Education". http://www.icce.rug.nl/~soundscapes/DATABASES/MIE/Part1_chapter06.shtml (accessed 26 January 2020).

Lawrence, Tim (2015). "How Loleatta Holloway Became Disco's Most Sampled Artist". http://www.electronicbeats.net/how-loleatta-holloway-became-discos-most-sampled-artist/ (accessed 24 November 2020).

Leonard, Marian (2007). *Gender in the Music Industry*. Farnham: Ashgate.

Leonard, Marian (2016). "Girls at Work: Gendered Identities, Sex Segregation and Employment Experiences in the Music Industries". In *Voicing Girlhood in Popular Music: Performance, Authority, Authenticity*, edited by Jacqueline Warwick and Allison Adrian, 37–55. New York: Routledge.

Lewis, Lisa A. (1990). *Gender Politics and MTV: Voicing the Difference*. Philadelphia: Temple University Press.

Liddington, Jill, and Jill Norris (1978). *One Hand Tied Behind Us*. London: Virago.

Lieb, Kristin J. (2013). *Gender, Branding, and the Modern Music Industry*. New York and London: Routledge. https://doi.org/10.4324/9780203071786

Lock, F. P. (1976). "Astraea's 'Vacant Throne': The Successors of Aphra Behn". In *Woman in the 18th Century and Other Essays*, edited by Paul Fritz and Richard Everett Morton, 25–26. Toronto and Sarasota: Hakkert.

Lorde, Audre (2018). *The Master's Tools Will Never Dismantle the Master's House*. London: Penguin Classics.

Love, Darlene (2013). *My Name is Love*. New York: William Morrow.

Lown, Judy (1990). *Women and Industrialization: Gender at Work in Nineteenth-century England*. Cambridge: Polity.
Loza, Susana (2001). "Sampling (Hetero)sexuality: Diva-ness and Discipline in Electronic Dance Music". *Popular Music* 20.3: 349–57. http://www.jstor.org/stable/853626. https://doi.org/10.1017/S0261143001001544
Lull, James, ed. (1992). *Popular Music and Communication*. London: Sage.
Madonna (1992). *Sex*. New York: Warner Books.
"Madonna's Secret to Making Music" (2000). Blog post. http://web.archive.org/web/20130618234026/http://transcripts.cnn.com/2000/SHOWBIZ/Music/11/10/wb.madonna.album/index.html (accessed 5 June 2020).
Malik, Nesrine (2019). *We Need New Stories: Challenging the Toxic Myths behind our Age of Discontent*. London: Weidenfeld & Nicholson.
Marsh, Charity (2018). "'When She Plays We Hear the Revolution': Girls Rock Regina – A Feminist Intervention". *IASPM Journal* 8.1: 88–102. https://iaspmjournal.net/index.php/IASPM_Journal/article/view/890 (accessed 23 September 2019).
Massey, Doreen (1994). *Space, Place and Gender*. Cambridge: Polity.
Massey, Howard (2000). *Behind the Glass: Top Record Producers Tell How They Craft the Hits*. London: Backbeat.
Massey, Howard (2009). *Behind the Glass II: Top Record Producers Tell How They Craft the Hits*. London: Backbeat.
Massy, Sylvia (2016). *Recording Unhinged: Creative and Unconventional Recording Techniques*. Milwaukee: Hal Leonard Books.
Mayhew, Emma (2004). "Positioning the Producer: Gender Divisions in Creative Labour and Value". In *Music, Space and Place: Popular Music and Cultural Identity*, edited by Sheila Whiteley, Andy Bennett and Stan Hawkins, 149–62. Farnham and Burlington, VT: Ashgate.
McClary, Susan (1989–90). "This Is Not a Story My People Tell: Musical Time and Space According to Laurie Anderson". *Discourse* 12.1: 104–128. https://www.jstor.org/stable/41389143
McClary, Susan (2002). *Feminine Endings: Music, Gender and Sexuality*. Minneapolis: University of Minnesota Press.
McKeage, Kathleen (2004). "Gender and Participation in High School and College Instrumental Jazz Ensembles". *Journal of Research in Music Education* 52.4: 343–56. https://doi.org/10.2307/3345387
McRobbie, Angela (1990). "Settling Accounts with Subcultures: A Feminist Critique". In *On Record: Rock, Pop and the Written Word*, edited by Simon Frith and Andrew Goodwin, 66–80. London and New York: Routledge.
McRobbie, Angela (1992). "Post Marxism and Cultural Studies: A Postscript". In *Cultural Studies*, edited by Lawrence Grossberg, Cary Nelson, and Paula Treichler, 719–30. London and New York: Routledge.
McRobbie, Angela (1993). "Shut Up and Dance: Youth Culture and Changing Modes of Femininity". *Cultural Studies* 7.3: 406–426. https://www.tandfonline.com/doi/abs/10.1080/09502389300490281 (accessed 14 January 2021).
McRobbie, Angela (2000). *Feminism and Youth Culture*. Basingstoke and London: Macmillan.

McRobbie, Angela, and Simon Frith (1978). "Rock and Sexuality". *Screen Education* 29: 3–19.

Middleton, Richard (2006). *Voicing the Popular: On the Subjects of Popular Music*. New York and Abingdon: Routledge.

Milner, Greg (2009). *Perfecting Sound Forever: The Story of Recorded Music*. London: Granta.

Moore, Allan (2002). "Authenticity as Authentication". *Popular Music* 21.2: 209–223. https://doi.org/10.1017/S0261143002002131

Mulvey, Laura (1975). "Visual Pleasure and Narrative Cinema". *Screen* 16.3: 6–28. https://doi.org/10.1093/screen/16.3.6

Murphy, Gareth (2015). *Cowboys and Indies: The Epic History of the Record Industry*. London: Serpent's Tail.

MusicTech (2018). "Mandy Parnell Interview – A Master of the Industry". 19 January. http://www.musictech.net/2018/01/mandy-parnell-interview/ (accessed 5 July 2018).

Negus, Keith (1999). *Producing Pop: Culture and Conflict in the Popular Music Industry*. London: Arnold.

Nehring, Neil (1997). *Popular Music and Postmodernism: Anger is an Energy*. Thousand Oaks, CA: Sage. https://doi.org/10.4135/9781483345475

Newman, Melinda (2018). "Where Are All the Female Producers?" *Billboard*, 19 January. https://www.billboard.com/articles/business/8095107/female-music-producers-industry-grammy-awards?utm_source=twitter&utm_source=t.co&utm_medium=referral (accessed 30 June 2018).

Nicholson, Rebecca (2015). "Chvrches: 'We could have sold 200,000 more records if we hid us boys out of view'". *The Guardian*, 20 August. http://www.theguardian.com/music/2015/aug/20/chvrches-we-could-have-sold-200000-more-records-if-we-hid-the-boys-out-of-view (accessed 3 January 2016).

O'Brien, Lucy (2012). *She-Bop: The Definitive History of Women in Rock, Pop and Soul*. London: Penguin [1995].

Odintz, Andrea (1997). "Technophilia". In *The Rolling Stone Book of Women in Rock*, edited by Barbara O'Dair, 211–17. New York: Random House.

Paglia, Camille (1992). *Sex, Art and American Culture: Essays*. New York: Vintage.

Palmer, Lisa Amanda (2011). "'Men Cry Too': Black Masculinities and the Feminisation of Lovers Rock in the UK". In *Black Popular Music in Britain since 1945*, edited by Jon Stratton and Nabeel Zuberi, 115–30. London and New York: Routledge.

Parker, Roszika, and Griselda Pollock (1991). *Old Mistresses: Women, Art and Ideology*. London: Pandora.

Pegley, Karen, and Virginia Caputo (1994). "Growing Up Female(s): Retrospective Thoughts on Musical Preferences and Meanings". In *Queering the Pitch: The New Gay and Lesbian Musicology*, edited by Philip Brett, Elizabeth Wood, and Gary C. Thomas, 297–313. New York and London: Routledge.

Pellegrinelli, Lara (2008). "Separated at 'Birth': Singing and the History of Jazz". In *Big Ears: Listening for Gender in Jazz Studies*, edited by Nichole T. Rustin and Sherrie Tucker, 31–47. Durham, NC and London: Duke University Press. https://doi.org/10.1215/9780822389224-003

Phillips, Anne, and Barbara Taylor (1980). "Sex and Skill: Notes towards a Feminist Economics". *Feminist Review* 6.1: 79–88. https://doi.org/10.1057/fr.1980.20

Pini, Maria (1997). "Women and the Early British Rave Scene". In *Back to Reality: Social Experience and Cultural Studies*, edited by Angela McRobbie, 152–69. Manchester: Manchester University Press.

Plant, Sadie (1998). *Zeros and Ones: Digital Women and the New Technoculture*. London: Fourth Estate.

Porcello, Thomas (2004). "Speaking of Sound: Language and the Professionalization of Sound-Recording Engineers". *Social Studies of Science* 34.5: 733–58. http://www.sagepub.com. https://doi.org/10.1177/0306312704047328

Potter, Sally (1997). "On Shows". In *Framing Feminism: Art and the Women's Movement 1970–1985*, edited by Roszika Parker and Griselda Pollock. London: Pandora.

Raphael, Amy (2019). *A Seat at the Table: Interviews with Women on the Frontline of Music*. London: Virago.

Reality Check Team (2018). "Festivals 2018: The Gender Gap in Music Festival Line-ups". *BBC News*, 3 July. https://www.bbc.co.uk/news/entertainment-arts-44655719 (accessed 3 June 2020).

Reddington, Helen (2012). *The Lost Women of Rock Music: Female Musicians of the Punk Era*. London: Equinox.

Reddington, Helen (2016). "Recorded Music". In *Music Entrepreneurship*, edited by Allan Dumbreck and Gayle McPherson, 141–62. London: Bloomsbury.

Reddington, Helen (2018). "Gender Ventriloquism in Studio Production". *IASPM Journal* 8.1: 59–73. https://iaspmjournal.net/index.php/IASPM_Journal/article/view/884

Reitsamer, Rosa (2019). "Alternative Histories and Counter-Memories: Feminist Music Archives in Europe". In *Preserving Popular Music Heritage: Do-it-Yourself, Do-it-Together*, edited by Sarah Baker, 91–103. London: Routledge.

Reynolds, Simon (1998). *Energy Flash: A Journey through Rave Music and Dance Culture*. New York: Pan Macmillan.

Roberts, Robin (1996). *Ladies First: Women in Music Videos*. Jackson, MI: University Press of Mississippi.

Rodgers, Tara (2010). *Pink Noises: Women on Electronic Music and Sound*. Durham, NC and London: Duke University Press. https://doi.org/10.1215/9780822394150

Rose, Tricia (2008). *The Hip Hop Wars: What We Talk about When We Talk about Hip Hop – and Why It Matters*. New York: Basic Books.

Rustin, Nichole T., and Sherrie Tucker, eds. (2008). *Big Ears: Listening for Gender in Jazz Studies*. Durham, NC and London: Duke University Press. https://doi.org/10.1215/9780822389224

Saidin, Khaliza, and Aizan Yaacob (2016). "Insider Researchers: Challenges and Opportunities International Seminar on Generating Knowledge through Research", UUM-UMSIDA, 25–27 October 2016, Universiti Utara Malaysia, Malaysia. http://ojs.umsida.ac.id/index.php/icecrs (accessed 4 December 2020).

Sandstrom, Boden (2000). "Women Mix Engineers". In *Music and Gender*, edited by Pirkko Moisala and Beverley Diamond, 289–305. Urbana and Chicago: University of Illinois Press.

Savage, Mark (2012). "Why are Female Record Producers So Rare?" https://www.bbc.co.uk/news/entertainment-arts-19284058 (accessed 30 December 2020).

Schmidt Horning, Susan (2013). *Chasing Sound: Technology, Culture and the Art of Studio Recording from Edison to the LP*. Baltimore: Johns Hopkins University Press.

Schmutz, Vaughn, and Alison Faupel (2010). "Gender and Cultural Consecration in Popular Music". *Social Forces* 89.2: 685–707. https://doi.org/10.1353/sof.2010.0098

Seabrook, J. (2016). *The Song Machine: How to Make a Hit*. New York: Jonathan Cape.

Sharpley-Whiting, T. Denean (2007). *Pimps Up, Ho's Down: Hip Hop's Hold on Young Black Women*. New York: New York University Press.

Shepherd, John (1991). *Music as Social Text*. London: Polity.

Shetterly, Margot (2017). *Hidden Figures: The Untold Story of the African American Women Who Helped to Win the Space Race*. London and New York: HarperCollins.

Sillitoe, Sue (1999). "Recording Cher's 'Believe'". *Sound on Sound*, February. http://www.soundonsound.com/sos/feb99/articles/tracks661.htm (accessed 19 March 2015).

Smith, Stacy L., Marc Choueti, and Katherine Pieper (2018). "Inclusion in the Recording Studio? Gender and Race/Ethnicity of Artists, Songwriters and Producers across 700 Popular Songs from 2012–2018". http://assets.uscannenberg.org/docs/aii-inclusion-recording-studio-2019.pdf (accessed 10 September 2019).

Spender, Dale (1990). *Man Made Language*. London: Pandora.

Spring, Alexandra (2015). "Listen Again: Gender Twist Reveals the Dark Side of Some Top Hits". *The Guardian*, 15 April: 17.

Stallybrass, Peter, and Allon White (1986). *The Politics and Poetics of Transgression*. New York: Cornell University Press.

Steward, Sue, and Sheryl Garratt (1984). *Signed, Sealed and Delivered: True Life Stories of Women in Pop*. London: Pluto.

Stewart, Catriona (2015). "Engineering a Girls only Course at Glasgow College". *Glasgow Times*, 3 September. http://www.eveningtimes.co.uk/news/13644875.Engineering_a_girls_only_course_at_Glasgow_College/ (accessed 3 June 2020).

Stras, Laurie, ed. (2010). *She's So Fine: Reflections on Whiteness, Femininity, Adolescence and Class in 1960s Music*. Farnham: Ashgate.

Stratton, Jon (2014). *When Music Migrates: Crossing British and European Racial Faultlines 1945–2010*. Farnham and Burlington, VT: Ashgate.

Tallon, Tina (2020). "A Century of 'Shrill': How Bias in Technology Has Hurt Women's Voices". *The New Yorker*, 3 September. https://www.newyorker.com/culture/cultural-comment/a-century-of-shrill-how-bias-in-technology-has-hurt-womens-voices (accessed 26 January 2020).

Tannenbaum, Rob, and Craig Marks (2012). *I Want My MTV: The Uncensored Story of the Music Video Revolution*. New York: Plume Books.

Tavana, Art (2015). "Democracy of Sound: Is Garageband Good for Music?" *Pitchfork*, 30 September. http://pitchfork.com/features/articles/9728-democracy-of-sound-is-garageband-good-for-music/ (accessed 31 January 2016).

Teichman, Eric (2018). "Something's Missing from My Jazz Band's Bulletin Board: An Autoethnographic Reflection on Making Space for Girls and Women in Jazz Education". *Canadian Music Educator* 59.4. https://www.questia.com/magazine/1P4-2135486790/something-s-missing-from-my-jazz-band-s-bulletin-board

Théberge, Paul (1989). "The 'Sound' of Music: Technological Rationalization and the Production of Popular Music". *New Formations* 8: 99–111.

Théberge, Paul (1997). *Any Sound You Can Imagine: Making Music/Consuming Technology*. Hanover, NH: Wesleyan University Press.

Thornton, Sarah (1995). *Music, Media and Subcultural Capital*. Cambridge: Polity.

Tomaz de Carvalho, Alice (2012). "The Discourse of Home Recording: Authority of 'Pros' and the Sovereignty of the Big Studios". *Journal on the Art of Record Production* 7. https://www.arpjournal.com/asarpwp/the-discourse-of-home-recording-authority-of-"pros"-and-the-sovereignty-of-the-big-studios/ (accessed 2 April 2020).

Toop, David (2005). "Sound Body: The Ghost of a Program". *Leonardo Music Journal* 15 (December): 28–35.

Toynbee, J. 2000. *Making Popular Music: Musicians, Creativity and Institutions*. London: Hodder Arnold.

Turkle, Sherry (1988). "Computational Reticence: Why Women Fear the Intimate Machine". In *Technology and Women's Voices: Keeping in Touch*, edited by Cheris Kramarae, 33–49. New York: Routledge.

Turkle, Sherry (2000). *The Second Self: Computers and the Human Spirit*. Cambridge, MA and London: The MIT Press.

Upton, George (1880). *Woman in Music*. Boston: Jr. Osgood.

Vernallis, Carol (2004). *Experiencing Music Video: Aesthetics and Cultural Context*. New York and Chichester: Columbia University Press.

Wajcman, Judy (1991). *Feminism Confronts Technology*. London: Polity.

Walkerdine, Valerie (2004). *Counting Girls Out: Girls and Mathematics*. London: Routledge.

Walser, Robert (1993). *Running with the Devil: Power, Gender and Madness in Heavy Metal Music*. Middletown, CT: Wesleyan University Press.

Walser, Robert (2000). "Forging Masculinity: Heavy Metal Sounds and Images of Gender". In *Sound and Vision: The Music Video Reader*, edited by Simon Frith, Andrew Goodwin, and Lawrence Grossberg, 153–83. London: Routledge.

Ward, Alison (2001). "Why Men Twiddle Knobs and Women Don't". Unpublished undergraduate thesis, University of Westminster.

Warwick, Jacqueline (2004). "'He's Got the Power': The Politics of Production in Girl Group Music". In *Music, Space and Place: Popular Music and Cultural Identity*, edited by Sheila Whiteley, Andy Bennett, and Stan Hawkins, 191–200. Farnham and Burlington, VT: Ashgate.

Waterman, Pete (2000). *I Wish I Was Me*. London: Virgin.

Weale, Sally, and Caelainn Barr (2018). "Female Scientists Urge Research Grants Reform to Tackle Gender Bias". *The Guardian*, 10 August. https://www.theguardian.com/education/2018/aug/10/female-scientists-urge-research-grants-reform-tackle-gender-bias (accessed 12 August 2018).

White, Hannah (2019). "'If I were a boy...' Gender Inequality in the Music Industry". https://www.bellesandgals.com/2019/11/01/if-i-were-a-boy-gender-inequality-in-the-music-industry/ (accessed 11 December 2019).

Whiteley, Sheila (2000). *Women and Popular Music: Sexuality, Identity and Subjectivity*. London and New York: Routledge.

Whiteley, Sheila, ed. (1997). *Sexing the Groove: Popular Music and Gender*. New York: Routledge.

Whiteley, Sheila, Andy Bennett, and Stan Hawkins, eds. (2004). *Music, Space and Place: Popular Music and Cultural Identity*. Farnham and Burlington, VT: Ashgate.

Williams, Alan (2012). "'I'm not hearing what you're hearing': The Conflict and Connection of Headphone Mixes and Multiple Audioscapes". In *The Art of Record Production: An Introductory Reader for a New Academic Field*, edited by Simon Frith and Simon Zagorski-Thomas, 113–28. Farnham and Burlington, VT: Ashgate.

Wilson, Elizabeth (2000). *Bohemians: The Glamorous Outcasts*. London: I.B. Tauris.

Wolfe, Paula (2012). "A Studio of One's Own: Music Production, Technology and Gender". *Journal on the Art of Record Production 7*.

Wolfe, Paula (2016). "'I write the songs. He's the eye candy': The Female Singer-Songwriter, the Woman Artist-Producers and the British Broadsheet Press". In *The Singer-Songwriter in Europe: Politics, Paradigms and Place*, edited by Isabelle Marc and Stuart Green, 95–109. London and New York: Routledge.

Wolfe, Paula (2019). *Women in the Studio*. London: Routledge. https://doi.org/10.4324/9781315546711

Women's Engineering Society (n.d.). http://www.wes.org.uk/statistics (accessed 17 March 2015).

Women's Liberation Music Archive (n.d.). https://womensliberationmusicarchive.co.uk/ (accessed 5 June 2020).

Zak, Albin (2012). "No-Fi: Crafting a Language of Recorded Music in 1950s Pop". In *The Art of Record Production: An Introductory Reader for a New Academic Field*, edited by Simon Frith and Simon Zagorski-Thomas, 43–55. Farnham and Burlington, VT: Ashgate.

Documentaries

The Joy of Disco. BBC 4 TV. Broadcast 27 September 2015. http://www.bbc.co.uk/programmes/b01cqt72 (accessed 12 August 2018) (currently unavailable).

Play Your Gender. Director: Stephanie Clattenburg. Nava Projects. https://www.youtube.com/watch?v=dH-Kjt8g9ow (accessed 24 September 2019).

Producer Biographies

Adrienne Aitken has worked predominantly in advertising, although she also had a hit with the song 'Wassup' in 1992. At the time of her interview she was a member of the Music Producer's Guild and also worked in higher education as a music technology lecturer. She is now a scriptwriter, developing ideas for features and crime drama series.

Dot Allen trained with London's Community Music organization and taught Music Technology at the Elizabeth Garratt Anderson School in Islington, London, while working as a session keyboard player for Lee Perry, amongst others. She now works at Edinburgh College teaching music production skills and plays in a blues band.

Helen Atkinson was studio manager and engineer at RAK studios in London at the time of the interview. She has since had a baby, and was working freelance as a live iTunes mix engineer for the *X Factor* TV programme. Engineering credits include Laura Marling, Rod Stewart, Editors and many more.

Laura B became a live sound engineer after serving an informal apprenticeship on tour with the Clash. Originally from France, she became a sound engineer in London working with Roger Waters and other high-profile artists. From there, she became a solo electronic dance music producer. She is currently working on a novel multi-speaker art form, teaching mixing on Ableton Live, and mixing/remixing artists, one of whom has been Grammy nominated.

Janet Beat studied music at Birmingham University in the 1960s where she studied composition with Alexander Goehr, and on graduating became a freelance French horn player. She had started experimenting with electronic music in the late 1950s, and established the electronic and recording studios at the Royal Conservatoire of Music in Glasgow (formerly RSAMD) while lecturing there between 1972 and 1996. Since then she has lectured at Glasgow University, and she was musical director at Soundstrata between 1989 and 1993. In 2019 she was given a Lifetime Achievement Award from Scottish Women Inventing Music.

Samantha Bennett holds audio and music technology degrees at Master's and PhD level. She worked as a recording engineer in numerous recording studios across London between 1998 and 2006, is a former director of the UK's Music Producer's Guild and an active member of the Audio Engineering Society. She is currently convenor of Music Technology at the Australian National University, where she recently refurbished the School of Music's recording facilities.

Isobel Campbell was a founder member of Glasgow band Belle and Sebastian. After that she released material as The Gentle Waves. Later, she produced the singer Mark Lanegan and they collaborated regularly between 2007 and 2013; their album *Ballad of the Broken Seas* was nominated for the Mercury Prize in 2006. She released a solo album, *There Is No Other*, in February 2020. https://isobelcampbell.com

Cathy Cuvelier was brought up in Marseilles and moved to London to become part of London's reggae scene, as well as spending time in Jamaica. She became a live sound engineer, working with artists such as Sugar Minott, before opening her own analogue reggae studio in east London. She also worked as a sound technician on the 2015 documentary, *Abandoned Adopted Here*.

Lauren Deakin Davies started out with her own studio at the age of 17 in 2012, and by the age of 18 she had achieved her first BBC Radio 2 play. A pop/indie record producer and songwriter, she recently won the European Pro Sound awards for Breakthrough Studio Engineer as well as (for the second year in a row) NMG's Producer of the Year award in 2017 and 2018. She has worked with artists as diverse as Laura Marling and Black Box. http://www.laurendeakindavies.com

Debbie Dickinson was a live sound engineer for jazz and 'World Music' bands before teaching music production at City University, London. Live sound engineering credits include touring with the jazz artist Jack DeJohnette. She was extremely active in furthering the careers of women in the live jazz world, and was adept at setting up collaborative partnerships between live music organizations. She died in 2019.

Chantal Epp started her music production career at University where she found a unique opportunity to combine her degree and her hobby of cheerleading to start a company making music for cheerleading and dance. She now caters for Team Netherlands, Team Jamaica, Team Canada and many more national teams attending Cheerleading Worlds competitions.

Olga Fitzroy is a recording and mix engineer. Her credits include Coldplay, Daughter, The Foo Fighters, and Muse. She has also recorded film scores by Hans Zimmerman and, more recently, the score of the Tim Burton/Christian De Vita film *Yellow Bird*. She has become a prominent campaigner for freelance women's parenthood rights. http://www.olgafitzroy.com

Isabel Gracefield Grundy studied a BA in Commercial Music at the University of Westminster, before internships in various small but influential recording studios in London led to a job as an engineer at RAK studios, where she has worked with artists such as Adele, Noisettes, Emeli Sandé and many more. She is based at RAK studios in London.

Saran Headman was working mainly in education as a production and engineer trainer at the time of her interview.

Terrie Harris co-founded Little London Studios in Hastings with her husband in the late 1990s. There, she engineered and recorded with, amongst others, the late Poly Styrene of X-Ray Spex. From 2005, she worked as a live sound engineer at Glastonbury Festival, working for artists such as Pete Docherty and Joss Stone. She has also worked at Guilfest and Trowbridge Festivals, and currently co-hosts a radio show, Little London Live.

Katia Isakoff has worked as a sound engineer and producer since the 1990s. She continues to experiment with electronic music, predominantly with other female artists in the field. She was a founder member of Women Produce Music and currently lives between London and Berlin, working on an experimental composer/producer music project called !N_K o L//\\B. https://www.katiaisakoff.com

Laura Leitch studied at the University of the West of Scotland. She has engineered recordings by her tutor's band the Pearlfishers and now works in live sound.

Felix Mackintosh was originally a bass player before 'inheriting' a Portastudio from a member of her now-defunct band. After working at Lewisham Academy of Music and Ovatones as a sound engineer, she moved into advertising. She now owns and runs her own studio where she works as a producer and re-mixer on predominantly dance music and electronica.

Masol (Marie-Solange Ndeley) is a multi-disciplinary music and mixtape producer who works in community settings, inspiring young people to become empowered through music technology skills development. https://masolartistry.net/

Ms Melody was one of London's original grime music producers, moving from 'girl band' to producer status. After running her own studio, she has now invested in premises to set up a production management business in south London.

Colleen Murphy moved from New York to London in 1999. Originally working in music radio, she has since become a DJ, setting up the pioneering company https://classicalbumsundays.com which specialises in vinyl listening events on high-end speakers. She also has worked as a producer and remixer and is a regular radio broadcaster.

'Natalie' is the pseudonym for a producer who lives and works in the north east of England. She did an apprenticeship in a large analogue studio before becoming independent, and now works from a studio in her home.

Mandy Parnell is one of Britain's most respected dance music mastering engineers, although she has also worked with artists such as Roisin Murphy. Björk is one of her most well-known clients. She founded Black Saloon Studios after 24 years of working as a sound engineer, and has won many awards and accolades. http://www.blacksaloonstudios.com

Jacqueline Pelham-Leigh (JPL) is an R'n'B producer who has worked with Alexandra Burke alongside male artists in the genre. She now mostly works as an executive producer.

Susan Rogers began her professional life as a sound equipment maintenance technician in California. She later moved to Minneapolis and became Prince's sound recording engineer between 1983 and 1987, working on all his major albums including *Purple Rain*. She is now primarily an academic, after gaining a doctorate in psychoacoustics and music cognition in 2012 from McGill University.

Eleonora Romano moved to London from Sicily in the 1980s to work in the music industry. She became a live sound engineer, originally at the Hope and Anchor, before moving to the (now defunct) venue The Astoria. She now tours with acts such as Yann Tiersen, doing live sound for him.

Rasha Shaheen embarked on a degree in creative music technology to make sure she had control over her sound as an artist. She mainly produces her own work; however, she has travelled on European tours as a sound engineer and has gone full circle in teaching music technology. Currently Rasha is the deputy principal of a music college in Brighton that explores the sustainability of creative people within the creative industries. http://www.rasha.co.uk

Sandie Shaw won the Eurovision Song Contest for the UK with 'Puppet on a String' in 1967. This was the first British entry to the competition. Unusually for a woman of her era, she was the producer behind her own songs. She had a string of hits in the 1960s, and has guested with various artists since then including The Pretenders and The Smiths, with whom she had a hit record. In 2017 she was awarded an MBE for services to music.

Yvonne Shelton has been involved in the production of many singles. She is currently principal vocalist for the Hacienda Classical albums, and tours, in various capacities. This multi-talented artist and entrepreneur runs and directs choirs, groups and has been involved in BBC productions for Music Live 1999 in Glasgow, co-ordinating artists such as Chaka Khan, the James Taylor quartet, Ce Ce Winans, and Deniece Williams' show on BBC Radio 2. She has also done a stint as a singer in American musical *I Have a Dream*, and local plays *Chaos By Design* and *The Windrush Series* for BBC Radio 4, the World Service. Artists such as Celine Dion and Gloria Estefan are on the roster of singers she has backed.

Sally Smith worked at Rooster Studios, north London, in the early 1980s as an assistant engineer. One of her early clients was Billy Bragg, at the start of his career. She later worked at Triple XXX studios in Harlesden, and as a live sound engineer for Helen and the Horns and other bands. She is now a primary school teacher and cello player.

Karina Townsend is an electronic and experimental music maker who took over and ran the music technology vocational course at the City Lit in London. After the course closed, she became a studio technician at the University of East London, while continuing to make music of her own.

Alison Ward became a web designer after her degree in Commercial Music at the University of Westminster. She returned to sound engineering and became the in-house live engineer for the respected London jazz venue, The Vortex, where she makes live recordings of the concerts.

Tina Weymouth was the bass player in Talking Heads and, later, Tom Tom Club. Both bands were inspirational for female bass players in punk music. She was a co-producer/engineer and worked with Black Grape on their album *Yes Please!* in 1992. At the time of the interview, she was on tour with Tom Tom Club, who had a female sound engineer with them on the tour.

Gemma Whitfield studied Music Technology and Production at the University of East London. She is now an electronic music producer in the Midlands.

Estimated breakdown of ages of interviewees at time of interview (culled from music genres/artists worked with):
5: 60+
11: 50–60
11: 40–50
4: 30–40
4: 20–30

Index

Abbey Road studios 1, 29, 46, 69
Adichie, Chimamanda Ngozi Adichie 17–18
advantage, gender 83–4
advertising (music) 70
AES (Audio Engineering Society) 161, 182
AIM (Association of Independent Music) 8, 103, 159
AIR studios 40, 46, 178
Aitken, Adrienne 15, 21–2, 45, 83, 109, 164, 207
Albini, Steve 53, 112
Allen, Dot 14, 57, 164, 207
Anderson, Laurie 143
Arab, Leila 92, 145–6, 157
Armstrong, Victoria 13, 57, 168
Art of Record Production, The (publication/conference) 1, 4, 102, 112, 194
Askar, Paris 104–5, 109, 112
Atkinson, Helen 14–15, 32, 51, 60, 69, 84, 115, 164, 173, 176, 178, 207
auteur producers 1, 5, 8, 10, 99, 102, 117, 121–3

B, Laura 14–15, 27–8, 34, 37, 41, 78–81, 84, 110, 184, 207
Bamz 93, 176
Bayton, Mavis 20, 23, 105, 113, 167, 184
Beat, Janet 9, 14–15, 20–2, 37, 56, 75, 78, 101, 172, 207
Belle and Sebastian 30, 43, 136, 208
Bennett, Joe 130
Bennett, Samantha 23, 45, 178, 208
Beyoncé 114, 120, 122, 130, 133, 148, 157, 188
bias, gender 3, 15, 83, 97, 119, 170, 179, 192–3
Bishi 93
Björk 6, 91–2, 112, 144–6, 157, 188, 210
Black Box 126, 208
Blauel, Renata 2
Bradby, Barbara 122, 125–6, 128, 133–4
Brown, Jennifer 68, 184
bullying 11, 74–7, 82, 89, 159
Bush, Kate 6, 116
Butler, Judith 9, 123

calmness 79

Campbell, Isobel 14, 30, 37, 43, 136, 174, 187, 208
Cava studios 43
cheer music 9, 15, 36–7, 68
Cher 128–9, 143
Chick, Stevie 136–7
Church, Charlotte 158
Classic Album Sundays 30, 71
classical music 7, 100, 112
Coles, Maya Jane 108
Colossus studios 45
Community Music (organization) 57–8, 207
country music 64
credit on a musical work 126, 130, 133
    women not receiving 6, 83, 157, 188
Cuvelier, Cathy 15, 24, 33, 50, 52, 85, 178, 188, 208

Davies, Helen 12, 101, 132, 148
Davies, Lauren Deakin 15, 30, 36, 47, 64–5, 80, 82, 91, 113, 134, 139, 178, 186, 208
Dickinson, Debbie 35, 59, 208
disco (music genre) 142, 151
DJs 25, 62, 71, 81, 97, 102, 108, 141–54, 174, 177
Doane, Mary-Ann 124

EDM (electronic dance music genre) 16, 50, 140–61
electronic music 5, 12, 20, 32, 57, 61, 75–6, 92, 95–6, 108, 125, 140–45, 149, 150–6, 173–7, 184–5, 192
electro-acoustic music 96, 173
Elliot, Missy 6, 92, 97, 104, 106, 159, 192
Empire, Kitty 103, 108, 157
Epp, Chantal 9, 15, 32, 36–7, 68–9, 173, 185, 187, 208
Exchange studio, the 39–40, 78

female artists (musicians) 3, 7, 16, 64–5, 74, 81–3, 87, 90–2, 97, 102–13, 121, 124, 131–9, 146, 155–7, 163, 184–7
feminism 7, 11–12, 84, 92, 95, 98, 101, 105, 113, 120, 126, 136, 146, 151, 154–5, 162, 173, 176, 180, 183, 193
    second wave 124, 147

Index

Fitzroy, Olga 15, 90, 116, 138, 178, 182, 209

Garageband 6, 107
gender advantage 83–4
    bias 3, 15, 83, 97, 119, 170, 179, 192–3
    division 100–1
    essentialism 91, 99–100, 163
    ventriloquism 119–39
gendered labour 97–100
girl groups 113–14, 121–5, 128, 133, 187
Gospel music 9, 15, 25, 36, 56, 65
Gracefield Grundy, Isabel 15, 50–1, 65, 101, 103, 115, 178–9, 186, 209
Graeber, Maggie 30
Grieg, Charlotte 121–2, 125
grime (music/scene) 53, 63–4, 83–6, 187, 192, 210
Grimes (artist) 93, 107–8, 135, 159
Guest Stars, the 35, 47, 59
Guichard, Daniel 41–2

"Hannah" (pseudonym) 138, 182
Harris, Terrie 2, 15, 35, 66, 80, 165, 195, 187, 209
Hassell, Felicity 191
Headman, Saran 24, 117, 176, 209
hip hop 58, 84, 92–7, 127, 130, 176, 192
Holland 121–2
homosexuality 139, 142, 152

Isakoff, Katia 14, 26–27, 46, 61, 64, 91, 172, 209

jazz (music genre) 23, 25, 35, 47, 59, 112, 119, 124, 168, 172
journalists
    female 154, 192
    male 92, 96, 127, 130
JPL 15, 44, 63, 85, 137–8, 161, 164, 182, 187–8, 210

Kenyon, Carol 5
Keys, Alicia 6, 106, 157
King, Carole 122–3
King, Jonathan 123, 125

Labine, Joanie 141
Lady Sings It Better 135–6
Lanegan, Mark 136, 187
laptop production 1, 47, 56, 68, 106–7, 112, 115, 184–5
Lavigne, Avril 134
Leitch, Laura 15, 172, 209

Levi, Mica 93
Lilith Fair 77
Little London studios 66–7, 209
location sound 71–3
Lost Women of Rock Music, The 11, 102, 174
Love, Darlene 123, 137
Lumsden, Martin 47

Mackintosh, Felix 2, 14–15, 29, 49, 52, 79, 85, 178, 182, 209
Madonna 16, 34, 91, 122, 130–2, 146–8, 153, 188
Mayberry, Lauren 134
male artists (musicians) 87–8, 104, 112, 161
    ear 107, 135
    producers 6, 10, 16, 64, 87, 92, 98, 102, 104–5, 108, 115, 118, 121–41, 143, 153–4, 161, 188
    voices (vocals) *see* voices, men's (vocals)
Marling, Laura 158, 207, 208
Masol (Marie-Solange Ndeley) 25, 209
Mayfair studios 41–2
Melody, Ms 15, 52–3, 63–4, 83, 86, 90–1, 94, 187, 189, 210
miming 125–6
Minogue, Kylie 132–3
misogyny 11, 77, 84–111, 139, 152–5, 159
Mitchell, Joni 92, 106–7
mom-ism 97, 102
motherhood 115–17
Motown 5, 43–4, 135
MPG (Music Producers' Guild) 62, 83, 102, 158–9, 183, 190
Murphy, Colleen 15, 30, 71, 81, 142, 154, 210

"Natalie" (pseudonym) 29, 37, 76, 210
Nwachukwu, Tony 177

O'Brien, Lucy 102, 125, 174
Obsidian, Black 93
Oram, Daphne 32, 192
Ovatones studio 49, 85, 164, 209

Parnell, Mandy 14–15, 26–8, 37, 39, 41, 54, 78, 82, 86, 92, 109, 112, 114, 117, 145–6, 157, 160, 182–3, 191, 210
pop (music genre) 102, 112, 117–26, 131, 134–5, 138–40
Prince (artist) 10, 54, 186, 210
punk (music genre) 3, 5, 28, 31, 62, 66, 113, 174, 212

racism 11–12, 74, 76, 94, 189, 192

Raincoats, the (band) 105
RAK studios 32, 50–1, 60, 69, 164, 178, 186, 207, 209
rave (scene) 142, 150
Rayner, Alison 47
Ritchie, Beryl 191
rock (music genre) 7–11, 27–8, 50, 56, 58, 84, 90, 109–12, 124, 131, 133, 138, 154–7, 170
  journalism 154
Rodgers, Nile 124, 161
Rodgers, Tara 12, 95–6, 117, 149, 154
Rogers, Susan 10, 15, 53, 83, 87, 109, 137, 161, 210
Roman, Eleonora 14–15, 31, 48, 77, 210
Ronika 108
Rooster studios 42, 211
Rose, Nadia 93, 176

SAE institute 25, 39
self-production, female 1, 47, 56, 68, 106–7, 112, 115–16, 184–5
sexism 17, 74, 78–9, 83, 111–12, 152, 170–2, 177, 179
  internalized 74, 84, 92, 110–11, 170–1
sexual abuse 11, 67, 88, 102
  harassment 15, 74, 88, 112
sexuality 105, 121, 126, 133, 136–8, 142, 146, 155, 163
sexualization 87, 97, 141–2, 151, 155
Shaheen, Rasha 15, 72, 211
Shaw, Sandie 9, 106–7, 211
She-Bop 102, 125, 174
Shelton, Yvonne 15, 36, 65, 211
Sigsworth, Guy 131–2
Smith, Sally 34, 42, 211
Spector, Phil 5, 122–3, 128, 132, 135, 137
Spice Girls, the 146–8, 153
Stock, Aitken and Waterman 5, 53, 132–3
Stras, Laurie 122, 187
studios
  Abbey Road 1, 29, 46, 69
  AIR 40, 46, 178
  Cava 43
  Colossus 45
  De Champs-Elysees 41
  Exchange, the 39–40, 78
  Mayfair 41–2
  Ovatones 49, 85, 164, 209
  RAK 32, 50–1, 60, 69, 164, 178, 186, 207, 209
  Rooster 42, 211
  Utopia 41
Styrene, Poly 66–7, 209
Summers, Isabella "Isa" 6, 85, 92, 104, 188
Svengalis 16, 91, 117, 132, 187

techno (music genre) 151, 174, 184
Townsend, Karina 15, 22, 58, 71, 211

Utopia studios 41

voices, men's (vocals) 86, 90, 136–43, 186
voices, women's (opinions) 3, 5, 13, 38, 120, 193
voices, women's (vocals) 5, 8, 46, 65, 72, 82–3, 86, 90–3, 114, 119–66, 136–43, 151–5, 180–1

Ward, Alison 23–4, 47, 60, 169, 211
Warwick, Jacqueline 20, 123, 125, 134
Welch, Florence 6, 85, 92, 188
Weymouth, Tina 10, 23, 212
White, Hannah 120, 136
Whitfield, Gemma 174, 212
Wolfe, Paula 6–9, 12, 20, 36, 56, 85, 101–4, 107, 109, 137, 140, 159, 162, 164, 166, 172, 179, 185, 188
women artists (musicians) 3, 7, 16, 64–5, 74, 81–3, 87, 90–2, 97, 102–13, 121, 124, 131–9, 146, 155–7, 163, 184–7
women's voices (opinions) *see* voices, women's (opinions)
women's voices (vocals) *see* voices, women's (vocals)

Yarborough, Camille 126

Zalon 137–8

www.ingramcontent.com/pod-product-compliance
Lightning Source LLC
Chambersburg PA
CBHW062026220426
43662CB00010B/1493